The transformation of South Korea

South Korea has undergone rapid economic development, originally under a semi-military, anti-communist government that banned trade unions and kept close checks on the economy. President Roh Tae Woo, from 1987 to 1992, however, introduced wide-ranging electoral and social reforms.

Robert E. Bedeski provides a thorough analysis of the institutions of government in South Korea under Roh Tae Woo and how they have been transformed by the introduction of political pluralism. The author shows how a strong state, created by previous presidents, allowed constitutional and other political reforms to be implemented. The new political parties are examined, along with their role within the South Korean political system. Also, the state reforms are compared with developments in Taiwan, North Korea, China and the former Soviet Union.

This book should be of great value to students of the politics, economics and development of East Asia.

Robert E. Bedeski has lived and worked in various parts of East Asia since 1959, has taught and written about the comparative politics and international politics of the region. He is now Professor in the Department of Political Science, University of Victoria.

The transformation of South Korea

Reform and reconstitution in the
Sixth Republic under
Roh Tae Woo, 1987–1992

Robert E. Bedeski

London and New York

To Chalmers Johnson
teacher, mentor, and friend

First published 1994
by Routledge
11 New Fetter Lane, London EC4P 4EE

Simultaneously published in the USA and Canada
by Routledge
29 West 35th Street, New York, NY 10001

© 1994 Robert E. Bedeski

Typeset in Times by LaserScript Limited, Mitcham, Surrey

Printed and bound in Great Britain by
TJ Press (Padstow) Ltd, Padstow, Cornwall
Reprinted by Intype London Ltd 1995

British Library Cataloguing in Publication Data
A catalogue record for this book is available from the British Library.

Library of Congress Cataloging in Publication Data has been applied for

ISBN 0–415–05750–7   ISBN 0–415–10604–4 (pbk)

Contents

Preface

Among developing countries of the world, South Korea remains an anomaly that defies conventional wisdom. Its traditional roots were shaken by imperialism, and in the post-1945 era, division and war seemed to destroy whatever was left of a functioning society. Few modern societies have had to endure such calamities, and yet were still able to survive – much less to prosper.

The present study attempts an explanation of the South Korean phenomenon in its latest adaptation. Out of destruction and abject poverty, the South Koreans have built one of the most successful economies in the world, and are now moving to more democratic institutions. Making their progress all the more astonishing is the furor and apparent chaos which have dominated the Korean political scene. To an outsider, the society seems frequently on the brink of anarchy – dissidents facing police have been a common image since 1960.

The explanation for the chaos of the Korean miracle to be offered is that it is an ongoing experiment – a pattern of trial and error in socio-political engineering. Each of the six republics of South Korea represents a semi-scientific project – a set of assumptions, hypotheses, and acts which have sought to improve a state with few deep-rooted institutions except family and faction. In turn, many state experiments have generated resentment among those who were abused or ignored. Ambivalently committed to an open society at its inception, the state was unable to contain or repress dissent without resort to overt force.

Nevertheless, the Sixth Republic has seen considerable sustained progress toward democracy and a return to the civilian rule of law. Much has been done to create a healthy and vigorous economy and society; much more remains to be accomplished. The remainder of the twentieth century will undoubtedly see more major changes on the Korean peninsula – especially with the continued decline of North Korea's viability as a rival. The disposition of the totalitarian DPRK will be the central challenge of the

viii *Preface*

present government in Seoul. If the past is any guide, the South Koreans will meet the challenge with energy and pragmatism.

My own interest in Korea began with a military tour of duty during the First and Second Republics. Teaching English part-time brought me into contact with students active in opposition to the Rhee government. Although my subsequent academic concentration focused on China and Japan, I continued my interest in Korean affairs. In 1981 I returned to Seoul after an absence of two decades, and was amazed at the transformation of a war-torn society into an industrial and commercial dynamo. Further investigations and visits enabled me to analyse the society more closely. The Far Eastern Research Institute of Kyungnam University in Seoul and the Department of External Affairs (Canada) provided me with funding to initiate the current project in 1988. The International Cultural Society of Korea contributed to a summer of research in 1990. The Social Science and Humanities Research Council of Canada (SSHRCC) and the Center for Pacific Initiatives (CAPI) at the University of Victoria assisted with further travel and research assistance.

Numerous friends and contacts in the Canadian and Korean academic and diplomatic communities facilitated the genesis and completion of the study. Valuable research assistance was provided by Gordon MacCague, Lori Pike and Tina Thomas. My wife Kathleen has patiently accepted long absences at the computer, in the library and in Korea, and to her I owe more than can ever be repaid. My daughter Pamela has been a wonderful distraction. The author alone is responsible for errors of omission and commission.

R.E.B.
Victoria, Canada
May 4, 1993

List of abbreviations

AFKN	Armed Forces of Korea (radio) Network
BPL	Basic Press Law
CBS	Christian Broadcasting System
CEMC	Central Election Management Committee
CIS	Commonwealth of Independent States
CNA	China News Agency
COCOM	Co-ordinating Committee on Exports to Communist Areas
ComEcon	Council on Mutual Economic Assistance
CPC	Central People's Committee (North Korea)
CPPCC	Chinese People's Political Consultative Conference
CPSU	Communist Party of the Soviet Union
DJP	Democratic Justice Party
DKP	Democratic Korea Party
DLP	Democratic Liberal Party
DMZ	Demilitarized zone
DNP	Democratic Nationalist Party
DP	Democratic Party
DPP	Democratic Progressive Party (Taiwan)
DPRK	Democratic People's Republic of Korea
DRP	Democratic Republican Party
DSPJ	Democratic Socialist Party of Japan (formerly the JSP)
EPB	Economic Planning Board
GNP	Gross national product
HDP	Han-guk Democratic Party
IAEA	International Atomic Energy Agency
JSP	Japan Socialist Party
KBS	Korean Broadcasting System
KCIA	Korean Central Intelligence Agency
KCNA	Korean Central News Agency
KDP	Korean Democratic Party

KFTU	Korean Federation of Trade Unions
KGB	Committee of State Security (USSR)
KJP	Korea Justice Party
KNP	Korean Nationalist Party
KWP	Korean Workers' Party
LDP	Liberal Democratic Party (Japan)
MBC	Munhwa Broadcasting Corporation
NARRKI	National Association for the Rapid Realization of Korean Independence
NATO	North Atlantic Treaty Organization
NCU	National Conference on Unification
NDP	New Democratic Party
NDPTR	New Democratic Party of the Third Republic
NDRP	New Democratic Republican Party
NIC	Newly industrializing country
NKDP	New Korea Democratic Party
NKP	New Korea Party (offshoot of DLP)
NPRP	New Political Reform Party
PECC	Private Economic Co-operation Council
PLA	People's Liberation Army (PRC)
PPD	Party of Peace and Democracy
PRC	People's Republic of China
PRI	Partido Revolucionario Institucional (Mexico)
RDP	Reunification Democratic Party
ROC	Republic of China (Taiwan)
ROK	Republic of (South) Korea
SDF	Self-defence Forces
SEZ	Special Economic Zone
UNP	United National Party
UPP	United People's Party
USSR	Union of Socialist Soviet Republics

1   State reform in South Korea

Introduction

Of all modern trends, equality has been the most dominant tendency in social and political relationships. Class differences have become weaker in industrializing societies – confounding the inheritors of the Marxist tradition. Male and female educational and income differentials become smaller as more women enter the work force. From the nineteenth century, the rights of citizenship were expanded to an ever-widening circle of inhabitants, and denial of rights and entitlements to aliens is increasingly regarded as unfair. Political equality has become the modern standard of performance for the modern state.

Internationally, diversity has been the rule, and any trend towards uniformity and equality has been only maintained in various international organizations, such as the United Nations. This has not, however, dictated a permanent hierarchy. The collapse of the USSR and other socialist regimes has radically altered the distribution of international power, while economic growth in East Asia has shifted expectations to this area for greater global influence. Disparities in national power are not growing smaller, but are radically redistributed almost every generation. Wars have certainly contributed to the emergence of new powers and the destruction of old empires. Equally, the combination of effective national strategies with fortuitous opportunities has permitted some societies to consolidate domestic cohesion and welfare, while amplifying their influence abroad.

Robert Tucker has written that the 'history of the international system is a history of inequality *par excellence*'. What has made it so have been various disparities in natural endowments and uneven development, but also 'the condition of society marked by the absence of effective collective procedures, competitive rather than co-operative, and lacking commitment to a common good that has ensured that differences in power and wealth will be employed to perpetuate inequality'.[1] In the early 1990s, however, these words require qualification – the perpetuation of general inequality remains, but the specific cases of inequality are changing rapidly. Power and wealth – at least outside the Western industrialized states and Japan – have not been self-sustaining and self-preserving. The Soviet Union's dissipation of its national power may provide the classic illustration of twentieth-century defeat without war.

The international system does make a contribution to inequality, and, as Tucker notes, is structured in a way which may help to preserve that inequality. But this structure does not rule out the possibility of nations moving from weak to strong, or vice versa.[2] One major motivation in contemporary arms races has been the perception that arms build-up is a short cut to national power. It is also recognized that unlimited arms spending leads to instability and bankruptcy.

The questions remain. Why are some societies poor and others relatively well-off? What can communities do to overcome poverty and a backward economy and to improve their lot? Is there a conspiracy among the industrialized states to prevent the emergence of new members of the chosen few? Must democracy be set aside or postponed for the achievement of modernization?

The South Korean phenomenon of rapid economic growth followed by a successful movement towards democracy poses some hard questions to those who may overestimate the permanence of power. Korea is a society which had been subjected to colonial repression for over a third of this century, and its two halves were formed by division of the peninsula. South Korea was practically destroyed in the peninsular war, and was threatened by the renewed outbreak of war until recently. Despite these monumental handicaps, the South Koreans have built a dynamic industrial economy, and moved towards greater democracy during the 1980s. A preliminary evaluation of this progress indicates a few key factors which include:

1 *A talented and resourceful population, able to draw on bonds of familial solidarity, and historical memories of a unique national identity with past major achievements as a source of inspiration.* The Confucian heritage strongly reinforced family values and stressed education both as a means of upward social mobility and as an agent of moral improvement.

2 *The relatively good fortune of alignment with the United States has provided a wealthy and eager market for Korean manufactures at a time of industrialization.* The US patronage has also enhanced the viability of the Republic of Korea (ROK) by reinforcing the defence shield against North Korean threats. While the United States has remained in Korea for its own strategic reasons, and has been a source of domestic and

international tensions, the net effect has been to preserve the security of the ROK against North Korea and its allies. The pan-Pacific Pax Americana has also enabled South Korea to maintain its autonomy *vis-à-vis* its former colonizer – Japan.

3 *Strong leadership has forcibly established and preserved South Korean sovereignty, and guided the country's economic development.* Under a firmly entrenched presidency, now under a fully civilian leadership, the country has been moving towards greater democracy.

These same factors had a negative side which cannot be overlooked. While giving due credit to Korean talents, Korea has also been a quarrelsome society, from leaders down to interest groups, and to individuals. Mutual animosity among top leaders has its counterpart in the regions of the country, as well as between labour and management, or between students and government. Compromise and accommodation often take secondary priority in Korean society. Regarding the pro-US alignment, many in South Korea deny it much positive value. The US military presence, according to critics, hardens the division of the Korean peninsula, and made the ROK a front-line state in the Cold War. Critics argue that access to the US market has been of dubious value because that market only tolerates products not in competition with domestic American producers. Strong leadership has meant dictatorship and repression under harsh authoritarianism, causing many Koreans to attack their government as a creature of military and police brutality.

These two sides of the South Korean phenomenon present a painful dilemma. If democracy and economic improvement are possible only with long years of hard work, sacrifice and repression, then are the benefits worth the exertion? The Korean developmental story certainly testifies to the difficulties which accompany economic growth. Rights and democracy were restrained to maintain internal order and to prevent premature distribution of the benefits of growth to the working class. If there was a less painful road of development – under the existing international circumstances – the alternatives were not obvious. The North Korean path of development has resulted in stagnation and bankruptcy, and virtually no respect for diversity and freedom.

Another option has been revolutionary socialism, with its even more intense concentration of political power and attendant abuses. The collapse of the USSR and its client states has been a clear signal that the modern totalitarian state has become a near-extinct species. The machinery of central planning abhors free markets and has not come anywhere near the efficiency of capitalism in generating wealth. While capitalism often fails in the short-term equitable distribution of benefits, it has at least demonstrated an ability to produce an increasing quantity of goods to distribute. Capitalism combined with democracy has also offered opportunity to the many to improve their class status – a phenomenon whose possibility was denied by Marxism, which sees class as a static condition. The failure of Soviet and Chinese communism has been economic as well as political, and their attractiveness as models for developing societies has practically disappeared.

South Korea represents a third option for developing societies. It is a society characterized by high growth and movement towards a more liberal and possibly more equitable society during the Sixth Republic. Instead of rigorous central planning, the state practises some 'guidance' through administration and legislation. Coercion has played a part in state techniques to ensure compliance with goals and plans, but there is little or no effort or ability to subordinate all of society to a single orthodox ideology, as in totalitarian states. It is perhaps this combination of state power and pluralist diversity that gives it viability and dynamism. It is a process of state-building I will call 'piecemeal socio-political engineering', borrowing from Karl Popper.[3]

In the first decade of its existence after World War II, the ROK was an unlikely candidate for successful political and economic development. The Korean peninsula had been subjected to a harsh colonial regime for half a century, then divided into two mutually hostile regimes at the end of World War II. From 1950 to mid-1953, South Korea bore the brunt of a most destructive war. Yet today it has become one of the most dynamic economies in the modern world, despite its insecure borders and a paucity of natural resources.

Critics charge that US patronage has been a major factor in this 'artificial' success, and some use a 'dependence' framework to explain the Korean case. United States aid, defence guarantees, and market access have been important, but would have meant little without South Korean determination to strengthen a sovereign state and to embark on rapid economic growth, which averaged 8.9 per cent from 1962 to 1987. To explain some of this success in economic development, we will examine how the formation of a strong state has been the crucial ingredient in South Korean development. With the strong state in place, authority has been decentralized, with major movement towards full democracy. This movement occurred hesitantly in the Fifth Republic, and more rapidly in the Sixth Republic under Roh Tae Woo.

The authoritarian state that emerged under Syngman Rhee and Park Chung Hee acquired a capacity to maintain the Republic against international threats. The Third Republic mobilized human and economic resources for rapid industrialization. One dilemma of modern South Korea is that the bureaucratic-authoritarian regime – which has sustained economic development – is less able to liberalize without undermining some of the strengths leading to its success. A more liberal policy towards labour unions, for example, has tolerated hundreds of industrial strikes, raised workers' wages, and has made South Korea less competitive in the world economy of low-cost labour. Dismantling the *chaebol* conglomerates has been a popular demand, but if carried out as government policy, it could endanger the steady growth of the economy in competition with international giant corporations.

The present study will examine the interrelationship between the bureaucratic-authoritarian state and South Korea's political economy, in order to understand the new challenges of the Republic as it moves from the status of 'developing' to 'developed' nation. One major challenge is to maintain the characteristics which fuelled its rapid development, while responding to a changing domestic and international environment. The Sixth Republic has also been notable for two additional achievements – establishing a sound basis for democracy, and expanding international contacts.

South Korea, a society which has already experienced a multitude of changes, has been undergoing unprecedented political transformation since June 1987, when Roh Tae Woo announced a major reform programme for the country. Until then, the country was an example of how a poor, undeveloped society could concentrate its human and material resources to industrialize. The Sixth Republic has continued this push for economic growth, but has added democratic development to its priorities – even on occasion risking economic growth for expansion of democracy. It would be premature to pronounce the experiment a success, but there has been a major effort to introduce more democratic institutions into the Korean political system. In this, South Korea's political reform is an important precedent for many developing countries, as they achieve higher economic growth. The South Korean example shows that economic growth can be a priority and can be achieved with perseverance and the right inputs. Beyond well-being, there is a universal sentiment for freedom that drives a civilization forward.

Recent political reform in South Korea has brought liberalization of state institutions – a reduction of reliance on state force as the major instrument for exacting compliance from citizens. The original state institutions evolved to concentrate power to maximize government ability to exercise the powers of sovereignty, achieve rapid economic growth, and maintain national security. Dissent from these goals has been present in Korean society since the Korean War, and concessions were made before 1987. With the Roh reforms, a new era of limited democracy was inaugurated. Some would argue that formerly explicit controls have been replaced by more subtle restrictions – including the dominance of money in relatively free elections.

Domestically, a new generation is emerging – one which did not know the repressive Japanese colonial regime or the tragic suffering of the Korean War. To a few in this generation, the nationalism of Kim Il Song in North Korea has had a certain attractiveness, despite the anti-communist indoctrination in South Korean schools and despite the overwhelming evidence that North Korean communism is economically stagnant and continues to sustain one of the most repressive regimes in the world. The south has a large middle class which wants social stability, economic growth, and greater democracy. The generals and coup-makers were often waiting in the wings if liberalization went too far, or if radical disruptions undermined South Korean security.

The South Korean state is a stepchild of the international system which dominated the Cold War period, and its existence was denounced by communist countries for decades. Through a combination of persistent diplomacy and good fortune, the Sixth Republic has, however, expanded diplomatic and commercial contacts with the communist world. Military and economic support from the United States has been a positive factor in South Korean viability and success, although trade disputes and popular discomfort with the US military presence – as well as American budget-cutters' enthusiasm to reduce foreign entanglements – have softened this relationship. Propinquity to Japan suggests much greater co-operation in that direction, but this is tempered by residues of anti-Japanese feeling among many Koreans, and potential rivalry for the future.

In addition to the importance of domestic political reforms for the South Korean state, there is a comparative dimension of analysis to be explored. Events on the Korean peninsula have been overshadowed by reforms elsewhere – notably in China and the ex-Soviet Union. Political reform has also successfully occurred in Taiwan as the mainland power elite increasingly shares power with the native Taiwanese, and has proceeded to the point where the ruling Guomindang has voluntarily changed election rules to permit intensifying challenges to its rule. These examples will illustrate the larger context of South Korean reforms – one in which democratization has vied with renewed nationalism as the dominant theme in the non-Western world for the remainder of the millennium.

The category of 'developing nation' may refer to subjective aspirations in the sense of goals of progress – as well as to an objectively measurable set of characteristics. 'Development' reflects progress, industrialization, democracy and improved health and living standards. Developing countries are characterized by lower economic and social indicators in comparison with the 'developed' countries. (In an age of language inflation, countries are called 'developing' even when they are stagnant or moving away from progress.) Political structures are usually less efficient in executing and co-ordinating government policy, and identification between citizens and government is sporadic, non-existent, or mutually suspicious. This condition is often correlated with governments which rely largely on a combination of patronage and coercion. The ideal of government accountability and citizen participation remains alien to many, if not most, developing countries.

Within this category of developing countries, South Korea belongs to a select group of 'Newly Industrializing Countries' (NICs).[4] These are characterized by successful modernization in economic growth, political stability, governments which support (or, in the case of Hong Kong, at least do not interfere with) private property and capitalist enterprise, and social development. The frequent expectation of economists has been that the process of modernization will be accompanied by increasing inequalities in the distribution of wealth, which may be necessary for capital accumulation. Two important variations have been (1) communist states, which have forcibly expropriated most private wealth, and claim to work for radical egalitarianism; and (2) a few societies, such as South Korea and Taiwan, where economic benefits have been distributed more equally than anticipated.

A major question in this study is the extent to which democracy is compatible with rapid development. One argument for the postponement of democracy is that pluralist interest groups inhibit economic growth because of parochial loyalties which slow the growth of a centralized state. Moreover, they are a distraction from material accumulation in that their reliance on pre-industrial modes of production limits efficiency, which in turn keeps surpluses low. The state must be able to mobilize significant resources to ensure economic growth. The free play of vested interests may interfere with the efficient allocation of inputs and outputs of the economy. The multi-party system of democracy may aggregate narrow local interests, but it also gravitates towards short-term gains, while making promises which dissipate scarce resources at the expense of vital accumulation. A free press, competing interests, consumer markets and other traits of a liberal democracy may substitute short-term for long-term benefits for the whole society, argue the authoritarian regimes. Once these undemocratic arguments have been accepted, the choice of government is reduced to that between authoritarian or totalitarian.

The argument in favour of democracy *and* development is that free markets are relatively efficient in accumulating wealth at individual and corporate levels, and so will strengthen the country generally. Major flaws in government policy will be detected earlier by the existence of a loyal opposition and institutions which impose accountability. A free press can debate major issues and strategies, and educate citizens in responsibility. In this view, concentrated power is a high risk – even when it promises broad-based prosperity in the future. In recent years, the collapse of totalitarian (or systems which aspired to be totalitarian) regimes in countries from Mongolia to Poland and Hungary, including the USSR, has demonstrated that fundamentally anti-democratic regimes have failed to be effective modernizers as the world economy increased in sophistication and as word of non-communist success reached their populations.

The tentative lesson of South Korean development is that authoritarianism, under certain conditions, may be a suitable environment for fostering, first, development, and then democracy, especially if economic development has proceeded sufficiently to allow the establishment of the necessary infrastructure – including education, communications, and an incipient opposition. A key feature of this developmental sequence is that some pluralism should be maintained and tolerated. Authoritarian regimes will find pockets of resistance which may grow from nuisance to threat, but the application of maximum force will prove counterproductive.

The South Korean experience has undoubtedly been affected by the Cold War. The state was established and preserved in part because of mutual tensions between two of the major world systems. It prospered under the Pax Americana in the Pacific, and it is finding new opportunities in the collapse of the Cold War. The same conditions also helped Taiwan – although US–PRC normalization in 1979 removed the American defence umbrella in that instance. In both cases, the existence of communist antagonists challenged South Korea and Taiwan to survive and prosper. The severity of their international environment provoked them to respond in what proved to be an effective, pragmatic, and appropriate manner.

Korean state development has been intimately linked with four major powers in the twentieth century: Japan, Russia/USSR, China, and the United States. Until the mid-nineteenth century, Korea's politics hinged on semi-vassal relations with China. Dynastic changes had generated domestic factionalism in Korea over shifting allegiance to a new ruling house. Nomadic expansion in north China and Manchuria exposed Korea to incursions as well. The decline of the Qing dynasty in the latter half of the nineteenth century increased the vulnerability of the Korean kingdom to the rising power of Japan as well as to the ambitions of other industrial states. After 1895, Korea fell under the sphere of influence of Japan, a trend culminating in the establishment of a colonial administration in 1910, and lasting until 1945. With the defeat of Japan in 1945, state development of Korea was dominated by the USSR in the northern Democratic People's

Republic of Korea (DPRK) and the United States in the southern Republic of Korea.

These historical experiences have conditioned modern Korean nationalism as a response to powerful external forces. Yang Sung Chul considered the survival of the Korean people a

> remarkable historical feat. That Korea has survived as a nation and has maintained its independent political entity, national identity and a high degree of cultural homogeneity despite incessant foreign invasions and domination by the Chinese, Khitans, Jurchens, Mongols, Manchus and Japanese is indeed extraordinary. Its artificial division in 1945 notwithstanding, the same unifying historical and cultural tradition persists against the strong currents of divisive ideological and political forces in both halves of the Korean peninsula today.[5]

Yang traces the idea of Korean nationalism to the Shilla dynasty (A.D. 668–935), the first united kingdom on the Korean peninsula.[6] In addition to scholarship through the centuries which contributed to Korean national consciousness, the masses adhered to and transmitted the old culture. This reinforced bonds created by kinship, periodic political and economic unification, and a common language. Military heroes in battles against invaders further strengthened national self-consciousness. A half-century of Japanese domination could not extinguish Korean nationalism, which was forced into two antagonistic semi-nation states after 1945.

Background of the modern Korean state

The modern Korean potential for unity and growth had its roots in pre-modern culture and kingdoms. But this potential was interrupted and postponed by international intervention. A tragic political geography, locating the Korean peninsula at the crossroads of Chinese, Russian/Soviet, and Japanese strategic interests and ambitions, would not allow Korea to remain outside international power politics.

Geography played a major part in predisposing Korean society to its characteristic history. The Koreans occupy a peninsula, so political boundaries on three sides are predetermined. Its fourth border, the Yalu and Tumen Rivers, was sufficiently clear to be conceded as the frontier between China and Korea. The relatively compact land mass also facilitated early communications among the tribes of the area. The nomadic tribal onslaughts and wanderings that affected the Chinese empire – except for the Jurchens, Mongols and Manchus – often bypassed Korea.

In contrast, the Shandong peninsula of China, opposite Korea across the Yellow Sea, failed to develop an independent character in large part because it was part of the emerging Yellow River culture in earliest times. The Chinese generally were not a seafaring people, so Korea was spared massive maritime colonization – except for a military colony during the Han dynasty.

Within the Korean peninsula itself, the two major zones, north and south, had some degree of influence on social evolution before the division of 1945. Although the people are ethnically and linguistically homogeneous, there is a 'waist' transition zone through the centre, running east and west, which has been variously defined by the 38th parallel, the Demilitarized Zone, and roughly the Han River. North of the central zone, topography tends to be more mountainous, and the natural resources needed for industry more abundant – a factor influencing Japanese investment during the colonial period. The southern zone enjoys a milder climate, less mountainous topography, and greater suitability for agriculture. It is closer to Japan and Shandong than the north, and was both the recipient and the exporter of culture. Its sedentary civilization was epitomized by the Shilla dynasty, in contrast to the more military Koguryo kingdom of the north.

Korean legend places the origin of the Korean people at nearly 4000 years ago – born from a bear which became a man by an act of will and persistence. Chinese histories date Korea later – when Chinese troops set up military colonies near present-day Pyongyang. Like the Japanese colonial regime of two millennia later, the Chinese imposed order brought a new civilization – and gave the Koreans an enemy against whom to unite.

Subsequent history witnessed the division of the peninsula and its reunification, until the great Yi, or Choson, dynasty (1392–1910). Korean unity and disintegration paralleled that of China. But unlike Chinese political/dynastic cycles, the Koreans left the idea of a mandate of heaven to the Chinese empire, where an impersonal cosmos bestowed transcendent legitimacy on the ruling house, ending the chaos of division. The Koreans had no illusions of grandeur that their kingdom or kingdoms had the universal significance claimed by the Chinese. Korean kings accepted subservience to the Chinese emperor, and derived their formal legitimacy from the Chinese monarchy.

This provides an insight into the Koreans' view of their place in the world. Rulers and cultural elites recognized Korean uniqueness, but also understood the need for protection in a continent often racked by nomadic invasions and new empires. The natural borders of the Yalu and Tumen Rivers provided a boundary between Korea and non-Korea, but were not nearly as effective as the sea moat surrounding Japan. The non-Korean world affected and threatened the peninsula and its peoples, and drove home the lesson that unity and co-operation were the best strategies in maintaining independence.

Numerous tribes had bordered China, attacked it, and were eventually either absorbed, assimilated, or dominated – with subsequent incorporation into the empire. The Korean rulers accepted the investiture rituals in which the Chinese emperor bestowed kingship on them as vassals. Tribute missions – which camouflaged a thriving Sino-Korean trade – further contributed to the appearance of superior–subordinate relations so valued in Confucian political philosophy. From the Chinese viewpoint, the fact that the Koreans accepted and used the Chinese writing system, and were devoted followers of the Sage, suggested that the Koreans were not a threat, and in time, would be integrated into the Chinese world system.

This adaptability, expressed as *sadae* ('serving the great'), was what the Japanese expected when they established their rule over Korea – anticipating that the Koreans would accept the hegemony of Japan as they had that of the Chinese. To the Japanese, Korean acceptance of Chinese cultural supremacy was taken as evidence that they were a people with a natural susceptibility to obedience to a strong power. Transferring that obedience to Japan was the objective of the colonial regime. There were, however, significant differences between Chinese suzerainty and the Japanese colonial regime, established in 1910. The Japanese may have failed to realize that, first, Korean relations with China were based not on abject subservience, but on Confucian notions of loyalty. With these came reciprocal obligations to protect and respect each other. This notion of loyalty was also dynasty-specific. Whenever an imperial dynasty was defeated, the Korean court agonized about whether – and when – to transfer loyalty to the new dynasty. Second, Korean political and cultural relations had evolved over centuries, and were tied to political ritual and culture. For the most part, these political relations did not penetrate far into society or the economy. In contrast, the Japanese military colonists sought penetration of Japanese control down to the lowest social and economic levels.

Third, the Chinese could tolerate a quasi-independent Korea on their flank because the peninsula was of only secondary strategic importance in the defence of the realm. Inner Asia remained the major source of invasions until the mid-nineteenth century, and Korea was a functional extension of the Great Wall – a loyal barrier in the north-east to prevent the incursions of Siberian and Manchurian tribes. Prior to the first Sino-Japanese war (1894–95), the Korean peninsula had once been an invasion avenue to China – in the sixteenth century, when the armies of Hideyoshi ravaged the country in preparation for an advance into the Chinese empire. At that time the Koreans proved their importance to the defence of the Chinese empire as a buffer, and bogged the Japanese armies down, forcing them to abandon dreams of continental empire for another three centuries. Japanese hegemony over Korea stemmed from ambitions of expansion – of offence, not defence, and Korean human and material resources were to be mobilized for purposes of Japanese imperial expansion on to the mainland of Asia. Unlike the Chinese *imperium*, independent Korean survival was not possible in the Japanese scheme of things.

Fourth, the Chinese had centuries of experience in dealing with non-Chinese neighbours – in war, in diplomacy, and as subjects of their conquests. If this did not make the Chinese cognizant of foreign sensitivities, at least it smoothed relations. The Japanese, in contrast, had emerged from centuries of isolation into an age of imperialism.[7] Despite the formal international environment of equality of nations, there was also the Spencerian view of nations as competing species, and the fittest proved their capacity by acquiring colonies.

Fifth, China represented a set of universal ideas and morals until the mid-nineteenth century. Nativistic culture remained for the Korean masses, but in politics, the symbols of government and learning were Sinitic. Japan's regime in Korea, on the other hand, derived from a mix of Japanese *shinto*, 'imperial way', and Western ideas. In particular, the idea of nationalism was Western-derived, so Korean nationalism was as valid as Japanese nationalism. Japanese suzerainty lacked the moral claims of the Chinese cultural dominance of the past.

Finally, Japanese dominance depended upon military prowess. Once this was defeated, the superior pretensions of Japan vanished. Thus the overlay of Japanese colonialism may have affected social and economic organization in Korea, and it no doubt stirred up Korean nationalism – but there was little transfer of social and political values. On the other hand, the Japanese work ethic, the drive to modernize, organizational skills, and military competence undoubtedly left their mark after the colonial period.

The external forces which shaped Korean nationalism have inhibited the evolution of a united Korean state. Through the period of Japanese rule, Korean nationalists at home and abroad worked and struggled for an independent and united Korea – a sovereign nation state which would provide a homeland for the millions of Koreans scattered abroad, and a society where Koreans would enjoy the benefits of peace and prosperity. It was the nationalist vision activated by Woodrow Wilson in his Fourteen Points, and delayed by the Versailles conference in 1919. In China the cession of German rights in Shandong to the Japanese sparked the May the Fourth Movement. The earlier mutual acceptance (1905) of US dominance in the Philippines and Japanese rule in Korea led to massive demonstrations and assassination attempts against the Japanese military rulers in Korea. Popular uprisings broke out all over Korea around the time of the First World War. When US President Wilson proclaimed the self-determination of nations as a principle of the post-war settlement, it was greeted by Koreans with great enthusiasm, as they wanted their own independence. The March First movement began with the promulgation of a Declaration of Independence in Seoul. It set off a great mass demonstration against Japan, although vengeance was not part of the document. The demonstrations spread throughout the country but were crushed by the Japanese police and military forces. A reported 7,509 demonstrators were killed, with nearly 47,000 arrested. The movement involved over two million Koreans, and was led by religious and educational groups. Although its goal of independence was defeated, its work was carried on with the formation of the Korean Provisional Government in Shanghai.

Japanese repression intensified as Tokyo tried to integrate the peninsula into the empire. Japanese rule in Korea – a colony seen as the forward advance base of empire into Manchuria – was harsher than in Taiwan, owing to the island's lesser strategic importance. Tens of thousands of workers were drafted in labour projects, and subjected to inhuman conditions, as Japanese males went to fight the Pacific war. Women from Japanese colonies and conquered territories were forced into prostitution as 'comfort women'.

While Korea was a Japanese colony there was relatively little international concern for its inhabitants. Benign neglect characterized the attitude of the major powers. At Yalta it was agreed that the Soviet Union would enter the war against Japan three months after the surrender of Germany, and that the United States and the Soviets would jointly accept the surrender of Japanese troops. Eventually the Koreans would be trained and educated to enjoy democratic rights and institutions.

Historically, the Western notion of sovereignty was alien to the non-Western world. As it developed in Western Europe, it referred to a single unified government and the locus of supreme legislative and executive power. This ultimate secular power could not be shared with other institutions, such as the Church or the aristocracy, and paralleled the termination of feudalism, with its local privileges and vetoes of centralized power. At the international level, sovereignty also assumed the legal equality of states under international law. With the concept of sovereignty, there also evolved a 'standard of civilization' which presumed to define the standards of the institutions and behaviour of 'civilized states' which could be admitted to the select circle.[8] But these moral considerations, as with Wilsonian ideals of national self-determination, were set aside in order to pursue *Realpolitik* as Soviet–American amity broke down after 1945.[9]

The Soviets proceeded to assist and guide the formation of a North Korean state based on communist doctrine and organization, while the United States helped to establish a South Korean government, but with less dedication than Moscow. United States indifference to the strategic importance of the Korean peninsula was expressed in Dean Acheson's speech to the National Press Club (12 January 1950), in which he pointedly omitted Korea from the scope of a US defence perimeter in the Pacific region. According to the Secretary of State, countries of the Asian mainland would have to depend on their own efforts and the UN for defence.[10] In the north, communist groups, sponsored by the Soviets, expanded their influence and power at the expense of democratic parties. As it happened, the divided peninsula with a quasi-free, non-communist republic preserved the possibility of a future democratic Korea.

If South Korea evolved under structures and goals ostensibly democratic and capitalist, the north was dedicated to rigid Stalinist socialism and uncompromising nationalism – even to the degree of attempting to unify the country by force. Pyongyang claims that the Korean War began with an attempted invasion by the south. However, evidence supports the contention that the north, under Kim Il Song, initiated the invasion when 'revolutionary uprisings' in the south failed to bring about the collapse of the Seoul government. The massing of North Korean troops along the 38th parallel in the weeks before the 25 June attack further indicated Pyongyang's preparation for attack. The invasion failed to drive US forces out of Korea after their deployment, and MacArthur's counter-attack at Inchon pushed North Korean forces out of the south and much of the north. But it also set off a Chinese 'counter'-counter-attack. The war settled into a long stalemate culminating in an armistice on 27 July 1953.

While overt conflict between the two regimes halted, intense competition and potential for conflict remained. The Korean War established the major parameters of the two Korean states for decades. Those characteristics can be summarized as follows:

1 A state of quasi-siege characterized both regimes – with high military spending and preparations for attack by either side. The south was less likely to initiate a resumption of the war, as it stressed economic development based on a civilian economy.
2 There has been a high degree of rivalry between the two regimes. Both have competed for foreign recognition at the expense of the other.
3 Both were dependent on outside support. The north has depended on Beijing and Moscow for crude oil and military assistance. In addition, contiguous continental territory between North Korea and its communist allies rendered assistance easier and more dependable. South Korea has US troops in place, and also depends on its ally for military assistance. After the Vietnam War, however, it was unlikely that the United States would commit itself to defending South Korea as

it had in the 1950s. The United States has also been a major source of aid in the past, and is now a key trading partner.

4 While overt conflict has subsided, there remain recurring acts of violence perpetrated by the north – including assassinations and terrorist acts. Until December 1991, with the joint north–south signing of the Agreement on Reconciliation, Non-aggression and Exchanges, and Co-operation, the two sides were technically at war.

Conflict and political reform

Buffeted by international changes beyond their control from the end of the nineteenth century to the 1950s, Koreans have taken command of their polity to.build two nation states which could resist future intrusions. The North Koreans built a totalitarian state whose form has changed little in the near half-century since peninsular division. The southerners constructed political institutions lacking long-range durability, but this has been compensated for by adaptation to a rapidly changing international environment. South Korea has responded to domestic and external pressures – if not with grace and efficiency, at least with enthusiasm and ingenuity. South Korea has rejected ideological dogma – such as the cult of Kim Il Song in North Korea – which might interfere with adapting to change. A succession of six Republics, each based on different leadership,[11] values and goals, has facilitated this adaptation to changing circumstances.

While the specific changes and reforms examined in this volume are unique to South Korea, they have occurred in an era of major political reform in other parts of the world. Indeed, the decade of the 1980s might be termed 'the era of political reform' by future historians. While these changes are *revolutionary*, they do not constitute *revolutions* in the classical sense that societies overthrew their governments and installed radically different political systems. The changes in South Korea, the PRC, USSR, and Taiwan, for example, were sparked by the need to revise the relation between government and society, to respond to changes in international relations, and to adapt to new conditions in the international economy. The North Korean leadership has been aware of these changes, but has so far spurned significant political reforms.

While popular dissatisfaction has played a role in compelling reforms in a number of countries, it has not determined the content of government-led measures. Reform in communist regimes has been ostensibly to adapt to new conditions. Following the reformist Fourteenth Congress of the Communist Party of China, discussions have emerged in China calling for structural revision and constitutional amendment to reflect the new line of moderate reform. Political reform is often a strategy to head off revolution or social breakdown by removing some of the aggravations which historically provided a catalyst for revolution.[12] It is also a means of adjusting to new socio-economic complexities – including failures of old dogmas.

Political reform and political development

Political reform is the modification of state institutions for the purpose of adapting to changes in the domestic and/or the external environment. A developing country seeks to enhance the strength of the state. State strength is related to the following factors:[13]

1 The ability to deploy effective force against threats at home and abroad.
2 The ability to execute commands and laws exacting compliance.
3 The ability to convince citizens of common interests between themselves and the state.

Political reform seeks to enhance the above three conditions. Each condition has one or several structures which help to achieve it:

1 For the most effective use of force, the armed forces and police are created and maintained.
2 An effective legal system requires structures of adjudication – especially courts. In many countries, the courts and legal system may be an arm of the structures of force, but the rule of law requires an independent judiciary.
3 The quality of system performance is conducive to enhancing state legitimacy. Mass media and education contribute to the shaping of public opinion.

Political development and economic development

Political development involves significant advances in all three sectors towards the achievement of sovereignty and legitimacy. The case of South Korea demonstrates that simultaneity is not likely and is probably not desirable. Moreover, it is essential that the state should accumulate sufficient material resources in order to carry out its incremental reforms and institution-building. If this is accomplished by state confiscation of private property – as in communist countries – a tentative legitimacy may be achieved. So far, market economies, by increasing the wealth of the state and broad sectors of society, appear to be most effective in supporting political development. Reform requires that the state should encourage economic development[14] but not dominate it. Excessive state intervention will restrict economic development by the politicization of a privileged private sector, as in the Philippines or Indonesia, while inadequate attention of the state to economic activity (a rare phenomenon) would deprive it of necessary financial resources.[15]

South Korea and the middle class market-oriented state

To amplify the phenomenon of political reform, we will examine the case of South Korea in some depth – especially the reforms of the Sixth Republic. Other cases of political reform in the past fifteen years will be compared. These cases include the Soviet Union, the People's Republic of China (PRC), and the Republic of China (ROC) on Taiwan. These, and South Korea, are selected from an increasing number of cases because they represent an epochal phenomenon at the end of this century – a development which will probably define states into the next century.

This phenomenon is that middle-class democracy, based on a market economy, is a reasonably effective mode of state organization for the future. It is effective because it is wealth-generating and stable, as well as able to elicit and utilize advancing technology, and allows an expanding number of citizens to enjoy the benefits of modern society. South Korea – perhaps of all developing countries – has most directly pursued this model. This pursuit has not been consciously articulated and the South Koreans have not fettered their drive to modernization with abstract or contrary ideologies.

Why has South Korea been a disciple of the middle-class, market-oriented state? Two powerful positive examples – the United States and Japan – and two negative examples – North Korea and the PRC – helped to define South Korea's path of political development. These were further sustained by trade and technology patterns which emerged out of military alliances and enmities. State socialism, an ideology epitomized by the fossilization of North Korea and the extremism of Mao's Cultural Revolution, was anathema to most South Koreans, except perhaps to a number of radical dissidents who remain disillusioned by the injustices and inequities of South Korean society.

Characteristics of political reform

A number of political systems are facing similar problems of adapting to demands for democratization and pressures for economic modernization. The democratization of a developed or developing country is a type of political reform which is marked by redistribution of political resources[16] in society, and it will entail empowerment of some groups at the expense of others, especially those which may have been excluded in the past. These groups may be political parties and their constituencies, or they may aggregate political interests or ethnic groups. A key determinant of political pluralism seems to be opposition party power, and the degree to which an opposition can realistically aspire to influence government policy without compromising its autonomy.

One set of six countries in north-east Asia has had intimate interaction and overlapping or competing interests in the decades after World War II. All but Japan are facing the challenge of major state reform. The other five are the USSR (now collapsed and reorganized as the 'Commonwealth of Independent States', or CIS, with Russia pursuing some of the national interests of the old Soviet Union), North Korea, South Korea, Taiwan, and the People's Republic of China. They fall into three types, based upon the changing strength of the opposition groups:

Type one   Significant expansion of opposition groups.

South Korea. Opposition parties existed from the beginning of the ROK, were briefly successful in 1960, and came close to capturing presidential power in late 1987, capturing a majority of legislative seats the following spring. Faced with a majority opposition in the National Assembly, the ruling party in early 1990 merged with two opposition parties – bringing them into government. This was followed by the expansion of local autonomy in the 1991 elections. There has also been divestiture of other government powers in the legal system, the media, and the economy. The military has also lost much of its influence. The urban middle class and farmers have made gains through the reforms.

Taiwan. After the shock of US de-recognition in 1979, the ruling Guomindang embarked on major restructuring of the state apparatus. This was done partly to restore its waning legitimacy at home, and also to regain the democratic lead it had enjoyed over the PRC. For the first time in Taiwan, opposition parties were allowed to participate in provincial elections. More Taiwanese were admitted into the highest levels of national government.

Type two   Expansion of opposition groups at the expense of central hegemony

USSR. In the Soviet Union, power was reduced or removed from the Communist Party, the bureaucracy, the army and the KGB – first as a result of Gorbachev's reforms, and in late summer of 1991, in the wake of a failed coup by hard-liners. The Communist Party lost its official dictatorship, and hundreds of opposition groups emerged. Soviet Republics have responded to the collapse of the centre by seizing autonomy from Moscow. Numerous opposition parties have emerged, but none strong enough to form a government. Boris Yeltsin maintains a tenuous hold on power in the face of fragmented opposition in 1993. (Huge outlays for defence also contributed to the impoverishment of the former Soviet Union.)

Type three Limited or minimal political reform, with prohibitions against the formation of opposition groups

PRC. In China, administrative power was shifted from the central Politburo to the various Ministries, to the producers and managers, and to the National People's Congress during the reforms of 1979–89. More open elections were introduced in 1979 at the local level, but genuine opposition groups were forbidden. The emergence of opposition was quickly, and often brutally, repressed. The Communist Party has retained its monopoly of power, although there has been significant economic reform. In June 1989 the Communist Party of China demonstrated its resolve to retain power with its massacre of dissidents in Tiananmen. In 1992, Deng Xiaoping toured the south and the Special Economic Zones, and decided that economic reforms had to proceed. Resumption of pragmatic economic growth was ratified at the Fourteenth Congress of the Communist Party of China in mid-October 1992.

North Korea. Despite the shocks of major reforms in the communist world, Pyongyang has refused to make any concessions to democracy or a market economy. The example of East German reforms, followed by accelerated pressures, and finally extinction of the state certainly tainted the idea of change. The ideology of Kim Il Song is the exclusive dogma of the state, and allows for no deviation. The personality cult of Kim's son, Kim Chong Il, provides symbolic and actual continuity of North Korea state ideology.

In these five cases, political reform began with a fixed supply of political resources represented by state power. When democratic political reform begins, it does not increase the quantity of political resources in the state, but empowers citizens at the expense of the government. In the case of the USSR, state power was eroded because decades of repression under a strong state created a vast reservoir of resentment against communist dictatorship and the denial of ethnic identities, and because of the gross inefficiencies of production and distribution of wealth.

State reform poses crucial dilemmas to rulers. It entails great risk to power monopolies because it requires the distribution of power resources to previously marginal or unempowered sectors of society – at the expense of the central party/government apparatus. However, failure to reform can bring about a much greater crisis in the future. State reform can also be premature: distributing powers before the consolidation of power has matured can weaken a state. The timing of state reform is crucial. It must occur when, and only when, society has a civic culture which can manage newly empowered groups, and not before. If government waits too long after a civil society has developed, it may face rebellion and revolution, which could severely weaken societal integration. While the development of a middle class is helpful in creating modern civil society, diffusion of its values (especially achievement and stability) may serve as a temporary substitute. In order to further identify the key elements of state reform, the case of South Korea will be examined. The following section provides an overview and background of the Roh Tae Woo reforms of June 1987.

The first five Republics: background to democratization

The early development of Korean nationalism undoubtedly contributed to the resilience of Korean society. Since 1950, this nationalism has taken two rival forms – communist and anti-communist authoritarianism with democratizing tendencies. (A moderate group of nationalists attempted to establish a middle ground, but failed to make much impact in the polarization following the Korean War.) Both built strong state structures to maximize nationalist appeal, and to prevent the other from winning the contest for legitimacy.[17] Both North and South Korea sought rapid methods of centralizing political power. Kim Il Song eliminated his rivals, and installed trusted friends and relatives into positions of power, while remoulding the state into a totalitarian dictatorship after the models of Stalin and Mao.

The south pursued a different state-building route. After Korean independence in 1945, various elites competed for authority and influence in the new order. The Korean War further consolidated Syngman Rhee as the supreme leader of the South Korean nation and key spokesman for the Republic. He built a personal dictatorship based on a dominant party, but was restrained by the democratic impulses of his rivals and the Korean people. Many had fled from the north before and during the peninsular war, and became fervid anti-communists as well as potential rivals to Rhee, who was also opposed by the Democratic Party. Sponsorship by the United Nations and United States, and aspirations to a more open society, further set limits on Syngman Rhee's autocracy. Mass demonstrations led to his overthrow in 1960. After the short-lived Second Republic led by Chang Myon, General, and then President, Park Chung Hee pursued a policy of economic development and institution-building in the two following Republics. The policy lifted the country out of its war-torn poverty into the status of a NIC, and also accelerated the formation of new elites and classes. He launched the Saemaul programme to retain rural support and ensure that agriculture would not lag behind industrial growth.

Park's Third and Fourth Republics also witnessed extensive expansion in higher education – producing graduates who learned about democracy in their living quarters, classrooms and university clubs, but saw the reality of authoritarianism in society. University education provided the credentials of middle class membership, but adequate employment opportunities were often lacking – producing alienation and opposition to the government. Park centralized and modernized the state apparatus, backing up his programmes with military force.

The First Republic and the Rhee presidency

The Korean presidency has been the focus of the state since the founding of the Republic in 1948. Four strong Presidents have personified the difficulties of forging a polity that would survive the challenges of development, conflict and sovereignty, while weak ones have succumbed to the pressures of party politics and military challenge within months of assuming power. Syngman Rhee's record of achievements is mixed. His contribution to the creation of the modern Korean state is undeniable, but his use of corrupt methods and force against opponents certainly damaged the prospects for democracy. His stubbornness with allies created rifts to the point where his own survival was endangered. But considering the post-war environment, where one Eastern European government after another was taken over by communists, and the growing threat of invasion from North Korea, Rhee was able to succeed where other, more liberal, leaders had failed.

The Korean War was the defining event of the post-war era, and it set the state agenda for subsequent regimes to the present. The war had at least three lessons for the Korean state in the south:

1 International, and particularly US, sponsorship was necessary for survival.
2 The north was the greatest threat to the existence of the south, so tight political unity was needed, and a strong defence force to resist future incursions had to be built up in the event that US support was weakened or distracted.
3 A strong centralized state was needed to tackle the challenges of economic reconstruction. Lacking democratic traditions, and requiring emergency powers, Rhee's determination to build a dictatorial presidency was not without reason.

Syngman Rhee was elected President of Korea under the First Republic. A nationalist who had fought for Korean independence for decades, he considered his countrymen unready for democracy. He regarded the communist regime in the north to be a dangerous enemy, and pursued vigorous anti-communist measures. He considered political parties to be divisive, but established the Liberal Party – based largely on his own personal following. The party did not survive his fall. At the outset of the First Republic, there was a major battle between the President and the legislature, and the National Assembly moved to impose limits on the presidency. After intense controversy, the legislature approved direct election of the President. In 1954, the Liberal Party passed a constitutional amendment which removed the two-term limitation on the office of President, and did it without the required two-thirds majority. Faced with these actions, the fragmented opposition united into a single Democratic Party in 1955.

In the 1956 presidential election, the opposition reduced the Rhee majority, and defeated his vice-presidential candidate, Lee Ki Boong, who lost to Democrat Chang Myon. In the National Assembly elections of May 1958, the Democrats won more than a third of all the seats. Rhee and his supporters moved to crush opposition in the name of national security. His supporters resorted to blatantly rigging the March 1960 election. By the end of the decade, popular reaction was generating widespread demonstrations over intimidation. This set off major student demonstrations, followed by repression and violence. Rhee was forced to resign on 26 April, ending the First Republic. One legacy of the Rhee years was a strong presidency which could oversee the polity and manage the levers of civilian power.

The Second Republic

Rhee was succeeded by Ho Chung, his Foreign Minister. The National Assembly passed a constitutional amendment establishing a Cabinet system in place of the presidential system to prevent dictatorship and to regain its own prerogatives. The Second Republic emerged after the National Assembly elections of July 1960. The Democrats had over a two-thirds majority, but were united only in opposition against Rhee. This coalition disintegrated into factions, and Chang Myon became Premier in August 1960 by a narrow margin.[18] Within less than a year, however, civilian rule was overthrown by military coup. Although nominal civilian rule was restored, former generals continued to rule until the end of the term of Roh Tae Woo in early 1993.

Is military intrusion an aberration or a characteristic of Korean society?

Historically, the combination of periodic external invasion and occasional intra-peninsular war among various tribes or kingdoms contributed to the growth of a military elite. The *hwarang* warrior elite, consisting of young men, formed the core of the military forces during the Period of Three Kingdoms and cultivated loyalty, filial piety and martial courage. During periods of peace, civil and military officials occupied equal places in court. Several kingdoms and dynasties had been founded by military leaders, and strong generals were a continued potential for coups against the state.

Thus the military played an important, and sometimes dominant, role in the evolution of the Korean state. A long period of tranquillity after the Manchu invasions of the seventeenth century left the Korean military ill prepared to deal with domestic rebellions in the nineteenth century, or with foreign incursions from Russia or Japan. The traditional protector, China, was also unable to provide much aid.

During the Japanese interregnum, all military and police functions were absorbed by the empire, and the Korean forces were dissolved. Some Koreans (including Park Chung Hee) were trained in Japanese academies. After independence, the United States provided training for the core of the new ROK military. It proved to be inadequate in resisting the North Korean invasion of 25 June 1950 as well as in other wartime operations. With significant US advice and aid, the Korean armed forces were upgraded and the officer corps was rebuilt – with the elite coming from the Military Academy. As the Argentines call their Defence Ministry their 'Presidential Factory', the South Koreans can point to the Military Academy with similar irony. Presidents Park, Chun and Roh have all been products of the academy, giving the government a decidedly khaki colouring.

The military influence has contributed to political repression of opposition and dissidence, anti-communist ideology, pro-US defence and foreign policy, and conscription. To its credit, the military has overseen intense economic growth and gradually liberalized politics and law after the demise of Park Chung Hee. However, the prominence of the military in government has been a source of conflict in South Korea. Claiming to defend the nation against North Korean communism and its subversion domestically, the army has been reluctant to dismantle the National Security Law. The repression of the Kwangju uprising in 1980 blemished the military as a force which could ignore its national defence mission along the Demilitarized Zone to attack its own citizens.

The Third and Fourth Republics: economic and social transformation under Park Chung Hee

The military coup executed on 16 May 1961 toppled the civilian government. Martial law was proclaimed and remained in force until late 1963. The military junta banned political parties and demonstrations. Faced in part by US displeasure, the military government made plans for a transition back to civilian rule by mid-1963. During this time, Park Chung Hee emerged as the dominant general. He retired from his military position, and relied on the Democratic Republican Party to carry out authoritarian rule. During the Park regime, economic development and state strengthening proceeded rapidly. As in many developing countries, the peasantry lagged behind, and the rural population poured into the cities. To improve the rural sector, Park launched a programme of rural reconstruction in 1971 (the *Saemaul Undong*). The economy attained an average annual GNP growth rate of 10 per cent, and was energized by prudent government planning, protection, and guidance. Policies also included credits on favourable terms to preferred types of industry, technology imports, and after 1965, US and other foreign credits, Japanese direct investment, and encouragement of able entrepreneurs.

Politics under Park Chung Hee

Park's presidential rule lasted over a decade and a half, through the Third and Fourth Republics. His policies expanded state power to dominate society. The conventional wisdom was that a weak and divided South Korea was no match for the growing power of North Korea. He initiated negotiations with Japan over normalization, and was met by student opposition, causing him to declare martial law again in July 1964. Nonetheless, normalization was concluded in 1965. Wishing to confirm his firm alliance with the United States, he sent two army divisions to Vietnam. In preparation for the presidential election of 1967, the opposition parties merged to form the New Democratic Party (NDP), with Yun Po Sun as their unity candidate. Park won by a larger margin than in 1963, and the Democratic Republican Party (DRP) won 130 of 175 seats in National Assembly elections. In the 1971 election, Park Chung Hee won with 53 per cent of the vote over Kim Dae Jung, who won 45 per cent. Following the election, he began negotiations with North Korea on unification.

Park's insistence on election for a second term hinted at his forthcoming plan to occupy the presidency indefinitely. Sporadic demonstrations, open opposition, and major political crisis resulted. National Assembly elections were held in December – for the first time in five years. The NDP won by a margin of 1 per cent in the voting, although this was not reflected in National Assembly membership. Park again proclaimed martial law in October 1972. The government suspended the constitution, forbade political activity, and imposed press censorship. According to the government, the measures were necessary in order to have unity in the dialogue with the north – which has complete control over 'everything the people say and do'. Park also stated that the constitutional revision was needed to cope with the major transformation taking place in the international sphere – including PRC–US rapprochement, Sino-Japanese normalization, and the deterioration of the situation in Vietnam. His insecurity was increased by the withdrawal of the US Seventh Division with its 20,000 military personnel as part of the Nixon doctrine – despite strong opposition from Park.[19]

Park introduced the Yushin constitution, which allowed the President an indefinite number of six-year terms. He was chosen indirectly by the electoral college – the National Conference for Unification (NCU). The NCU barred members of political parties, and it had the power to nominate one-third of the membership to the National Assembly (seventy-three of 219 seats). The President could dissolve the National Assembly. In a referendum, 92 per cent of the voters approved the new constitution, which established the Fourth Republic. Park lifted martial law, and was elected President without opposition in December 1972. The National Assembly elections gave the opposition parties 42 per cent of vote versus 39 per cent for the DRP. The DRP won half the seats, with the opposition vote concentrated in cities.

In essence, Park was dictator for life. His government engineered the abduction of his main critic, Kim Dae Jung, from Tokyo in August 1973, an affair which strained Japanese–Korean relations. Park was shaken by the fall of Vietnam in 1975, and disturbed by Jimmy Carter's emphasis on human rights – two developments signalling the vulnerability of US-supported dictatorships. The alliance with the United States was looking less dependable. The National Assembly elections in December 1978 gave Kim Young Sam more elected seats than the DRP. There was growing widespread opposition to the Yushin constitution.

Opposition leader Kim Young Sam said he wanted to meet Kim Il Song to open talks on reunification. Acting the responsible statesman, he met US President Jimmy Carter on his visit to Korea, in the hope that the NDP popular base, unrest among students, official US favour, and initiating dialogue with North Korea might help him to challenge the Park government. He also counted on the political neutrality of the army.

The government instigated a court case against Kim Young Sam, alleging voting irregularities, and he was expelled by the National Assembly in October 1979. In protest, all opposition members resigned from the National Assembly. There followed violent demonstrations against the police by over 5,000 students and unemployed workers in Pusan, Kim Young Sam's political base. The turmoil spread to Masan, where anti-Rhee demonstrations had started. Park was losing control.

Crisis of the Fourth Republic

A new round of student demonstrations began in March 1980 in Seoul. Kim Jae Kyu, head of the Korean Central Intelligence Agency, tried unsuccessfully to arrange a meeting between Park and Yun Po Sun to restore political order. Fearing that he was about to be removed, Kim invited Park to a party. He assassinated Park and five others in the entourage. He was subsequently arrested by the army and executed.

Choi Kyu Ha became acting President under the constitution and proclaimed martial law. The NCU formally elected Choi President, and he later granted dissidents an amnesty. The investigation of the Park murder was carried out by Major General Chun Doo Hwan, head of the Defence Security Command, who was later to become President of the Fifth Republic. Chun took over the KCIA in April 1980. The military retained control over government, fearing the return of Kim Dae Jung to politics, renewed activity in North Korea to subvert the south, and more student demonstrations.

Violent demonstrations broke out in the south-west. The most disaffected region was Cholla, which included the city of Kwangju, where Kim Dae Jung's support was strongest. Students issued an ultimatum over the repeal of martial law. The government responded by imposing 'extraordinary' martial law on 17 May 1980. In Kwangju over 2,000 demonstrators called for an end to martial law. Troops were driven out of the city centre, and succeeded in retaking it only with high casualties. In the wake of the Kwangju incident, the government targeted the opposition leaders, removing them from politics. Censorship was reimposed, and over 170 journals were closed down. The government blamed Kim Dae Jung for stirring up the Kwangju incident, charged him with sedition, and sentenced him to death.

Transition to the Fifth Republic

The government of the Fifth Republic moved to recognize and accept the social changes, but not fast enough for expanding groups in business, management, the media, and education. Among the leadership there was a sense that Park Chung Hee had been successful in strengthening the South Korean state, but that he had held on to power too long. General Roh Tae Woo assumed control of the Defence Security Command. Political parties were legalized, and there was 'purification' of the media, with the dismissal of hundreds of journalists. President Choi resigned on 16 August, taking the blame for the crisis. Supporters of General Chun Doo Hwan started a movement to get him elected President now that he had retired from active duty. Members of the National Unification Conference nominated him, and on 27 August he was elected President of the Republic

A new constitution was introduced as an amendment to the Yushin constitution. It centralized power in the presidency. In a referendum held on 22 October 1980, it passed with 91.6 per cent approval, with 95.5 per cent voter turn-out. The new constitution established the Fifth Republic. On 24 January 1981 President Chun ended martial law, but reminded Koreans that the need for stability was as great as ever.

Three elections were held shortly after the end of martial law – for the electoral college, the presidency, and the National Assembly. These elections included several new political parties. Domestic politics remained stable during the first half of the Chun regime, but was punctuated with strikes and demonstrations. Outrage simmered over the Kwangju incident, and the military continued to repress dissidence. With parliamentary elections in 1986, there were renewed outbreaks of violence. In mid-1987, in order to restore peace and ensure that the 1988 Summer Olympics could take place in Seoul as planned, Chun's heir-apparent, Roh Tae Woo, announced a sweeping programme of reform, which was carried out in the autumn.

The Sixth Republic and the Roh presidency

The 1987 presidential election provided a peaceful transfer of power. It was the first direct popular vote in sixteen years, and set the stage for successful hosting of the Olympics. According to the government, the main priority was to eliminate past vestiges of authoritarian rule. The government moved to declare amnesties, and revised 1,673 laws and decrees to remove undemocratic provisions. Freedom of the press was expanded during the first several years of the Sixth Republic. Press censorship was abolished with the repeal of the Basic Press Law. Campus autonomy was introduced. Restrictions on overseas travel and restraints on artistic creativity were lifted. Intervention in the private sector of the economy was reduced. In 1990, the government ended or eased control of 576 categories of economic and business activities.

In early 1990, the government party and two opposition parties merged into the Democratic Liberal Party (DLP). The government claimed that this party merger ended the government stalemate, caused by a legislative logjam due to a minority party having to deal with three disparate opposition groups which had a combined majority in the National Assembly. The Roh reforms also increased autonomy at the local level. To increase the financial self-sufficiency of local governing bodies, a cigarette excise tax and other new taxes were created as additional sources of revenue for them, along with a system of grants-in-aid from the national government. Some authority and power of the national government also devolved to local governments.

Summary

The broad thrust of state development in South Korea has generally been positive in augmenting social development – from abject poverty, insecurity, and repression, towards moderate well-being, self-confidence and democracy. Although there are problems in the distribution of wealth and the stability of politics and democracy, the South Koreans have done well compared with most other nations in the developing world. From the perspective of early 1993, the turbulence of the South Korean Republic during the post-World War II decades culminated in successful development. It is premature to suggest that the future will be easy, but the Koreans have accomplished what most developing societies only imagine – a strong state, a dynamic economy, and steady movement towards democracy.

Stepping back from the historical narrative of state-building, we see a rough-and-tumble experiment in socio-political engineering at work. No single actor or regime was in full control, nor does each Republic represent a discrete set of trials and errors. Some elements of democracy were overlaid by the exigencies of authoritarian control throughout the period from 1948 to the present, but gradually – and occasionally with violence – these seeds have taken root, pushing aside overtly repressive elements of the state. We may be witnessing the rapid growth of a healthy democratic seedling in South Korea which may develop into a sturdy plant in the future. The plant metaphor should not obscure the active political process of trial and error conducted by governments in Seoul. Confrontations between government and student dissidents were trials of countervailing force representing different ideals, or at least contradicting visions, of the Korean state. Out of these encounters has emerged a political system still evolving, but one which has solved several severe problems of a developing country under siege.

2   The institutions of government

Foundations of the modern Korean state

Strengthening the Korean state has been the primary goal of political, military, and economic institution-building. But US and UN sponsorship of South Korea has pressured government to be more accountable and amenable to liberal democratic pressures than was the case in North Korea, where the drive to hegemony has had few external inhibitions. The impact of outside pressures should not be exaggerated, but South Korean dependence on co-operative relations in trade and defence has made the state responsive to non-Korean demands. An educated sector – many having had an education abroad, or under instructors with a foreign education – was reinforced with a fairly open system of information.[1]

At the constitutional level, Syngman Rhee established the national presidency at the centre of the South Korean state when he assembled the levers of state power during the First Republic. The transformative potential of the South Korean Republic was enhanced during the regime of Park Chung Hee. For much of the post-World War II period, the presidency has held the commanding heights of the South Korean state. Under Park, presidential power was based on the army and the security apparatus – including the KCIA. As Han Sung-Joo has written: 'What the state has exercised in an effective way is a *negative* control aimed at preventing antigovernment activities rather than a *positive* control of the totalitarian type designed to elicit explicit and total support for the government in power.'[2] A slow process of shifting coercive control from the military to the civilian administrative and party apparatus also occurred from the late Third Republic to the Sixth.

This chapter examines some of the institutions which have contributed to the concentration of power in the Korean state. An important general characteristic of the modern state is that there must be rudimentary manifestations of administrative, executive, and coercive/defensive institutions prior to democratization. These institutions are necessary to mobilize human and material resources, set authoritative priorities, and maintain political and social order. Smaller communities may be able to pursue immediate democracy but, perhaps, at the expense of rapid modernization. The scale of the modern state requires impersonal institutions which tend to negate – or interfere with – individual freedom. Without modern rational organization, the modernization of other sectors of society cannot be accomplished.

Background

Korea's modern political evolution can be explained by the continuing attempt to build a strong state.[3] The modern nation state emerged from the European Renaissance and Reformation, when sacred and secular realms separated. The development of the European multi-state system and the competitive expansion of states into the non-Western world brought continents into the Europe-initiated framework. Dynastic and religious conflict expanded into a global setting as new technology and the commercial dynamism of capitalism enabled and motivated vast new opportunities for risk and gain.

North-east Asia was one of the last areas to be subjected to European imperialism – until the weakness of the Chinese Empire was well evident. The kingdom of Korea initially confronted the Western challenge, but was pressured more by Russia and growing Japanese expansionism. Korea had survived as a nominal vassal of China for centuries, and the weakening of the Qing empire left it vulnerable to pressures from Japan and other expansionist states.

Pre-modern nationalism had emerged early on the Korean peninsula. A common language, significant cultural achievements (including the first development of movable type printing in the world), and well defined territoriality contributed to a strong sense of national identity among the Korean people. This nationalism was periodically tested as Chinese, central Asian, and Japanese invaders tried to dominate the peninsula. Endemic Korean factionalism usually prevented a unified response, but invasion and occupation never led to the extinction of Korean nationalism.

From 1895 to 1910 the Japanese grip on Korea tightened, until it became a colony under a Japanese governor-general. From 1910 to 1945, Korea was a nation without a state. It lacked sovereignty until 1945, but division into two halves left it an international ward of the major powers. Initially, the peninsula's strategic position in the Cold War was underestimated by the United States, but the Korean War placed the country at the centre of attention in East Asia. During and after the war, American aid helped to establish a viable economy and polity in the south, and to provide stability and security on a peninsula which had been a bridge between Japan and continental Asia. South Koreans and Americans had a common interest in building a stable, strong and prosperous country to resist North Korea and to offer a non-communist alternative to Koreans. It was far from the ideal of an independent and unified Korea that several generations of nationalists had hoped to establish, but it was more open than the totalitarian regime in the north.

The nearly four decades since the war's end for South Koreans witnessed the phenomenal growth of political, economic, and military strength. Within the inconclusive legacy of the 1953 armistice, South Korea has become one of the world's most dynamic economies, and is taking a lead in the reunification of the peninsula. This could not have happened without the continuous application and extension of force and leadership. Rather than see it as a linear growth of force, Han Sung-Joo's notion of a cycle of authoritarianism in Korean politics is helpful.[4] The First and Second Republics represented the first full cycle of power, with Rhee emerging as dictator upon consolidation of his power as President. Upon his downfall, the backlash against dictatorship swung towards free-for-all democracy, resulting in legislative hamstringing of the executive branch of government. The second cycle occurred with the Third and Fourth Republics of Park Chung Hee, which consolidated dictatorship even more than Rhee had accomplished – adding the military reinforcement to presidential power. The undoing of the Park regime came with his assassination, followed again by tendencies towards the unravelling not only of military dictatorship but of the South Korean state itself. There was a brief period of hope of democratic release, but this was closed when Chun Doo Hwan and his junta seized power and set up the Fifth Republic.

The concept of a cycle, however, implies a return to the starting point and a recurrence of past patterns. Perhaps 'spiral' is more accurate, if the metaphor conveys the learning that occurs from past mistakes and setbacks. A cycle represents a trap of doomed repetition – which has not been the case with South Korea. Learning from past mistakes of overconcentration of power, the Chun constitution of the Fifth Republic in 1981 limited the President to a single seven-year term. This promised a more peaceful transfer of power than had occurred in previous Republics. It also addressed the concern that presidential centralization of power had led to major abuses. A limited term was a compromise between those who wanted legislative supremacy with a Cabinet system, and those who felt that a strong President was needed to carry on the struggle for economic development and the potential battle with North Korea.

Nevertheless, a third cycle of authoritarianism appeared likely when the

Chun regime faced increasing popular opposition in the 1986 legislative elections. Popular demonstrations threatened peaceful achievement of the 1988 Summer Olympics. Confronting a major state crisis, Chun's successor Roh Tae Woo stepped in and announced a programme of major reforms, culminating in a new constitution and his election as President in the new Sixth Republic. Roh and his advisers had learned from the cycle of authoritarianism. Unless concessions were made to the growing demands for democracy, the polarization of society would accelerate and destroy the existing political system.

The introduction of major political reforms in June 1987 met several key demands of the opposition, and allowed the regime a second chance to continue its programmes and policies with a minimum of interruption – if it could win the election of December 1987. The reforms were subsequently implemented, the new constitution was approved, and Roh Tae Woo won the December 1987 election for the presidency. While full democracy remained to be implemented, even holding the presidential election on schedule was a major step forward towards constitutional democracy. A number of democratic reforms occurred during the Roh administration, culminating in the peaceful transition to civilian government under Kim Young Sam in early 1993. The prognosis towards further institutionalization of democracy is promising.

State-building in South Korea

The Korean state will remain incomplete as long as the Korean peninsula is divided, but within the limitations of this division, Seoul has pursued four main avenues of state-building over the past decades:

Political reform The South Korean Republic began as a weak and besieged nation – a condition which prompted the autocratic South Korean presidents to pursue the centralization of power. This generated counter-movements from both organized and unorganized opposition – i.e. opposition parties as well as student dissidents (who have practically institutionalized their anti-government protests). The government confronted periodic crisis by major constitutional revision which involved a modest redistribution of power to the civilian sector after the demise of Park Chung Hee.

From the beginning, Syngman Rhee had been concerned primarily with building a strong state through the consolidation of loyal civilian power. With Park Chung Hee, the military gained control over the state. With help from a Western-educated elite, he generated parts of a developmental state which maintained its security against domestic opponents and foreign (especially North Korean) threats. Chun Doo Hwan reconstituted the South Korean state on the foundations established by Park, but recognized that the military had to withdraw from the centre. The Kwangju affair tainted the legitimacy of the Fifth Republic, but the principles of civilian rule and limited presidential tenure were carried further with Roh Tae Woo in the Sixth Republic.

The pattern of development can be characterized as (1) building a strong state, (2) enhancing economic growth with industrialization and export-led development, (3) gradually placing constitutional limits on government and, in the Sixth Republic, (4) broadening democracy, including access to power by a wider range of political groups with increased disengagement of the military from political power. Unlike numerous new nations, where independence brought immediate democratic institutions, followed by subsequent entrenchment of autocracy, South Korea has had only brief experiences with democracy – specifically in the wake of the overthrow of Syngman Rhee. Those democratic institutions did not take hold, and incremental evolution has followed. The result has been that, during much of modern Korean development, the prospects for democracy have seemed dim. However, viewed over several decades, the movement towards pluralism, multi-party competition, expanding freedoms, and the rule of law has been slow and steady. The international environment of Korea has played a part in this movement.

Diplomacy A modern state requires acceptance by other established states. For over a century, Korea has been tossed by the waves of international disputes and conflicts. Since 1950, South Korean governments have been increasingly skilful in adapting to the international environment and utilizing it to reinforce state-building policies. The involvement of the United States in the Korean War and subsequent defence assistance made South Korea an immediate client. The end of the Vietnam War in 1975, and America's subsequent re-evaluation of its role in the Pacific region, forced South Korea to plan for the day when the US presence would be reduced. Simultaneously, Japan has emerged as an economic superpower rivalling the United States, and has been providing more technology and investment capital for the Asian region. Although the United States continued to provide a major market for South Korean products, diversification into the developing world has been a key strategy. When the PRC embarked on the post-Maoist economic reforms, the South Koreans recognized an opportunity, and have made major penetrations of the Chinese market. They concluded the normalization of diplomatic relations to further cement the economic relationship on 24 August 1992 – to the chagrin of their long-time Taiwan allies.

The collapse of communism in Eastern Europe and the Soviet Union has given Seoul a new range of opportunities. Large projects have been undertaken in the former Soviet bloc – and even in Vietnam. In September 1990, Gorbachev shocked the world by normalizing relations with the Republic of Korea. The extraordinary train of events, beginning with the diplomacy of hosting the 1988 Summer Olympics in Seoul, began in the Park regime, when South Korea pursued diplomatic relations with a range of non-aligned countries. All these factors have contributed to the international acceptance of South Korea, and diminished the appeal of Pyongyang as a viable alternative.

Economic development The modern state requires an industrial base to provide the material goods for economic needs. South Korea has concentrated its meagre resources on transforming the war-torn agrarian society into a modern industrial economy. Not only has growth occurred, but so has far-reaching restructuring of society and the economy. The South Koreans have successfully mastered many of the techniques of the industrial economy and are now moving rapidly towards post-industrial society, where a preponderant portion of the labour force is engaged in service and knowledge sectors.

Without escape from poverty, the modern state may lack adequate resources for its activities, and must rely on the goodwill of patrons or the exigencies of international politics. Industrialization has been a primary vehicle for enriching modern states. Creating a manufacturing base is more effective than external military expansion – which often generates opposition from jealous rivals and the target peoples of imperialism.

Park Chung Hee understood the importance of economic development as the most effective means of combating the influence and strength of North Korea in the Third World. With economic growth, the security of the Republic was also enhanced. It also enabled South Korea to deal with Japan and the United States from positions of industrializing success rather than as an aid supplicant. Economic success further helped South Korea to display its new strength to the world in the Asian Games (1986) and Olympics in 1988. Both became occasions for pursuing the diplomacy of *Nordpolitik*.

Military modernization Defence of national territory is a primary purpose of the state. The Chinese ideograph for state, *guo* (*guk* in Korean), consists of three radicals or elements which convey the ancient meaning: a fortress wall, weapon, and people. From earliest times, the state has required a military component. The traditional Korean state evolved in response to war and invasions. The *hwarang* were aristocratic warriors who served the central court, in contrast to the Japanese samurai, whose loyalty was to feudal lords. Civil and military officials in the last dynasty, the Yi, were of roughly equal status. While Confucianism had great impact on Korea's intellectual development, it did not reduce the status of the military, as it did in China. Nevertheless, the Koreans lost their independence to Japan in part because their military forces were still no match for the Meiji expansionists.

After World War II, the North and South Koreans created new armies, which went to war against each other in 1950. With American assistance and training, the ROK army became a modern fighting force. In 1961, seeing the Republic falling into turmoil, the soldiers seized power – hoping to turn it into a country capable of resisting the north. A weak Republic would invite a second invasion if Kim Il Song thought he could unite the peninsula by force. These perceptions of North Korean threat have underlined the importance of national defence for the past four decades. For South Korea this has required a state of war readiness not unlike that of Israel. However, where Israel faces an implacable enemy defined by religion and culture, South Korea's enemy is a part of the same nationality, but of a very different ideology.

Until detente with the Soviet Union, South Korea was in a condition of semi-war – preparing for conventional conflict against North Korean attack with modern weapons and training. Seoul relied on the presence of US forces for moral support and as a guarantee of American commitment to the sovereignty of South Korea. The transfer of US weapons and military technology was also intended to offset the arms that North Korea received from its Soviet and Chinese patrons. South Korean regimes have faced threats of domestic subversion – partly from North Korea, which seeks opportunities to weaken the regime, and from a frequently alienated student population. The massive student demonstrations of the past, however, have declined in the Sixth Republic as various reforms and external developments have eroded the issues of discontent. These events include domestic democratic improvement, the decline of the North Korean threat, the disintegration of communism, and continued economic growth.

Government structure – weak *v.* strong institutions

Centuries of pre-modern state development under the Yi monarchy produced a relatively strong Korean state prior to the mid-nineteenth-century government control over society.[5] Today, a major distinction between states lies not in the form of their institutions, but in the degree to which government actually governs. South Korea has overcome a major weakness of many developing states in state-building success. While the international arena has been a crucial influence on South Korea, it does not determine the fate of the state. In the domestic arena, the government has tried to maximize its autonomy. According to Joel Migdal, 'The major struggles in many societies, especially those with fairly new states, are struggles over who has the right and ability to make the countless rules that guide people's social behaviour.'[6] There is fundamental conflict over which organs in society – state or other organizations – should make these rules. These struggles are not over *which* laws, but over the sovereign power to make laws. They are struggles over whether the state will be able to displace other organizations in society that make rules against the wishes and goals of state leaders. The purpose for which leaders employ the state apparatus is to seek predominance through binding rules. Pre-eminence is not permanent, and accommodation is usually necessary. This struggle for predominance and the accompanying accommodations are the bedrock of politics in the Third World. The desire for the strong state partly explains the popularity of socialism among developing countries, which has been due to the belief that it delivers centralization and rapid industrialization as it seemed to do in Russia and China.

The six Republics of South Korea have been experiments in constitution writing and state renewal. Each constitution has attempted to structure relations between government and society in a way permitting a semblance of democracy, while building a political order to sustain stability. Both the 1972 Yushin constitution and the 1980 Fifth Republic constitution were pushed through by military leaders under martial law, and under bans on activities by political parties. President Chun failed to revise the constitution in 1987 to introduce a Cabinet system. Had he succeeded, his chances of retaining power might have increased dramatically.

The constitution of the Fifth Republic was more liberal than the Yushin constitution of Park Chung Hee, but its supplementary provisions negated the rest of the document. Article 51 presented no serious obstacle to prolonged emergency rule by the President, since emergency rule could be lifted only with the concurrence of a majority of the total members of the National Assembly. According to Article 57(1) the President had the right to dissolve the National Assembly, but only after a year had passed since its formation. In the event of dissolution, general elections had to be held within sixty days.

Article 66 provided for an Advisory Council on State Affairs. It was speculated that this could be the vehicle by which Chun Doo Hwan would have access to decision-making when his term was over. The article stipulated that:

1 An Advisory Council on State Affairs, composed of elder statesmen, may be established to advise the President on important affairs of state.
2 The outgoing President shall become the Chairman of the Advisory Council on State Affairs. In the absence of an outgoing President, the President shall appoint the Chairman.
3 The organization, function and other necessary matters pertaining to the Advisory Council on State Affairs shall be determined by law.

This last clause left open the function of the council which could make it a significant power. The Constitutional Committee (Articles 112–14) had the power to dissolve parties, and decide on the constitutionality of laws. Its nine members were appointed by the President. Other articles of the constitution also served to strengthen the central government. The US influence, with the tripartite division of powers, has much been in evidence, but, reflecting the vulnerability of the state, emergency powers have also been vested in the presidency.

Liquidation of the legacy of the Fifth Republic

As he approached assumption of state leadership in mid-1987, Roh Tae Woo faced a key constitutional problem: to forge a new constitutional order which would move the country away from the authoritarian heritage of Rhee, Park and Chun. Roh's 'June 29 Declaration' announced the intention of democratization, and laid the foundation for the Sixth Republic. Yet he could not abandon the cumulative achievements of the previous Republics. Syngman Rhee had established the parameters of the sovereign Republic with an identity distinct from that of North Korea. Park Chung Hee had set the course for successful economic development, and Chun Doo Hwan moved towards guided constitutional democracy. Since the early 1960s, the army had been a major force in the South Korean state, and its return to the barracks was a precondition of full democracy. Roh's own career had been in the military, and his close association with Chun seemed to disqualify him from civilian leadership. By promising democratic reforms in his declarations, he held out the promise of both controlling the military and moving the country towards liberalization.

After the legislative elections in April 1988, when the opposition parties gained a majority in the National Assembly, they pressed for settlement of issues left over from the Fifth Republic. Discussions were aimed at compensation for victims of the Kwangju incident and the revision of unpopular laws from the Fifth Republic. The government party, the Democratic Justice Party (DJP), opposed political revenge and any political punishment not in accord with legal procedure. The stress on legality was also to protect many party members who had been officials in the previous Republic. The opposition wanted key figures from the Fifth Republic to be removed from their official posts – a demand strenuously rejected by the DJP. A major issue was the format of testimony by ex-Presidents Choi Kyu Ha and Chun Doo Hwan. The DJP wanted closed-door hearings by a special commission.[7]

Stalemate between the DJP and opposition increased. The three opposition leaders, in a rare united front, agreed to seek the ousting of the Roh government unless democratic reforms and Fifth Republic legacy liquidation were completed by the end of the year. The three leaders, Kim Dae Jung, Kim Young Sam and Kim Jong Pil, identified six 'core leaders' to be punished in connection with the rise of Chun Doo Hwan to power. They also called for the freeing of hundreds of dissidents who had been 'unjustifiably' arrested. Another demand was revising the National Security Law and the law governing the Agency for National Security Planning. The three opposition Kims demanded that the government should apologize to the people, accept responsibility for the Kwangju civil uprising and enact a law to compensate the victims. Unless it did so, the opposition would block the passage of next year's budget. With this opposition co-ordination of its strategy, the Roh government faced a major challenge.[8]

The opposition parties insisted that settlement of the Fifth Republic issues must precede their co-operation with the government. However, this threatened to lead to government stalemate if no progress was made. Furthermore, it was a thinly disguised struggle between the executive and legislative branches of government. The opposition targeted a close associate of President Roh, Representative Chong Ho-yong, for expulsion from the National Assembly. They held him responsible for the military suppression of the 1980 Kwangju uprising as commander of the Special Warfare Command. These troops had been mobilized in the fierce quelling of the demonstrations. Chong had helped Roh become President and was an important figure in the DJP.[9]

Ten days later, a DJP resolution indicated that no progress had been made on the issue in over a year of negotiation. Several inter-party conferences failed to 'liquidate the Fifth Republic irregularities'. On 15 December 1989, President Roh and the chief opposition party leaders met and hammered out an agreement to settle the outstanding issues. The agreement worked out a compromise on Kwangju, the budget, political prisoners, labour discord, the testimony of former presidents, and the question of lawmaker Chong Ho-yong.[10]

Government and opposition were anxious to put the protracted controversy behind them. Former President Chun had been living in a temple near Mount Sorak, in the eastern part of South Korea, since 1988. He was to testify before the National Assembly concerning his seven years of rule and how he came to power on 12 December 1979. While Roh Tae Woo was concerned about the impact his testimony would have on the presidency, especially regarding the legal relationship between the executive and legislative branches, the party was uneasy over the impact his replies would have on the political world. Chun had reportedly supplied large sums of money during the DJP campaign to elect Roh President in December 1987, and there was also an allegation that large amounts had been funnelled into the opposition camp to split it. The National Assembly was most interested in who had issued the order to fire at Kwangju in 1980.[11]

In order to achieve political stability, former President Chun and President Roh were required to 'open the books' on the Fifth Republic – an act which few if any democracies had experienced. On 3 January 1990, following Chun's testimony, Roh declared the conclusion of the Fifth Republic issues, as he promised to carry out the other agreements of 15 December. The testimony of the ex-President both fascinated and disappointed millions of Koreans who watched it on television.[12] His answers on Kwangju were regarded as self-serving when he claimed that the troops had fired in self-defence. On political funds, he said that 'No ruler in the world reveals how he spent his political funds after leaving office.' The testimony angered the public and many opposition members, but his appearance had conformed to the letter of the agreement, and many were eager to put the past behind and tackle the challenges facing the country.

If the opposition had wanted to shatter those who had participated in the government of the Fifth Republic, it was disappointed. A number of Chun's relatives were prosecuted for corruption and abuse of power, and some officials were removed.[13] In January 1990, the government party regrouped and formed a coalition with two opposition parties to form the Democratic Liberal Party – a mega-party coalition consisting of the former DJP and the opposition parties of Kim Young Sam and Kim Chong Pil. By the end of 1990, political analysts were seeing signs of a possible alliance between Fifth and Sixth Republic politicians – including former President Chun.[14]

The controversy over the Fifth Republic and its legacy went to the centre of the legitimacy claims of the Sixth Republic. The connections between Chun and Roh were personal and political. The question for Koreans was whether a leadership so closely linked with the authoritarianism of Chun, which had been the target of uprisings and demonstrations, could really liberalize the political system. By pushing to 'liquidate the Fifth Republic legacies' the opposition may have won a Pyrrhic victory. It had forced the ex-President to testify to the National Assembly and be humiliated by accusations, but it had also convinced the government that its own authority would never be secure as long as it was a minority. Nor would it be able to govern effectively as long as opposition parties held the balance of power. From its perspective, the government needed more authority – but without authoritarianism. The result was a coalition of the government and two opposition parties – the Democratic Liberal Party (DLP).

Constitutional reform in the Sixth Republic: the presidency and local government

The heart and brains of the South Korean Republic has been the presidency. When it weakened under the Second and after the Fourth Republics, the country fell into turmoil, resulting in military intervention. As the command centre of the Korean ship of state, the presidency has been the object of ambitions as well as constitutional reform.

Under the constitution of the Sixth Republic, the President represents the state and heads the executive branch of government. He has the responsibility and the duty to safeguard the independence, territorial integrity and continuity of the state and constitution. It is also his duty to pursue the peaceful reunification of Korea. He is the chief of the armed forces and may proclaim martial law and grant amnesty. By law the President is directly elected by universal suffrage in an equal, direct and secret ballot. His term of office is five years, and he cannot be re-elected.

The presidential office has a number of agencies to assist the President in his tasks. The Presidential Secretariat is run by a secretary-general who has Cabinet rank, and has seven senior secretaries who are in charge of protocol, political affairs, the economy, civil affairs, public information, general affairs and administration. The Board of Audit and Inspection inspects the revenue and expenditure of the government and related agencies, and reports to the President and National Assembly.

The former Korean Central Intelligence Agency was renamed the Agency for National Security Planning in 1981, in part because of its director's part in the Park Chung Hee assassination and partly because it was linked with the repression of dissent. It now gathers information on espionage and subversive activities, and co-ordinates national security and intelligence-gathering activities. The President heads the eight-member National Security Council, which considers diplomatic, military and domestic policies related to national security before they are deliberated in the State Council. The President also consults the Advisory Council on Democratic and Peaceful Unification, which was established in 1981 and reorganized in 1988. The Twenty-first Century Committee has a five-year term of operation and is preparing policy recommendations for Korea in the next century. The National Economic Advisory Council advises the President on policies to develop the national economy.

For Korea, there have been two major dilemmas for democratic reform. The first is that a country facing rapid economic, political, and diplomatic change needs strong and flexible leadership. A powerful presidency, however, always brings the possibility of dictatorship unless balanced by other institutions. The National Assembly has been too fragmented by factions and regional interests to form much of a counterweight, especially after the amalgamation of the government and two opposition parties as the DLP. Nor does the judiciary carry much weight against the executive branch. In frustration over presidential autocracy, many citizens have taken to the streets on occasion, or have sought solace in regional opposition to Seoul.

The second dilemma has been the rule of law. Without the rule of law, democracy may wither on the vine as rights and freedoms are withheld or reduced by centralizing government. Until the Sixth Republic, many laws were highly restrictive, and aimed at protecting national security. Under President Roh, a number of draconian laws were liberalized. However, due in part to the influence of the Confucian heritage, the 'rule of man' has had an importance at least equal to the 'rule of law.' Choosing the right men for government – men who are competent and loyal – remains a core technique in Confucian statecraft in Korea. Furthermore, men who are related by blood or marriage – part of the extended family – may have a higher claim on presidential patronage than the merely competent.

A case in point is former first Minister of State Park Chul-un, who emerged as a man of considerable power in the ruling circle. Park is related by marriage to President Roh and was being groomed as Roh's successor for the next election. Park was at the centre of Roh's *Nordpolitik* and reunification efforts. By late 1989, there were reports of a 'Stop Park' movement within the party. He had allegedly interfered in the 26 April 1988 elections to prevent key Fifth Republic figures from getting party endorsement. DJP members claimed that his activities had lost votes in the election. There was also discontent over his 'one-man diplomacy' in Eastern Europe.[15]

Another contender at the top has been Kim Pok-tong, a Military Academy classmate of Roh, and brother-in-law to the President. He failed to run in the 1989 election because of Roh's campaign pledge to have 'no presidential relatives in government'[16] – a pledge made in response to the scandals of the Chun Doo Hwan family. The example of crass nepotism in North Korea's 'Kim dynasty' has also induced the south to avoid the political involvement of family members. To reduce popular suspicions, the President has tried to run a more open government. In a press conference on 10 January 1990, he dismissed speculation that he would be succeeded by either Kim Bok-tong or Park Chul-un. He also engaged in frequent dialogue with the major opposition leaders. Roh met Kim Dae Jung the following day and acceded to the proposal that the opposition parties should play a role in opening the dialogue with North Korea.[17]

By the first half of his five-year presidency, Roh Tae Woo had achieved significant progress in his promised reforms, but his decision to renege on a promise to hold a referendum on his performance was roundly criticized. Despite numerous labour–management disputes and continued street demonstrations by student activists, the economy was growing at a rate of 12.1 per cent during his first year in office. In legal reform, his government modified laws, procedures and practices considered detrimental to democratization. The government also liberalized restrictions on overseas travel, and selectively allowed more information about North Korea to be published. With summit diplomacy, Roh Tae Woo enhanced relations with Japan and the United States. The policy of *Nordpolitik* saw normalization of relations between the countries of Eastern Europe and Seoul. The government also addressed welfare issues, with a minimum wage system introduced in 1988, and medical insurance that covered the entire population by July 1989.[18]

The end of 1989 saw the liquidation of the vestiges of Fifth Republic authoritarianism, and implementation of the northern policy (*Nordpolitik*). The 29 June 1987 Eight Point Declaration[19] led to the first direct presidential elections for sixteen years, and to subsequent shifts from authoritarian rule to democracy. His decision to form the DLP, which was designed to create a more stable regime, led to further confrontation as the remaining opposition, chiefly Kim Dae Jung, boycotted the National Assembly.

The Cabinet system

Another issue faced by the Sixth Republic was the debate over constitutional revision to introduce a parliamentary Cabinet system. The issue has recurred throughout South Korean history, as powerful Presidents have resorted to authoritarian rule, and critics have called for a trimming of their power.[20] Kim Young Sam called for a Cabinet form of government during the rule of Chun Doo Hwan, in large part to limit the scope of presidential power. He proposed a figurehead President, with real power vested in the Prime Minister. The military would be less attracted to intervention, and a retired general might even occupy the presidency.[21]

Soon after the formation of the DLP, its leaders began discussing a dual system – a compromise between the presidential and Cabinet systems.

Power would be divided; in times of crisis, the system would shift to dominant presidential authority, and in normal times, the Cabinet would exercise administrative power, answerable to the National Assembly. The party leadership had the dual executive system of France as their model.[22] The Cabinet scheme was once considered by Chun Doo Hwan as a way to stay in power after his single seven-year term had expired, but his desire to rewrite the constitution was thwarted by the massive demonstrations of June 1987.

The 1987 presidential election demonstrated other weaknesses of a system which gives considerable power to the chief executive by reinforcing the 'winner-take-all' mentality. The National Assembly remained an institution which could interfere with executive initiatives when an opposition majority existed. A Cabinet system, in contrast, would allow parties in the Assembly a greater share in national governance. Cabinet government also has the merit of making political succession less of a crisis, since there could be greater collegiality and equality between the Prime Minister and Cabinet members (when a single party is in control), and a wider pool of talent is theoretically trained and prepared for selecting the head of government.

During the Chun presidency, a Cabinet system was advocated as a means of protecting DJP power in the face of a presidential race certain to go against it. If the opposition parties had presented a united front, with a single candidate, they most probably would have won the election of 1987. The Chun government opposed a direct presidential election system, and demanded that the opposition should either accept the Cabinet system or keep the existing indirect presidential election system. The opposition wanted the direct presidential system, hoping it would field a single candidate and win. As it happened, Kim Young Sam and Kim Dae Jung could not agree on which would be the single candidate, with the result that they ran against each other, and split the opposition vote (with Kim Jong Pil as the third major opposition candidate) – handing victory to Roh Tae Woo and the DJP. By failing to unite in the 1987 election, the opposition parties had snatched defeat from the jaws of victory.

The 1990 proposal for a Cabinet system too closely resembled the proposal of the Chun regime in 1987 (which was more an option than a formal proposal). The Party for Peace and Democracy (PPD) of Kim Dae Jung opposed it as an attempt to maintain a DLP monopoly of power. He called the notion of political restructuring a reversion to the politics of the Fourth and Fifth Republics: 'The ultimate goal of this political re-structuring was to revise the constitution for the Cabinet system, and through this system, to enable President Roh to stay in power, taking charge of military, diplomatic, security, and unification affairs single-handed.'[23] Subsequently, he modified this position, saying that the present National Assembly had been elected under the presidential system of 1987, and it would be premature to modify it. Decades of military rule, he claimed, made it necessary for a completely civilian President (not a general turned politician like Roh) to establish the precedent of civilian control over the military, and then to introduce a Cabinet system.

Regarding civilian control over the military, some argued that a President with a military background, at least under present circumstances, was better suited to keep the military from reasserting itself in politics. The constitution of the Sixth Republic provided for the presidential form of government, with the Cabinet assisting the President – a modified adaptation of US precedent. Cabinets were shuffled and reshuffled according to the needs of the executive office, and not as a reflection of changing political realities in the legislature. The DLP was more stable than a coalition of the three parties which had joined to form it, and the Cabinet system would provide top positions for the faction leaders.

The ruling DLP launched a trial balloon on constitutional revision soon after its formation. The party platform called for full parliamentary democracy 'in which the National Assembly and the Cabinet shouldered responsibilities together'. The proposed change in constitution was part of the plan for intra-party consensus, especially in the post-Roh era, starting in 1993. The power structure was to represent the three major wings of the DLP, with Kim Young Sam in command. The plan addressed three centres of power: the Republic presidency, the office of Prime Minister, and the DLP party presidency.[24] Popular and press response to the proposal was not positive. *The Korea Times* editorialized that it was a result of the need of Kim Young Sam and Kim Jong Pil to 'assuage skepticism over their true motivation for their joining in the ruling camp'.[25] The Seoul *Hangyore Sinmun* was even more critical:

> It is clear that the politicians are manoeuvering for the DLP's prolonged stay in power by way of a constitutional revision in favor of a cabinet responsibility system. They have differences in views on a cabinet responsibility system to a certain degree. However, they are only differences in political interests among factions.[26]

Within a few months, the DLP was distancing itself from the proposal. Kim Young Sam, chairman of the party, stated that the constitution could be changed only with the support of the people.[27] The proposal was debated in a special session of the National Assembly. Kim Jong Pil's supporters called for Cabinet government, while Kim Dae Jung's PPD saw the plan as a DLP move to retain control with power and money.[28] The credibility of the proposal was further undermined in October with publication of a 'secret agreement' on a constitutional amendment for a Cabinet government. This was signed on 6 May 1990, by Roh Tae Woo, Kim Young Sam and Kim Jong Pil, shortly before the two opposition leaders joined the DLP.[29] Kim Dae Jung suggested a constitutional amendment to establish a vice-president. His proposal was reiterated at the PPD's third anniversary. He also suggested run-off elections for the next National Assembly. Both measures would probably help consolidate the opposition's unity.[30]

Joining with the DLP had not assured Kim Young Sam as clear a road to the presidency as he may have hoped. He and his followers, who had joined the 'mega-party', found themselves in competition with old members of the DJP, who remained the core of the new coalition. Possibly to indicate that he had other options, he joined in a five-point agreement with his old ally/opponent Kim Dae Jung in April 1990 to end the 'chronic confrontation between their home regions, Cholla and Kyongsang'. The two agreed to maintain the current election system of one lawmaker from each district. They also agreed to co-operate on other issues as well.[31]

Kim Dae Jung proposed that a vice-president be added to the executive branch in order to dilute presidential power and combat provincialism. Since his own appeal had been limited to the south-west region of the country, it would help his own presidential chances to have a running mate from another region. It was speculated that he had made this suggestion with his next presidential campaign in mind, when he could name Yi Ki-taek, leader of the splinter Democratic Party as running mate. This could help the chances of a merger between the two opposition parties. The DLP rejected the Kim proposal, saying it would be the same as a dual executive system (President and Prime Minister.) Moreover, the DLP floor leader, Kim Tong-yong, said that Kim Dae Jung had opposed a vice-presidency during negotiations on revising the constitution in 1987. He added that constitutional revision required a resolution of the National Assembly, and it was improper for Kim Dae Jung, whose entire party had resigned from the Assembly, to propose such a revision. He should rejoin the National Assembly and then discuss revisions.[32]

Although some quarters wanted a Cabinet system to implement a more democratic polity, others argued that such a move would be premature. In 1987, direct presidential elections had been restored after a hiatus of sixteen years, and the public was looking forward to further campaigns of high-profile individuals such as Kim Young Sam and Kim Dae Jung. A Cabinet system would short-circuit this. Also, there was the sense that it was 'un-Korean' and out of tune with Korea's Confucian culture and tradition of centralized authority. The last time a Cabinet government had been installed was in 1960, under Chang Myon, and it was overthrown after less than a year by a military coup. Nevertheless, there were reports of a presidency with reduced powers and a Prime Minister responsible to the National Assembly. Kim Jong Pil, who had served as Prime Minister, argued that the current system needed overhauling. Many people wanted a government more responsive than the strong presidency could provide. Even Kim Dae Jung opposed the dual system of power-sharing between President and Prime Minister, stating that it would tempt the military to intervene against an assertive Parliament.[33]

During the first year of the Sixth Republic, the President inaugurated a Committee on Administrative Reform (chaired by former Prime Minister Shin Hyun Hwack). Although the committee was unable to make recommendations on either the presidency or the office of Prime Minister, it did suggest changes in the Agency for National Security Planning, and in the area of Ministry consolidation. A call for the abolition of the Sports Ministry set off a reaction from the formidable sports lobby in the country.[34]

The debate over a strong presidency *v.* Cabinet system, or the compromise on a 'dual executive', reflected the struggle for power under way in the Sixth Republic. The presidency has been the paramount prize in South Korean politics, and the devaluation of the prize was a very sensitive issue. Constitutional reforms in 1987 opened up the office to numerous contenders, who tried to increase their chances of winning the 1992 election. In 1990, with the formation of the DLP, Kim Young Sam was brought closer to the prize. Previous Presidents had pushed through constitutional revisions in order to retain their power, and were successful under conditions of martial law. Chun had failed in 1987, in part because he could not return to more direct military rule without seriously compromising the promise of open elections and risking the high national penalty of calling off the Olympics. Roh Tae Woo has taken the road of democratization, and any return to the old ways of military authoritarianism will be a profound betrayal of the tentative trust he created. During the first five years of the Sixth Republic, liberalization occurred in numerous fields, and citizens have an increased level of political consciousness and stake in democratic politics.

The State Council is the highest policy-making organ of the government, and is composed of the President, the Prime Minister, and fifteen to thirty other members. The President serves as chairman and the Prime Minister as vice-chairman. The President appoints the Prime Minister, who takes direct responsibility for administrative acts. He reports to the National Assembly on governmental affairs, recommends the appointment and removal of State Council members, and supervises the administrative activities of the various Ministries. Included in the Prime Minister's office are the Secretariat, the Office of Administrative Co-ordination, and the

State Ministry of Political Affairs. The Ministries of the government are the following:

Economic Planning Board
National Unification Board
Ministry of Foreign Affairs
Ministry of Home Affairs
Ministry of Finance
Ministry of Justice
Ministry of National Defence
Ministry of Education
Ministry of Culture
Ministry of Sport and Youth
Ministry of Agriculture, Forestry and Fisheries
Ministry of Trade and Industry
Ministry of Energy and Resources
Ministry of Construction
Ministry of Health and Social Affairs
Ministry of Labour
Ministry of Transport
Ministry of Communications
Ministry of Information
Ministry of Science and Technology
Ministry of Government Administration
Ministry of the Environment
Ministers of Political Affairs[35]
Office of Patriots and Veterans
Office of Legislation.

A Constitutional Court was created under the Sixth Republic to rule on the constitutionality of laws and on constitutional petitions. It consists of nine adjudicators, subject to presidential approval. Three are chosen by the National Assembly, three by the Chief Justice, and three by the President for a six-year term. They may be reappointed, and can be expelled only by impeachment or a sentence of imprisonment.[36]

Chapter Three of the constitution vests legislative power in the National Assembly. Members have terms of four years and cannot hold any other office. The legislature decides upon the budget submitted by the executive branch. If it is not passed by the beginning of the fiscal year, then the executive will disburse funds in accordance with the previous year's budget – thus weakening the power of the legislature to hold up operations. One-third of the National Assembly membership may also propose a motion for the impeachment of officials of the executive, and the motion requires approval by a majority of the total members. In the case of presidential impeachment, a motion requires a majority of members, and approval by two-thirds.

The Korean presidential system favours the executive over the legislative branch. As long as the ruling party dominates both branches, its hegemony remains unchallenged. The prospect of 'gridlock' appeared with the legislative elections in April 1988, and was broken with the amalgamation of the DLP. The price of democracy at the central level has been a decrease in government ability to maintain social order and economic leadership. While many Koreans complain about authoritarianism, they are not willing to risk past gains with a gamble on returning to the relative chaos of the Second Republic. Moreover, significant gains have been made under the presidential system.

Local autonomy

For centuries of Korean history, the centralized state, or the goal of a strong state, was a persistent characteristic. Harold Hinton suggested that:

Presumably because of Korea's comparatively small size and relative ethnic and cultural homogeneity, and in spite of the existence of a high level of village autonomy . . . regionalism has not been an important influence on Korean political development. Korea was probably the most centralized and uniformly administered state in traditional Asia.[37]

The events of 1987 – reforms and the presidential election – contradicted this judgement when localism emerged as very strong indeed. Localism and regionalism proved to be important factors in the presidential and legislative elections. The Kwangju incident, where hundreds of civilians were killed or injured, was a turning point in increasing Cholla antagonism towards the central government. Democratization is a process which emancipates local units from central control, and the Roh reforms of 1987 promised local autonomy and local elections. As the local sentiments find political expression and autonomy in the Korean state, violence has subsided.

Regionalism remains strong, and Korean political scientists see it as remaining an important part of the political landscape – especially as political parties exploit mutual antagonisms to gain electoral advantage. A University of Pusan survey of 1,500 respondents in Cholla and Kyongsang found 39 per cent considered regional antagonisms a serious problem, with 56 per cent saying the problem was 'extremely serious'. Inter-provincial understanding has not been helped by the practice of filling posts with officials from the same province: in Kwangju, 92 per cent of the officials were natives of the region. In Chonju, the position was similar, with 90 per cent in Pusan and 82 per cent in Taegu.[38]

Initially, the passage of legislation to implement local autonomy seemed unlikely in November 1989. Nearly three decades had passed since the short-lived system of the Second Republic had been abolished by the 1961 military coup. The DJP and the three opposition parties feared their political credibility might be affected by local election failure, or if they were unable to nominate enough suitable candidates. Another obstacle was that the DJP wanted the central government to maintain full authority over local administration to ensure continuity and the use of professional civil servants. The party DJP also argued for strong executive leadership and supervision over local councils by mayors and governors. The opposition saw it as an issue to use against the government, and argued for local independence, with minimum supervision from the central government.

Party endorsement of local candidates was also controversial. The DJP perceived that possible candidates tended to be local leaders who favoured it as the government party. Leaders argued for political neutrality, and that the unhealthy elements within the four-party structure should not be repeated in local politics.[39] The opposition argued for disclosure of candidates' party association – at least in the campaign posters. The government party favoured multi-representative mixed electoral districts (similar to Japan's), while the PPD supported small-sized districts, and the other opposition parties (the DRP and NDRP) favoured medium-sized districts.

Public opinion also had reservations concerning party participation in local elections. A survey in 1990 indicated that 71 per cent of respondents opposed political parties fielding candidates in the upcoming local elections. An even higher number (73 per cent) expected corruption in the election, but around 80 per cent saw the local elections making a contribution to democratization.[40] Despite the reservations of the parties, local autonomy was restored by the National Assembly in late December 1989. Debate in the Assembly centred on whether candidates would run on party tickets or as independents. Objections to the party affiliation system included concern that wasteful bickering and intensified parochialism would result – compromising the possible benefits of local autonomy for Korean democracy.[41]

The DLP remained reluctant to introduce local autonomy, despite the 1987 promise of Roh Tae Woo to implement it. For one thing, the party feared an aggravation of regionalism – which had expressed itself as protest in the vote for Kim Dae Jung. For another, local elections would require a large amount of money – both for administrative expenses and for party campaigns. The government party also worried that its popularity had plummeted owing to internal quarrels since the merger and the forced passage of certain bills. Moreover, there had been *en masse* resignation of opposition representatives from the National Assembly over strong-arm tactics. The parties based their strategy and positions on considerations of how local autonomy would affect their power.[42] The PPD argued that, even during the Korean War, there was some degree of local autonomy, and so DLP claims that the system was premature were not valid.[43]

The opposition members resumed their Assembly seats (November 1990) after a four-month boycott. The return was made possible by an agreement between the DLP and PPD to implement local autonomy. They agreed to hold local council elections in 1991 and gubernatorial and mayoral elections in 1992. Parties would be allowed to nominate candidates, but only in large districts such as provinces and cities.[44] Once the Local Autonomy Bill was passed, the city and county governments began preparations. The central government set aside a budget allocation for building offices and paying election expenses. In addition, local regulations had to be revised to accommodate the transfer of powers from the provincial and central governments to cities and counties. Local autonomy required the development of local financial resources, and new taxes, tourist development schemes, and even licensing changes were introduced to help the local areas.[45]

With the Local Autonomy Law in place, the labour unions prepared to participate. The Korean Federation of Trade Unions (KFTU) stepped up its activities. It was limited by Article 12 of the Labour Union Law, which prevented union participation in political action, but the KFTU planned to appeal against the law in the Constitutional Court. The Federation planned to run candidates in industrial areas, especially local labour union presidents. The provision against labour union participation in political activity had been added to the law in 1963 by the military regime. The article was eliminated by the National Assembly in 1989, but the motion to repeal was vetoed by the President[46]

New groups were formed outside the mainstream parties for the local contests. A group of 325 activists founded the Conference of Citizen Coalition for Participation and Autonomy. Advisers included former Deputy Prime Minister Yi Han-bin, the poet Kim Chi-ha, various professors, feminists, and lawyers.[47] Another 'Party for the Masses' was formed in Seoul, but faced formidable problems of financing.[48]

The new local autonomy system called for the establishment of local assemblies, elected from medium-sized electoral districts, with two to five members each.[49] In preparation for the 1991 election, the National Assembly Subcommittee on Local Autonomy allocated seats for representatives. Cities, counties and districts with 300,000 or fewer population would have three seats, with one additional seat for each 200,000 population over 300,000. Other allocations were made for other types of districts. The country was divided into 297 local assembly districts, with a total number of 848 assembly seats.[50] Despite the expectations, controversies and manoeuvring, popular interest in balloting remained low. Voter turn-out was 55 per cent in the first round of local elections on 26 March 1991, when 443 districts were uncontested. This represented 12.4 per cent of the total 3,562 districts in small cities, counties, and wards in big cities. The large-unit local council elections were held later in June. In Seoul, eighty-three or 5.8 per cent of the total seats were uncontested. Eleven of seventeen uncontested districts were in the high-income district of Kangnam. Officials of the Central Election Management Committee (CEMC) attributed the lower competition to 'public distrust of politicians caused by scandals, strict restrictions on campaigning, and lack of public knowledge of the local self-government system'. Less than 1 per cent of the candidates were women. Official candidates from the DLP (although there were no party nominations) comprised 45.2 per cent of the total, compared with 12.6 per cent for the PPD. Another 39.3 per cent were listed as independent, although more than half were actually pro-DLP.[51]

The second round of local elections was held in June. The DLP sought to repeat its success in the small council elections, which produced control of 210 of the local councils.[52] Public apathy was evident but declining in the second local election as well, with a higher turn-out at 58.8 per cent of eligible voters.[53] Voters cast their ballots on 20 June 1991 for 866 local councillors in six major cities and nine provinces. With two-thirds, or 564 seats, the DLP declared a landslide victory. Critics feared that the ruling party now had too much power.

Two incidents probably affected the results of the second election. One month after the first elections, police beat a college student to death during a demonstration. This set off more demonstrations and generated public support for the dissidents. Then, three weeks before the second election, Prime Minister Chong Won-sik visited a university to present a lecture, and was attacked by students with eggs and batter. The assault alienated older Koreans, who thought the students had gone beyond decency. The affair allowed the government to justify a stronger posture in dealing with dissidents, and remained fresh in the minds of many older voters, who supported the regime's law and order approach. The same event may have moved the younger voters to abstain as a means of expressing their civic concern.[54]

President Roh Tae Woo expressed a moralistic view in a post-election speech:

People from all social strata should spontaneously participate in the campaign against social disorder, to build a new order and life. By doing so, they should try to develop a campaign on the national level to establish a correct view and morality suited to these times.[55]

These two constitutional issues – the presidency and local autonomy – represent major elements in the institutionalization of the South Korean state. The presidency continues to be the sovereign expression of state power, strongly influenced by past office holders and military manipulation. It serves as the anchor of order and stability – and the lightning rod of opposition. The President has been the head of the police and the army, the antagonist of the legislature, and the voice of the Korean state in international affairs. The first presidential term of the Sixth Republic has been a transition from military to civilian dominance, and the election of Kim Young Sam in December 1992 marked the first full civilian in the presidency since 1962, when President Yun Po-son resigned in protest against the military government.

At the local level, despite widespread pessimism and cynicism, the return to autonomy has been settled. The question remains whether the move will merely extend some of the negative features of national politics to the local level, or whether the expansion of political participation can reinforce democratic aspirations.

The 1992 presidential elections

Candidates and platforms

In reaction to the presidential dictatorships of Rhee and Park, the one-term presidency has become the rule. The constitution of the Sixth Republic prohibited Roh Tae Woo from seeking a second term. After some in-fighting in the DLP, the party nominated Kim Young Sam as presidential candidate. His reputation had been built on years of opposition to military authoritarianism, in alliance with Kim Dae Jung. Competition for the presidency in 1987 shattered that coalition, and lost the office to Roh. The frustrations of opposition and the opportunities for gaining the presidency in the next election induced him to join with the government party in the DLP in 1990. It was at some risk to his ambitions, since it appeared that his reformism was eclipsed by opportunism at the time. The move enhanced his image of pragmatism, and isolated Kim Dae Jung as a regional leader. The reforms of the Roh government and moves towards reunification took some of the wind out of the opposition sails. In the months prior to the 1992 election, a new, well financed party (the United

National Party) emerged under the leadership of Chung Ju-yung, the founder of Hyundai. Like Ross Perot in the United States, he offered *chutzpah* and success in business. Nevertheless, the prospect of an ambitious tycoon moving on to the political scene was a new phenomenon with ramifications for a broad spectrum of choices for voters. The government was not amused, and launched investigations into Hyundai finances, claiming irregularities.

Other candidates included lawyer Lee Byong-ho, the founder of the Korea Justice Party, whose platform was 'to free the country from its hardship and decline'. The New Korea Party, an offshoot of the DLP, advocated a parliamentary system and multi-member districts for National Assembly elections. Another candidate, Park Chan-jong, ran for the New Political Reform Party, and stood for a generational change in politics. Paek Ki-won, a former dissident, ran as an independent. A female candidate, Kim Ok-sun, member of the National Assembly, called for justice in the political system, and encouraged women to take a role in politics. With diversity and liberalization, there was no major candidate from the military. The long struggles since the demise of the Second Republic saw the re-emergence of civilian-dominated politics.

To avoid tainting the election campaign with charges of presidential interference – which would have been seen as indirect military meddling – Roh Tae Woo resigned from the DLP shortly before the campaign so as to create a neutral presidency and Cabinet to oversee the election process. He sought to maintain his neutrality, run fair elections, end civil servant interference in elections, and stop the practice of using money and gifts to buy support. Although the elections occurred without major incident, some candidates began their campaign too early. With the election scheduled for 18 December, campaigning before 20 November was prohibited – a sanction honoured more in the breach than in the observance. The campaign was further notable for the use of innuendo, rumour, and negativism in attacking rivals.

The economy was the major issue in the election. The high growth rates of the past were not maintained, and fell to 3.1 per cent in the quarter preceding the election. Unemployment was up to 2.3 per cent, and business bankruptcy was growing. It was a situation serious enough to prompt the central government to suspend local government elections out of concern for instability.

Kim Young Sam's campaign advocated clean politics, national reconciliation through amnesties for political prisoners, no retaliation against former political rivals, and international accommodation. His economic plans called for stable growth and reducing inflation. Interest rates would be lowered, he promised, and more spending on research and development would help maintain South Korean competitiveness. Kim Dae Jung presented himself as the only alternative to DLP rule, but his platform was not readily distinguishable from the other parties'. He pursued some of the grass-roots techniques which seemed to work for Clinton's United States campaign, such as bus travel to press the flesh with voters. He advocated Korean reunification, especially for divided families, arms control, and development of the Demilitarized Zone as a tourist zone. Appealing to youthful voters, reform of education was high on his list of changes, and he called for the reduction of mandatory military service to eighteen months. He wanted the voting age reduced to eighteen. Kim Dae Jung blamed the DLP for the economic slowdown, which was especially hurting small businesses, and he called for easing bank loans to them. He wanted the government to: purchase more rice from farmers, never liberalize the rice market, establish a full-fledged market economy, provide a national pension system, ensure job security, lower housing rents, encourage technology, slash taxes by 40 per cent, and peg annual price indexes at a low level.

Chung Ju-yung provided some diversion in the campaign with his claim that the UNP was the only party to be solely concerned with economic issues. Chung hoped to translate his business success into economic prosperity for his whole country. His grand plans included ending Korea's trade deficit, raising the income of the people, stabilizing consumer prices, lowering interest rates, promoting small and medium enterprises, ending the power of the *chaebol*, and providing mass housing. In addition, Chung was fighting the dominance of politics by the two Kims and corruption in politics. Chung wished to develop more four-year colleges to alleviate the pressures on universities, develop tourist areas, and bring the idea of a constitutional reform to the people. Chung promised that, if elected, he would use his own fortune to finance good service projects.

The election results

Kim Young Sam's lead in the polls translated into victory on 18 December 1992. He took 42 per cent of the popular vote, while Kim Dae Jung trailed with 34 per cent, against Chung Ju-yung's 16 per cent. A turn-out of 81.9 per cent expressed high interest in the election, which was remarkably honest. Only one problem was reported – Kim Dae Jung's name was printed in red ink on the ballots of one area in Kwangju. Polls were closed for several hours while this bias against Kim was corrected. After his defeat (his third unsuccessful bid for the presidency) he resigned his legislative seat and decided to leave politics.

The future for tycoon-turned-candidate Chung Ju-yung appears to be as rocky as his campaign. Accused throughout the campaign of having bought votes and of using Hyundai funds and workers illegally for his campaign, Chung Ju-yung continued to fight allegations after losing. Chung promised to remain in politics and to continue to work to achieve clean politics. Crisis, however, continued to rock the United People's Party and its leader. The 'coalition against the Kims' union of the UPP with the New Korea Party ended in bitter divorce immediately following the election defeat. Admissions by Hyundai workers and UPP campaigners of irregularities and vote-buying led, ultimately, to the summoning of Chung himself by the prosecutors. Chung lost even more of his characteristic self-confidence when he had to be barred from leaving the country when he was caught at the airport bound for Japan. Business leaders expect that the economy will top Kim's priorities as it did throughout the campaign and hope to find a sympathetic ear in the Blue House, reminding him of his economic platform. Kim began work on his reforms early by encouraging the DLP to establish close ties and hold frequent meetings with business leaders.

Upon his election, Kim faced the task of dealing with the military, who long dominated Korean politics. As a former opposition candidate he has had difficulty in winning their acceptance. To carry on the democratic reforms initiated by Roh, he must control the military with a firm hand. Kim began his administration with the reinstatement of teachers fired because of their association with an illegal union, allowing an amnesty of some political prisoners in early 1993, seeking to reduce the role of the Agency for National Security Planning to an information-gathering group on foreign economic conditions and considering labour unions to participate in government. One of Kim's greatest challenges lies in maintaining the democratic momentum of reforms started in the Sixth Republic. He will have to balance the demands of economic growth with the need to retain control over some levers of economic co-ordination. The problem of North Korean succession will be a major crisis not only for Seoul and Pyongyang, but for the entire region. The collapse of communism in North Korea will certainly accelerate the pace of reunification, but will also be a major distraction if the south must divert its resources to reconstruct a bankrupt system.

3 Political parties and South Korean politics

The character of political parties in South Korea

Precursors of modern Korean political parties existed prior to the twentieth century. Before the collapse of the monarchy, proto-parties existed at court and among the elites. Political issues affected the distribution of offices, foreign policy, and in the nineteenth century, the response to Western, Russian and Japanese challenges. There was a political culture in this 'homogeneous' society which tacitly endorsed political groupings as a means of influencing government policy and working for political power.[1]

Modern Korean political parties originated in the struggle for independence against Japan. The first leftist society emerged in November 1919 – the League of Great Unity. Its goal was the implementation of socialism in Korea: 'Several communist factions competed against one another, and were broken up by the police as fast as they were set up. In April 1925 the Korean Communist Party was formed, but collapsed in November with the arrest of some 100 communists.'[2]

The struggle for independence intensified the importance of parties, as they became vehicles for elite pursuit of national ideals. In the absence of elections until after World War II, it was hardly possible for the parties to develop a democratic outlook. Heroic resistance to Japanese imperialism nurtured the pre-independence parties, and personal leadership was as important as any party platform. The will to power seemed to become the measure of party effectiveness, and Confucian virtue was expressed in the perception of compromise as corruption.

When the US military took over administration of South Korea in 1945, they attempted to unite irreconcilable factions:

> In order to soften the constantly increasing Korean antagonism, General Hodge, on 5 October 1945, created a Korean Advisory Council headed by Kim Song-su, a moderate nationalist, to assist the American military government. The Americans, unfamiliar with Korean history . . . made

vain attempts to bring about a unity of moderate Nationalists and leftists who were not communists, and thereby antagonized the conservative right wing Nationalists. Meanwhile, the number of political parties and social organizations with various political ideologies grew by 1947 to 350, creating a chaotic political situation.[3]

Political parties in developing countries can play a key role in the institutionalization of governmental and electoral processes. They can serve as links between society and the state by the aggregation of interests, recruitment of candidates for office, and articulation of political issues. In a country where conflicts threaten the fabric of society, political parties have a potential to provide non-violent means for the reconciliation of differences. However, when a society is faced with major challenges which may be beyond the ability of government to solve, expectations may be raised which cannot be met. Where parties appear to differ only in small ways, or represent local interests, or depend upon the bonds of a personal leader with his followers, a broad popular mandate may not be possible, and no party is able to gain legitimacy.

This has been the dilemma of the South Korean political parties since 1945. They have formed, dissolved, and re-formed with facility, seemingly unconcerned about electoral consequences. When the civilian opposition parties had their great opportunity in late 1987 to unite and elect a President, they fielded several candidates and split the vote, enabling the ruling DJP to elect Roh Tae Woo with less than one-third of the popular vote. In his study of the Second Republic, Han Soong Joo contends that a crucial factor in the collapse of the Chang Myon government was 'acute ideological and social polarization. Such polarization, which was never conspicuous during the period of the Syngman Rhee government (1948–1960), became important because of the free atmosphere it offered to all forms of political activity.'[4] The civilian opposition parties have been creatures and captives of Korean circumstances. The National Security Law severely limited the scope of free speech in the Assembly and in elections by prohibiting any statements which could give aid and comfort to the North Korean side. Until June 1991, there had been no local elections for nearly two decades – depriving the parties of an important sector of activity and recruitment.

A major weakness of the Korean party system has been the strength of the government party. Under Syngman Rhee, Park Chung Hee and Chun Doo Hwan, the government party had been far more than an organization to compete for votes. Rhee's Liberal Party, Park's Democratic Republican party, and Chun's Democratic Justice Party had the full force of autocracy behind them. In the latter two, this also included the military. In addition, there were hints that the government funded splinter parties to further weaken the major opposition. Small wonder that Korean voters have been cynical of party politics. Despite this, the opposition parties were able to make a credible showing in major elections.

By January 1990, Kim Young Sam and Kim Jong Pil had decided that further opposition was futile, and joined the new government party, the Democratic Liberal Party. The DLP now provides a device for the moderate opposition to be incorporated into the ruling establishment. The DLP has also been the vehicle by which civilian control over the presidency was re-established in 1992 after a line of military Presidents.

South Korea's situation as a semi-garrison state, facing an implacable enemy in the north, contributed to the key role of the military in politics. From an ill trained, poorly equipped and demoralized force which was decimated by the North Korean onslaught in 1950, the South Korean military has become a modern fighting force. The drift to disorder in the Second Republic convinced the generals that they needed to take control of the state. The Kwangju uprising two decades later revived the same argument, with the result of military take-over and the Fifth Republic. Once involved in politics, the army was politicized – even though key leaders resigned from their military positions. The government party became the civilian instrument of military rule. The possibility of further intervention has continued to affect parties and elections. One factor influencing the candidacy of Kim Young Sam for President in 1987 was that he was moderate enough to be amenable to the military, while many perceived Kim Dae Jung as too radical, and unacceptable to the generals.

Military intervention has been endemic to South Korea since the coup by Park Chung Hee on 16 May 1961. Subsequently, the army has played a major role in setting national priorities and exercising control over civilian society through direct and indirect means. The large size of the army (550,000 out of a total regular armed force of 650,000) makes it a force to be reckoned with – even when it is not playing an overt political part. Spending on defence takes nearly one-third of the government budget. Military intervention in Korean politics has been explained as fairly typical of developing nations – related to rapid industrialization, and defence against a rising militant working class. Lee Su-Hoon suggests that South Korea, as a 'peripheral state', depends upon foreign capital as a major source of revenue, and must therefore create an environment conducive to the continuous flow of that capital. 'This task entails keeping the local labor docile and keeping wages low. This necessitates the expansion of the coercive organization of the state in the periphery.' He finds a causal link between military budgetary expansion, interstate competition (with North Korea), and the flow of foreign capital.[5]

A simpler explanation may be that the army was activated by some patriotic motives. Its leaders saw the deterioration of public order during the Second Republic as politicians bickered among themselves while ignoring the growing threat from Kim Il Song. The US–Soviet stand-off was accompanied by 'people's wars' throughout Asia, and fear of subversion by North Koreans was no imaginary paranoia. The soldiers understood that the civilian government in 1961 could have collapsed into social turmoil which invited the north to step in, or at least allowed a pro-north government to emerge. No doubt, the access to political power which emerged from civilian crisis transformed the attitudes of several generals, who increasingly saw their mission as preserving the state in the face of political mismanagement. Graduates of the Korean Military Academy became brokers in a system where party politics had dissipated some of the military's legitimacy to rule. Nominally under the United Nations Command, the Korean military establishment was bolstered by support from the United States through the Mutual Security Treaty, with the effect of reducing the appreciation of the American presence, and identifying it as a reinforcement for military dictatorship.

The continuing civilian concern over secret military conspiracy was illustrated by the revelation of the existence of a private organization of junior army officers – the Aljahoe. It was inaugurated with a membership of twelve, modelled after the twelve Apostles. Non-members were hostile to the Aljahoe because it seemed to give its members a special inside track in promotions, and it echoes an earlier secret club, the Hanahoe, which was dissolved by Chun Doo Hwan, who was also an earlier member.[6] Members of the Aljahoe were reassigned after a semi-public stir. It appeared to be a case of elitist camaraderie which was suspect because it undercut the hierarchical structure of the military. Also, the presence of a *hwarang* elan had contributed to the self-confidence of coup-makers in the past Republics of Korea.

Institutionalization of political parties

A common phenomenon in developing countries is the proliferation of political parties, especially at the time of independence. The democratic forms of participation provide multiform opportunities for the advancement of ambitious individuals as well as various regional interests and intellectual programmes. Countries diverge on the extent to which there is institutionalization of the parties. Where diversity of parties persists and interferes with orderly government, the military may be tempted to intervene and restore 'stability'. In this context, institutionalization is a more relevant concept than development. It is 'the process by which organizations and procedures acquire value and stability'.[7] Sometimes political order takes priority over 'progress' when unfettered change threatens to become anarchy.

According to Ahn Byong-man, the degree of institutionalization is determined by the amount of 'adaptability, complexity, autonomy and coherence of organizations and procedures'. There were over 160 political parties participating in legislative elections between 1945 to 1972. Up to 1977, only five parties survived more than two of these elections: the Democratic Nationalist Party, the Liberal Party, the New Democratic Party of the Third Republic, and the Democratic Republican Party. Most Korean political parties were organized only at election time for the goal of electing a few important individuals into office and then disbanded. Thus most Korean political parties lacked adaptability owing to their weak coherence, autonomy, and complexity in organization and administration.

Korean parties have been slow to generate and maintain sufficient broad public support through elections. Moreover, constitutional revision has had the effect of changing the rules of elections. In 1958 and 1971, the opposition parties obtained more than one-third of the seats and thus were able to resist constitutional revision temporarily. Subsequent political changes – the demonstrations which brought down the Rhee government in 1960, and the Yushin constitution of 1972 – interrupted the institutionalization of the competitive party system.[8]

In Western liberal democracies, political parties have sought to institutionalize political conflict into regular elections within the confines of the state constitution. Leon Epstein defines a political party as 'any group, however loosely organized, seeking to elect governmental office-holders under a given label'.[9] This definition centres on the electoral purpose and environment of political parties, and excludes organizations in non-democratic systems which designate themselves as parties. We can suggest a broader definition to include non-democratic party phenomena – 'any organized group which seeks to place its members in positions of official political power'. This may be done through elections, mass mobilization, or revolution, although elections are usually held as the final validation of a party's legitimate control of state power.

This broader definition, in addition to widening the scope of political parties beyond elections, also directs our view to the actual functions of parties. Roskin *et al.* summarize several functions of parties in democratic systems, including 'aggregation of interests', 'integration into the political system', 'political socialization', 'mobilization of voters', 'organization of government', and 'setting government policy.'[10] This approach provides a function-oriented perspective, based on mediation, compromise, and the propagation of a civic culture in which voters make choices based on belief in individual autonomy. It is an approach which postulates the democratic political system as an equilibrium.

The development of political parties in South Korea

The origin of modern Korean political parties precedes the Korean War and even the Japanese colonial period. While the state provides structure and procedure to political life, parties give it adaptiveness, and formulate choices in a way to make democracy meaningful beyond the top-down policies of bureaucrats. A diversity of views in any polity is inevitable, and party pluralism can help to formulate and debate policy. For South Koreans, the challenge has been to tame the personalistic tendencies of party life so that political organizations can modify the autocratic tendencies of the leadership – especially the proclivity towards military interventionism. The continued imbalance between the increasing power of the state and the inability of the opposition to supply credible long-term leadership beyond protest has been a stark feature of the Korean landscape. The presidency of Kim Young Sam has only emphasized this character with the inescapable message that only collaboration with the government party – or its destruction through protest and revolt – can lead out of the cul-de-sac of political impotence.

The First Republic and the beginning of party politics

Pre-modern political parties had existed in Korea for centuries. Gregory Henderson's thesis was that Korean homogeneity and mass society militated against cohesive groups.

> The formation of more or less identical factions and councils that compete despite the absence of natural cleavage or issue creates its own inner demand for hostility. When to this hostility is added the fundamental component of atomized mobility – when, for example, a man will always place his personal desire for power above the value of remaining with his group and helping it gain power – a political culture is produced in which groups are perceived by the participants as unworthy of loyalty or continuity. As a result, the effort to form groups and keep them intact becomes one of the most frustrating and repetitious tasks of the culture.[11]

Three main types of parties existed at the time of liberation in 1945: (1) groups which had worked abroad to fight for national independence; (2) groups which had worked underground against the Japanese; (3) groups which had remained in Korea, and had co-operated with the Japanese

colonial powers. Among the last, the most prominent was the Posong
Group, a collection of landowners and associates with roots in Cholla-do.
Immediately after liberation, one of the group moved to form the Korean
Democratic Party (KDP), but sought leadership outside the Posong ranks
because of its association with the Japanese.[12] By November 1945, a
coalition of various groups from a wide spectrum of political shading was
breaking up. An alliance between Rhee and the rightists in the KDP was
taking shape against the communists. Within a year, the Rhee-led
movement[13] claimed a membership of 7 million.

The KDP was one of the first two major conservative parties to emerge
as a competitor for political power after World War II. It was typical of
party politics in that it relied on informal forces of regional identification
and lineage to provide access to political power. Political parties became
personalistic organizations, and under Syngman Rhee the government
party was a major vehicle for access to political office. Part of this could be
attributed to a Confucian culture which traditionally emphasized kinship
loyalties over loyalty to government.

In the first Korean elections after independence, political parties did not
play a central role.[14] 'Facing the growing repressive tactics of the
government, and looking towards the 1950 National Assembly elections,
they merged with other groups and formed the Democratic Nationalist
Party in February 1950.'[15] Prior to 1951, Syngman Rhee insisted that
political parties were not desirable in Korea.[16] In February 1949, Speaker
Shin led a large part of a seventy-member confederation of politicians (the
Korean Nationalist Party) into the Han-guk (Korean) Democratic Party. It
was the first Korean group formed with the explicit purpose of being an
opposition party, and remained the most cohesive and stable political force
in the country until 1952. By the end of the first National Assembly, the
independents, numbering more than one hundred, had dropped to
twenty-nine. The centre of gravity for political parties had shifted. From the
early 1950s, they originated in the capital as factions providing alternate
ladders to executive power, not as bodies concerned with separate
legislative functions. They had no local functions, and, by the same token,
localities had few local demands to make on them or expectations to
communicate to them.

Although Rhee had allied himself with the KDP and used its support in
elections, he was reluctant to share the spoils of victory. The party
subsequently turned its efforts from the presidency to the legislature.[17] The
KDP sought a Cabinet form of government, in line with its new role as a
parliamentary party. It now focused on changing the constitution to realize
its goals.[18]

During the Korean War, the shape of Korean polarization between government and opposition was taking place. An outside observer would have expected the parties and factions in South Korea to suspend their quarrels during the war, but such was not the case. In August 1951, Rhee sought to emasculate Assembly power over executive tenure. He intended to propose a constitutional amendment providing for direct, popular election of the President and another for the formation of a bicameral legislature. Despite his distrust of political parties, the coming struggle required him to have a party to back him up in the legislature.[19] Thus the Liberal Party was inaugurated in December. It was a state party, resembling the PRI of Mexico, and the precedent for subsequent government parties in South Korea.

The party had no ideology except to maintain the authority of Syngman Rhee. The Liberal Party was comprised of five 'core social organizations', which resembled the 'mass organizations' of communist states. Central political power penetrated deeply into these 'voluntary' organizations, preventing them from exercising much autonomy.[20] The Liberal Party's chief role was to defend the presidency from opposition and public discontent. It worked reasonably well for much of Rhee's tenure, and in 1954 became the first party to win an absolute majority.[21] The emergence of the ruling Liberal Party sparked the opposition parties to coalesce, with the NDP at the core, into the Democratic Party (Minju-dang) in September 1955.

The emergence of a two-party system affected the voting population by providing clearer democratic choices in elections. Two distinct alternatives were emerging in Korean democracy – the pro-government Liberal Party and the anti-government Democratic Party. Voters found it easier to choose with clear selections, and mobilized citizens expressed their preference for the party acting in accordance with their new-found democratic values. In the 1956 election, the Rhee majority fell from 80 per cent to 56 per cent. Political parties were emerging as the dominant force in politics. Hopes for the permanence of a two-party system proved to be premature, as the growing opposition began to threaten government control over legislation. At the end of the Rhee regime, arrests and threats mounted, and popular feeling against the government – especially in urban areas – reached a high pitch.[22] However, the ability of the Democratic Party to mobilize the public for protest demonstrations was limited by its factionalist splits as well as by its conservative outlook.[23] The Democratic Party claimed some responsibility for mobilizing demonstrations against the Rhee government in April 1960, but the leadership was not effective in following up to form a more permanent base of popular support.[24]

The Democratic Party won a majority in the elections of July 1960. After the overthrow of the Rhee government and the establishment of the Second Republic, the opposition parties lost the enemy which had helped to define their goals. Rivalries within the ruling Democratic Party, and between the other parties of the left and right, contributed to serious instability. The Premier shuffled his Cabinet three times between September 1960 and May 1961, but failed to strengthen his leadership, or gain in popularity.[25]

During the events of 1960, the military remained neutral. The officers were generally pro-American and depended on US military support.[26] Also, many of the high-ranking officers had no strong ideological proclivities one way or another, and preferred to distance themselves from politics. Rebuilding the armed forces after the war was sufficiently distracting. There was also a lack of cohesion among the high-ranking officers and between the higher and lower officers.[27]

Political parties in the Third and Fourth Republics, 1962–72

The Second Republic collapsed in 1961 under pressure from a military coup, when General Park Chung Hee took command of government. The fragmentation of the opposition parties facilitated the coup and made continued control easier. The generals established the Democratic Republican Party as its organization to wield power – just as Rhee had created the Liberal Party as his instrument of rule. Park and his military colleagues, many from the eighth class of the Korean Military Academy, founded the party, which remained the government's major tool for mass mobilization during Park's regime, although other, less obvious, political programmes were also used for this purpose.[28] A constitutional amendment in late 1962 replaced the bicameral system of the First and Second Republic with a single National Assembly, and provided for presidential elections through direct voting. In the presidential election of 15 October 1963, with a turn-out of 85 per cent, Park was elected with 46.6 per cent against 45.1 per cent for the opposition.

Within the DRP, Park depended on Kim Jong Pil as his chief of staff, whose power base was the KCIA. Kim had been forced to resign as Premier in 1964 because he was too closely identified with the conciliatory policy towards Japan, and a reconciliation between Kim and Park took place in 1969. Until 1973 the KCIA was headed by Kim's chief rival, Lee Hu Rak, and became involved in a number of dubious activities, including the Unification Church and the kidnapping of Kim Dae Jung in Tokyo. Park then replaced Lee with Kim Jae Kyu as head of the Agency – the man who was to order the President's assassination on 26 October 1979.

Fifth Republic: Chun Doo Hwan

The death of Park released social forces kept in check for almost two decades. According to the constitution, Park's successor was the premier – Choi Kyu Ha – who initiated a few political reforms. Kim Jong Pil resumed the DRP presidency, and Kim Dae Jung was released from house arrest.[29] A coup by General Chun Doo Hwan installed a military junta on 12 December 1979, and overthrew the caretaker government. Reaction against the military take-over culminated in the Kwangju uprising and massacre on 18 May 1980. Student dissidents took over Kwangju and were crushed by special military forces. Chun used the incident to consolidate his power, and purged the KCIA. A new constitution was introduced, and the regime created a new ruling party, the DJP.

The Chun government was a continuation of the Park regime with a change of personnel. There was general agreement that the Yushin constitution had to be scrapped, and the major parties agreed to co-operate in drafting a new constitution. Intrigues proliferated, but the operating assumption was that the country was in transition to civilian democratic rule. Lee Hu Rak challenged Kim Jong Pil over party control. There was a falling out between Kim Young Sam and Kim Dae Jung over charges that the former had been too accommodating to the Park government.[30] In March 1980, President Choi restored Kim Dae Jung's civil rights. The rivalry polarized the NDP temporarily into two factions, and the three Kims prepared to fight each other over the presidency. Demonstrations, protests, arrests, the resignation of the Cabinet, and the reimposition of martial law ensued, and Kim Dae Jung and Kim Jong Pil were arrested.[31]

According to Peter Moody, 'the opposition was too willing to find any pretext not to cooperate and showed this propensity by blaming everyone else for the failure to cooperate'.[32] Kim Young Sam remained president of the New Democratic Party. Other opposition politicians reorganized themselves into splinter political parties. The pattern of opposition politics had emerged. Facing an authoritarian and militarist government, the opposition adopted a posture of stubborn resistance. Moderation often brought charges of compromise. When the government tried concessions, it was interpreted as an expression of weakness, and was followed by further demands. The politics of pluralism and compromise had been poisoned by years of authoritarianism, and would require new modes of adaptation.

In the legislative elections of March 1981, the government DJP won 151 of 276 seats. The DJP mandate eroded rapidly, and when the twelfth National Assembly elections were held on 12 February 1985, the opposition vote increased significantly. The overthrow of Marcos in the

Philippines further encouraged the South Korean opposition to push for reforms. They adopted a more militant strategy, in part to overcome their own internal dissensions. Radical protests by students and workers in the spring of 1986 made compromise less likely. Chun wanted to keep the electoral college system for the next presidential election, and to amend the constitution to make the government into a Cabinet system. This would have allowed him to rule indirectly, according to critics. The opposition called for a strong presidency elected directly by and accountable to the voters.[33]

The authority crisis of 1985

In the 1985 legislative election, the opposition parties flexed their growing strength. The February parliamentary election was preceded by the establishment of the New Korea Democratic Party (NKDP), led by politicians who had been removed from a political black list. Its roots were in the major opposition party of the 1970s – the New Democratic Party. Lee Min Woo, a close associate of Kim Young Sam, was elected party president. The two major opposition figures, Kim Dae Jung and Kim Young Sam, were still barred from political activity. The new party rejected the legitimacy of the current government and constitution, while the other parties of the opposition were considered to be creations of the government for the purpose of unbalancing the real opposition. Although the government engaged in direct and indirect harassment of the NKDP, the DJP was expected to win a sizable share in the National Assembly election. In anticipation of the 1987 elections, the NKPD sought to change the constitution to allow direct popular voting for the presidency.[34]

This time, the DJP won only 35.3 per cent of the popular vote and eighty-seven seats, while the new opposition scored 29.2 per cent, and fifty seats. To its chagrin, the government lost the five largest cities,[35] and the NKDP became the largest opposition bloc in the twelfth National Assembly, sweeping the urban centres of Seoul, Pusan and Inchon. It captured seats in fifty out of ninety-two local constituencies, and 30 per cent of the national vote – winning a total of sixty-seven seats out of 276. In the campaign, the opposition parties constantly referred to Chun as a military dictator. The Democratic Korea Party (DKP), winning 20 per cent, suffered from a perception that it was a government-created party. On March 6 the government removed the ban on several prominent politicians, but excluded Kim Dae Jung. A Cabinet shake-up followed, and Roh Tae Woo was named as party chairman. In early April, thirty legislators left the opposition DKP to join the NKPD. Subsequently, the NKPD absorbed the DKP to form a united bloc of 106 seats against the DJP's 147 seats.[36]

With growing opposition strength, constitutional change was becoming more likely. The Chun government stated it had no intention of changing the indirect presidential system into a direct one before 1988.[37] In the spring of 1986, the government adopted a more tolerant attitude towards popular demonstrations, but still ordered the house arrest of some 200 opposition party members. The crackdown was denounced by the US State Department, and was extremely unpopular at home. Events in the Philippines raised the cry of 'people power' in Seoul.[38] This set the stage for the opposition parties to organize a popular movement to pressure the government for radical reforms.

On 13 April 1987, Chun Doo Hwan halted the debate on constitutional revision until after the 1988 Summer Olympics, to be held in Seoul. He claimed that consensus among the opposition parties was not possible – making the settlement of outstanding issues difficult – and time was running out before the elections.[39] The government offered a parliamentary system as a compromise, while the opposition wanted a return to direct presidential elections. Lee Min-Woo said that his party would consider the government offer if the ruling party adopted seven major political reforms. This initiative was rejected by Kim Dae Jung and Kim Young Sam, who criticized the attempt to compromise, broke away and formed their own party, once again splitting the opposition and raising doubts over their ability to handle power responsibly.

Opposition parties

A general hurdle which opposition parties face is their credibility to form a government if they have never had the responsibility of running the state. These parties may be popular expressions of protest against existing injustices and may threaten the dominant party, but there is reluctance among voters to entrust an untested organization with the reins of power. Moreover, if an opposition party is perceived to behave in a way that indicates an incapacity to provide orderly government, its chances at the polls will be decreased. The slow progress of the Japan Socialist Party towards winning the confidence of the electorate – despite the relatively low popularity of the governing Liberal Democratic Party – reflects some of this burden of opposition parties.

By 1986, the opposition parties in South Korea had become serious rivals for power. The presidential election was scheduled for the end of 1987, and the two Kims were the strongest opponents against the DJP. Both had worked in the opposition during the post-war period and had strong popular appeal – in contrast to the stern Confucian military leadership provided by Park Chung Hee and Chun Doo Hwan.

Party organizations have not been very durable in South Korean political life. Until 1987, even ruling parties did not last much longer than their leader's hold on power. The Democratic Justice Party had been established as a vehicle for military participation in national politics after the demise of Park Chung Hee and his DRP. In anticipation of the 1987 election, civilian party members urged that it should become distinct from government and less dependent on the military. It had been an instrument of Chun Doo Hwan and his closest advisers.[40]

A central issue for the parties was the method of electing the President. The government insisted on indirect election, while the opposition wanted direct election, which would be a more accurate representation of public opinion, and also favoured the opponents of the DJP. Lee Min Woo's compromise formula for democratization only succeeded in weakening his own position in the party. The two Kims feared that any appearance of compromise would weaken their party *vis-à-vis* the DJP.[41] Chun claimed that he wanted to keep the office of national President above party politics, and so delegated full party powers to the DJP chairman and his heir apparent, Roh Tae Woo. Chun was reluctant to designate his successor too early, since that could have weakened his authority in advance of the election, and perhaps stimulated subtle defection from his support to the heir designate. Political power remains personalistic rather than institutionalized, as party dynamics have illustrated.

Street demonstrations in the spring of 1987 faced large numbers of riot police. As James Cotton emphasized, the middle classes – especially the managerial and professional classes of Seoul – played a part in the student-led protests.[42] Their participation was probably more important than that of other sectors which had continually joined in protests in the past. To the rest of the world, it appeared that the stability of the Olympics' host country was in question. The government pondered its international image, and dreaded a recurrence of the student-led riots which had overthrown Syngman Rhee in April 1960. Demonstrators were also supported by the growing labour movement, which had not shared in the fruits of the Korean economic miracle. The government feared recriminations over the Kwangju incident – which had discredited the Fifth Republic domestically and internationally. Demands for democracy were mixed with yearning for economic justice and retribution. South Korean society seemed to be drifting into two mutually antagonistic camps in early 1987.[43]

The opposition dealt from a position of weakness – against the entrenched government and its use of officials in its service. A $1.2 billion loan to fishermen and farmers in 1987 strengthened government support in the countryside. A viable opposition required unity of the two Kims, so before leaving the NKDP, Kim Dae Jung had backed the more moderate Kim Young Sam to replace Lee Min Woo as party president.

Other issues of contention between the government and opposition included the demand for the release of political prisoners, reintroduction of the local government system which had been suspended in 1961, press freedoms, an end to police brutality, and the repeal of draconian anti-communist laws. The opposition also demanded equitable redistricting to reflect population shifts into urban regions. A drift of migrants into the cities since 1981 had strengthened the popular support of the opposition parties but this would not be translated into National Assembly strength without district changes.

June 1987: Roh Tae Woo's eight point declaration

The DJP convention of June 1987 was scheduled to be a smooth transition of power from Chun to Roh. Within his own party, Chun perceived strong consensus for conciliation and the resumption of talks on constitutional reform. The United States was also calling for dialogue between rival forces to avert a breakdown which might invite North Korean intervention. The atmosphere was one of increasing public violence; students were joined by other groups – including middle class members – in urban Korea. Without a solution to the impasse, the Olympics were hostage to political instability.

On 29 June Roh Tae Woo reversed Chun's refusal to compromise with the opposition, and conceded their major demands – including direct presidential elections and an amnesty for Kim Dae Jung. Two days later, Chun conceded the reforms which he had previously refused. Other items of Roh's eight-point package included the freeing of all political prisoners except those charged with serious crimes; guaranteed human rights; a free press; local autonomy; freedom for political parties; and a campaign against crime and corruption.[44] The abrupt change in government policy was affected by over two weeks of clashes. Rallies on 26 June had drawn hundreds of thousands of demonstrators and there was even a revolt within the DJP.

By adopting the main demands of the opposition, Roh seized the initiative in the approaching election. He turned mass opposition to his candidacy into a new legitimacy, and began isolating the radical students from Catholic Church and middle-class support. The granting of an amnesty to Kim Dae Jung suddenly made him a viable candidate, and intensified the rivalry between the two Kims which paralysed their efforts to unite in the presidential election.

The 1987 presidential contest

Negotiations between the government and opposition parties cleared several major obstacles during the nineteen rounds of closed-door talks by the eight-member negotiating panel. The opposition wanted the President to serve a four-year term, with the option of running for a second term, while the DJP fought for a single six-year term. The panel compromised on a single five-year term. In a major concession, the ruling party agreed to drop the President's power to dissolve the National Assembly. The DRP wanted the voting age lowered to 18 to give university students, who were in the vanguard of the movement for democratic reform, the right to vote. However, the DJP remained firm, and the opposition agreed to leave the issue until new election laws were drawn up.[45] The voting age was later set at 20. In late October the new constitution for the Sixth Republic was approved by 93 per cent of voters.

The two Kims ran against Roh as well as against each other. Kim Dae Jung was the favourite son of South Cholla – the rice basket of the nation and a south-west province frequently bypassed in the past two decades of industrialization. The incident in Kwangju, the major city in the province, had further increased hostility towards the government. The people of Cholla perceived Kim as their regional hero.[46] Both Kim Dae Jung and Kim Young Sam called for the end of military rule, referring to the army background of Chun and Roh. Nevertheless, Kim Young Sam was supported by the former four-star general Chung Sung-hwa – a signal that he could work with the military establishment more effectively than the Kim from Cholla.

As the race heated up, other elements sought recognition of grievances. Labour became more militant, and staged over 3,500 strikes and demonstrations in the three months after 29 June. Wages rose by 20 per cent, and business feared the end of Korea's successful export drive.[47] In the election scheduled for 16 December, Roh was the only candidate heading a party not founded to further a leader's political ambitions. Kim Young Sam and Kim Dae Jung had held leadership positions in the newly formed Reunification Democratic Party, and failed to agree on a single candidate to oppose Roh. Kim Dae Jung later told this author that he could not guarantee that his followers would support Kim Young Sam even if he did. The fierce loyalty of his Cholla backers was expressed in the landslide majority he received there, and could not be traded away. Kim Dae Jung formed his own Party for Peace and Democracy.

Many Koreans were frustrated by the spectacle of opposition candidates' inability to allow national interest to transcend individual aspirations or growing regionalism. Roh was virtually assured of election when the two Kims failed to co-operate. Between them, they won and split 55 per cent of the popular vote to Roh Tae Woo's relative majority of 37 per cent. Strong regional loyalties to Kim Young Sam and Kim Dae Jung reduced their respective capacity to co-operate.

The opposition parties were determined not to repeat their mistakes in the April 1988 election for the National Assembly.[48] Under the new constitution, the legislature regained powers lost under previous regimes. Once again, the election system, which favoured the government party through the proportional representation scheme, had to be revised. Negotiations broke down and the DJP rammed through a law based on single-member districts, calculating that the PPD (Kim Dae Jung) and Reunification Democratic Party (RDP) (Kim Young Sam) would split the opposition vote. A system was set up in which the National Assembly consisted of 299 seats, with 224 to be filled through the single-member district system and the remaining seventy-five 'at large' (national constituency) seats to be allocated by a proportional representation scheme.[49]

After a lively campaign – not clean, but one of the freest[50] – 75.8 per cent of the eligible voters cast their ballots. It was a stunning setback for the government party, which won only eighty-seven of the 224 constituencies, against fifty-four for the PPD,[51] forty-six for DRP, twenty-seven for the NDRP, and nine for the independents. In terms of popular votes, the DJP won 34 per cent, the DRP 23.8 per cent, the PPD 19.3 per cent and the NDRP, formed by former Premier Kim Jong Pil, 15.6 per cent. Kim Dae Jung's PPD emerged as the largest opposition party, replacing his rival Kim Young Sam.

Voter turn-out was higher in rural areas, and lower in urban areas. The pattern of partisan support was for rural voting in favour of the government party and urban endorsement for the opposition – *yochon yado*. Kim Hong Nack's analysis indicates that the government's unilateral change in the election system was not a major factor in its defeat.[52] (Park Chan Wook, however, considers that Kim Young Sam was hurt by the changed rules.[53]) Rather, there appeared to be a strong desire among voters to strengthen the opposition in the legislature. Other factors included revelations about corruption in the DJP, the inability of the government party to attract the support of young and well-educated urban voters, and candidate blunders. A deepening sense of regionalism, evident in the 1987 elections, also affected the government's fortunes.

After the election, the government faced a National Assembly dominated by the opposition parties. President Roh's attempts at consultation and reconciliation eased some friction but did not spare his government setbacks and demands for the settlement of abuses suffered in the Fifth Republic – especially the Kwangju incident. Former President

Chun Doo Hwan's testimony and apology cleared away this logjam, and set the stage for a new realignment in South Korean politics. The DJP, DRP, and NDRP merged into a single 'mega-party' – the Democratic Liberal Party, which reduced the PPD to a minority opposition in the National Assembly. Domestically, the move reduced the choices available to voters in the next election, and was viewed as a backward step from the democratization under-way in 1987 and 1988. The consolidation did improve the ability of the legislative and executive branches to co-operate more in reviving a slowing economy and in providing a more unified front in diplomacy with the United States and communist countries. However, the deep-seated factionalism of Korean politics has also threatened to erode the stability of the alignment.

Creating a new ruling party

The DJP had hoped to maintain power for a decade or more when it came to power in 1980. An attractive model to emulate was the Liberal Democratic Party of Japan, which had been the ruling party from the merging of conservative forces in 1955 until its defeat in the 18 July 1933 election. The DJP's power was precarious as a minority party in the National Assembly after the 1988 election. Speculation on a possible merger between the DJP and Kim Young Sam's RDP centred on whether Kim could make the transition from leader of a major opposition group to member of the ruling party.[54] On 28 December Pak Chun-kyu, chairman of the DJP, announced the coming merger of three political parties (the DJP, the NDRP of Kim Jong Pil, and the RDP of Kim Young Sam) into one party.[55]

Corroboration of the merger came from Kim Young Sam and Kim Jong Pil, who announced in early 1990 their intention to join their forces into a single party.[56] They stated the need for restructuring in the face of coming local elections. A by-election defeat for the RDP in August may have been the catalyst for Kim Young Sam to reassess his party's declining fortunes and the means to salvage his own fortunes.[57] The opposition parties missed their chance in the 1987 presidential election, and were having little effect on the DJP's policies in the National Assembly – except as a nuisance factor and stalemating legislative procedures. To regain its effectiveness, the party leaders argued for merger with the DJP in order to take over government from within.

A more compatible merger would have been with Kim Dae Jung's PPD, but both he and Kim Young Sam had strong ambitions on the presidency, and the 1987 election had demonstrated their inability to co-operate. If Kim Young Sam could merge with the DJP – a party without a strong presidential candidate in the wings when Roh Tae Woo's term ended in

1992 – he could bargain for succession to the presidency. This would benefit the DJP, which could capitalize on Kim Young Sam's popularity and the existing RDP organization. Both parties planned to use each other and each hoped to get the better bargain.

Kim Young Sam's problem was that merger was a high-risk proposition: entering the lion's den of the DJP would involve him and his followers in the factionalism of the ruling party – and probably place them at a disadvantage as newcomers. In addition, by compromising with the regime he had opposed, he risked becoming damaged goods by collaborating with the group he had denounced so vehemently from the opposition.

The joint declaration on the formation of the DLP stated that 'the present four-party set-up has been found to be incapable of effectively meeting domestic and international challenges confronting the nation or of furthering the goal of shaping a bright future for the country'. The four-party system was portrayed as due to personal connections of the leaders rather than the choice of voters, and served to 'deepen divisions among the people by carving up the electorate by region, rather than organizing public opinion and harnessing national capabilities'.[58]

The new party resulted from a coalition of three major leaders – Roh Tae Woo, Kim Young Sam and Kim Jong Pil – and marked an end to the era of one-man authoritarianism of the past. Nevertheless, it has not ended the factionalism of Korean parties. The merging of the three parties brought the organizations under a single umbrella, but the succession to Roh loomed large. Kim Young Sam faced opposition from Park Chul-un, who had built up his own following in the government party under Roh. Kim Hakjoon, adviser to the President, justified the merger as an event in which the ruling party dissolved itself and formed a new party in conjunction with opposition parties. It was a move which enabled the parties of Kim Young Sam and Kim Jong Pil to share more power in the next election, thus paving the way for a peaceful transfer of power.[59]

Kim Hakjoon was correct that the multi-party system had intensified regionalism. Each of the opposition parties had a loyal regional constituency in the 1987 and 1988 elections. The formation of the DLP was an attempt to create a single national party. However, the problem of effective representation of the provinces remains. Kim Dae Jung's PPD had the most dedicated following – the more rural and underdeveloped Cholla provinces of the south-west. Without effective regional representation, the threat of Seoul domination of government remained a larger possibility, while centralization of power could alienate parts of the country.

Geographically and politically, the Seoul–Taegu–Pusan line is the axis of the South Korean state, with a political centre of gravity in Taegu. The

'Taegu clique' has been an elite in the political life of the country, although Seoul serves as national capital, as well as the commercial, industrial, cultural, and educational centre of South Korea, with more than a quarter of the nation's population in its environs. Pusan, Kim Young Sam's power base, is the regional centre of southeast Korea – and the country's second city in industry and commerce. Partly as a result of this concentration of power, the resources of development have been unevenly distributed, with the north-east and south-west regions underprivileged in comparison to the central (diagonal) axis.

Political parties and liberalization

During the Sixth Republic, a major transformation of the South Korean political system has taken place. A rigid – but far from totalitarian – government has modified its authoritarian autonomy from society, and upgraded the legislature to a more equal status with the executive branch in the new constitution. Repressive laws have been revised and the opposition party is now closer to influencing legislation and holding the government accountable for its actions. In the future, much will depend upon whether actual and prospective party coalitions co-operate or re-fragment.

The role of parties in political liberalization has been important, but not critical. The opposition parties have often been outmanoeuvred by strong governments, or have been vulnerable to internal factions and regrouping. The South Korean population has not seen parties as offering much beyond self-interested politicians – except perhaps in the case of support for Kim Dae Jung. The opposition parties have kept up pressure on government, and have focused attention on issues and constitutional solutions to popular grievances. The existence of organized and disorganized opposition has narrowed the margin of authoritarian discretion – subjecting it to continuous criticism and threats to its stability. We can recapitulate the stages of South Korean liberalization and the involvement of political parties as follows:

First preparatory stage – authoritarian regime control of state and society

The state apparatus consisted of coercive institutions, including the police and army, to protect the polity from North Korean attack and subversion within. It also included the state bureaucracy which co-ordinated economic development. This period lasted from the early 1960s through 1987. Although opposition parties existed in the National Assembly, their impact on government policy was minimized by disunity and government restrictions.

Second preparatory stage – popular reaction against government

Through the years of the South Korean Republics, opposition was frequently expressed in student demonstrations. In early 1987 students were joined by a broader cross-section of society. This convinced the regime leadership they could not maintain social order and control during the coming election or in the 1988 Olympics. Public opinion was increasingly rejecting the dominant DJP, and would consign it to the role of opposition party unless reforms were initiated.

Political reform, stage one: government takes the initiative and negotiates with the opposition

Faced with increasing social disruption and the prospect of economic difficulty, the government leadership acknowledged the crisis. Roh Tae Woo's eight-point proposal for reform on 29 June was a major tactical shift. To resume control, government opened contacts with representatives of the opposition, thereby granting them and their grievances a greater degree of legitimacy. This stage saw negotiations and consultations over changing the rules of the political system – especially the electoral process and the distribution of power – while the government tried to minimize risk to its monopoly of power.

Political reform, stage two: implementation

Having agreed to make changes, the government provided a clear agenda of its intentions and was obligated to implement them and abide by the outcomes of the new rules. Two crucial keys to South Korean political reforms have been the existence of a viable opposition which pressured for reform and liberalization, and an urban citizenry which was cynical and antagonistic towards continued authoritarianism. Without popular pressure, mediated by the opposition parties and often led by student radicals, political reform would probably have been postponed, or been slow in implementation, or even sabotaged by military and reactionary elements.

Liberalization – widening the power base

The liberalization occurred in South Korea when the political reforms were demonstrated to work in favour of responsible government and the increased possibility of power transfer to an opposition-dominated government. This prospect was indicated in the 1987 presidential election, and nearly realized in the April 1988 parliamentary elections. That a transfer did not occur was due at least as much to the divided opposition as to any aborted liberalization in the South Korean state.

When two major opposition leaders, Kim Young Sam and Kim Jong Pil, joined the DLP, the likelihood of a transfer of power to an active opposition party became even more distant. The South Korean DLP consolidated and co-opted the moderates into a single, Japanese LDP-style, coalition. While the long-run viability of the super-party remains unclear, it does not seem to bode well for democratic institutions in the sense of a system in which a political opposition aggregates demands, holds the government accountable for its actions, represents various interests in a plural society, and offers an alternative set of personnel and policies to voters. At the moment, it appears that the South Korean political reforms have led to liberalization, but not full democratization. At this stage of economic development, however, the emergence of limited democracy may be more positive in light of the need for security and order.

Liberalization of modern dictatorship is a late stage in the reduction of state autonomy from society. An organized opposition is crucial as a counterweight to the state power of the government. Without it, as in the former Soviet Union or China, the state remains the instrument of the regime, with little prospect of change except through violent revolution or grudging concessions which may be withdrawn when crisis has passed. This liberalization is expressed, enshrined and implemented in the constitution, the legal system and its enforcement, the accountability of government to a free electorate, the redistribution of power, and the possibility of a non-regime group taking control of government.

Authoritarian liberalization may also be characterized as the change from 'hard' to 'soft' authoritarianism. It has occurred in Taiwan, where elections have increased the number of opposition representatives in the legislature, and in late 1992, there was an open election for the Legislative Yuan.[60] These developments stop short of liberal democracy, but are an important step towards full democracy. Without justifying authoritarianism, it should be kept in mind that both South Korea and Taiwan have been in a state of semi-war with highly militarized states, and cannot be expected to allow full democracy to emerge until unification or stabilization/normalization has been completed.

Conclusions

The South Korean liberalizing reforms are significant because of their success in facing up to the authority crisis by making fundamental changes in the political regime, and bringing part of the opposition into government via elections. These reforms were generated by mass dissent and an opposition which mediated between popular demands and government concessions. Through the changes after the Roh reforms, the economy has maintained its growth. Presidential succession occurred on schedule in late 1987, and the Olympics were held with hardly a break. In the years since the 1985 legislative elections, a strong and responsible opposition facilitated the reforms by negotiating with the government as potential partner in the state. However, this liberalization cannot be guaranteed as permanent. Much has depended upon the character of the major actors – a cast which could change at short notice. Yet it has gone too far to be turned back easily, and this is no small achievement.

In the context of modern oligarchies, South Korea represents a tentatively successful case of reform and liberalization. There are several characteristics which make its experience unique – including its ethnic homogeneity, geographical compactness, tradition of factionalism, and acceptance of US influence. Unlike communist totalitarian/authoritarian systems, South Korea has rejected Leninist methods of single-party dictatorship and a single utopian ideology which rule out any role or legitimacy for opposition parties.

4   The economic context of reform

Introduction

The South Korean economic miracle has been well documented as a case of successful development. Its sustained high growth from a war-torn infrastructure has been an unsurpassed example of rehabilitation and growth, despite lurches of instability exacerbated by popular uprisings and military coups. The achievement was all the more significant given the hundreds of thousands of impoverished refugees who fled from North Korea before and during the war. The divided nation faced severe hardship with the loss of the industrial and resource capacity of the north.

The war ensured that South Korea would not be ignored by the major powers – it was the frontier in the Cold War and had to be maintained with infusions of international assistance along with domestic sacrifices and work. South Korea rebuilt its economy, and subsequent rivalry with North Korea challenged the south to pursue the most effective path of economic development. Early on, the government decided to build an export-oriented strategy, rather than import substitution, which was popular with economists in the 1950s and 1960s.

Co-ordination of the South Korean economy required a strong state and major investment in human resources. Leaving economic growth to market forces alone could not succeed in pushing the economy forward. Insecurity was a driving force in South Korea. *First* was the insecurity of poverty. Living standards were among the lowest in Asia after the war, and severe dislocations and destruction had to be overcome. *Second* was military insecurity – the presence of US and UN military forces reduced South Korean vulnerability, but those forces could not be depended upon indefinitely, so the North Korean threat of a second invasion stimulated national reconstruction. *Third*, insecurity of national identity required positive action to overcome some of the attraction of the nationalism advocated by Pyongyang. Ideological unity has not been a strong point of the pluralist Republic of Korea, and governments have relied either on coercion, the threat from the north, or vague historical nationalism.

Park Chung Hee inherited three major tasks – military security, economic development and state-building. North Korea was an unmitigated threat, and failure to confront this challenge could lead to the elimination and absorption of South Korea. Starting in 1962, Korea's development record has been astounding by any standard. A series of Five Year Development Plans transformed the country from a largely agrarian economy into an industrial one in less than three decades. Difficulties were compounded by war devastation, the large defence budget, lack of natural resources, and the exclusion of half the nation's territory in the north. In 1961, population was growing at 3 per cent annually, *per capita* GNP was about $82, and savings were negligible.[1] Population density has increased from 284.3 persons per square kilometre in 1964 to 403.6 in 1983.[2] Population growth alone necessitated rapid economic development.

By 1970, high economic growth was largely self-sustaining. When Park initiated economic policies of growth, South Korean *per capita* GNP was about $675 in current dollars. By 1990, it was $4,550, about four times that of North Korea. Longevity has also increased from 58 years in 1965 to 70 in 1990. Virtually all Koreans finish elementary school, and 37 per cent receive some higher education. Rural incomes have risen to urban levels. Unlike most developing countries, Korea has reduced income inequalities.

From 1962 to 1984, the economy grew at an average annual rate of 8.5 per cent – despite a negative 5.6 per cent in 1980 due to a convergence of oil crisis, domestic turmoil, and crop failures. During the same period, the industrial manufacturing sector grew from 14.3 per cent of GNP to 30.9 per cent, with proportional declines in agriculture, forestry and fishing. Exports of manufactures increased from 22 per cent to 92 per cent of total exports.[3] Capital deficiency was evident in low savings, which in turn were due to poverty. In 1963, domestic savings constituted 8.7 per cent of GNP. By 1986 the figure was 31.4 per cent.

South Korea has suffered inflation and instability. The Fifth Republic regarded inflation as a formidable enemy. Stiff monetary restraints were introduced, government budget deficits were cut, and there was a reduction of balance-of-payment deficits. Wage increases were limited. By 1982, inflation was reduced to less than 3 per cent. By 1986, the country had achieved a trade surplus of $4.2 billion. Exports grew at annual rates ranging from 13 per cent to 20 per cent in the years 1983–86, and wage increases stayed below 6 per cent per year.

Some of the social factors contributing to Korean growth included social consensus, which induces cohesion over the need to work together to achieve higher levels of livelihood. This consensus came from a society whose members had experienced colonial repression, division of land and families and modern war. It was not an artificial solidarity which had been manufactured by an authoritarian leadership. The consensus was reinforced by alternatives inherent in the past and the present. The poverty of the past, tied to a rural subsistence economy, was a choice that few would embrace.[4] The other Korea – the Democratic People's Republic (DPRK) – became a stagnant, repressive system from which many of the present generation of South Koreans escaped in the late 1940s or early 1950s. The price of failure for the Korean experiment would be very high for all. In addition, Koreans do not want to continue their military dependence on the United States, nor do they want to be overshadowed and dominated by Japan.

Alice Amsden notes how the traditional state model was continued as a means of rapid economic growth:

> the military regime pasted together particular policies to form a model of accumulation that was rooted in the past. At the heart of the model were subsidies offered by the state to private enterprise in exchange for higher output of exports and import substitutes. The wheeling and dealing, horsetrading, and trafficking that characterized this process were reminiscent of the reciprocity that characterized relations between the state and the privileged classes under dynastic rule. The critical difference lay in the tip of the balance of power towards the state. However clumsy at first, the state used its power to discipline not just workers but the owners and managers of capital as well. A larger surplus was extracted, and this was invested rather than consumed.[5]

Without a strong state, this function of discipline could not have been carried out.

Towards balanced growth: maturing of a developing economy

The goal of economic growth in Korea has been to create a strong state. While socialist totalitarian strategies may have promised quicker results, for the south, US sponsorship and the Cold War environment excluded such choice. Following the war, dependence on the United States was the likely future. An alternative model of military authoritarianism and directed capitalism has been followed with considerable success. This pattern enabled the state to deal with national insecurities, which remained the foundation of economic planning. Vulnerability to North Korea and opportunities in the United States-dominated international economy inspired the early stages of planning. Stress on economic growth meant that planners tended to neglect other aspects of development, especially in public welfare and environment. With the Fifth and Sixth Republics, more attention has been paid to balanced growth and expanding the welfare state.

During the Fifth Republic, economic reforms in China and the continuous growth of the Japanese economy shifted Korean attention to greater opportunities in East Asia. In the Sixth Republic, the collapse of Soviet communism after 1989 and the isolation of North Korea have decreased the security threat. This, and a quarter-century of steady growth, have allowed South Korea to embark on the transformation of the economic system. The Soviet collapse strengthened the argument that a relatively free domestic market, not rigid central planning, was the more effective road to prosperity. Furthermore, curtailing the power of the *chaebol* and liberalization of labour reinforced the political democratization image of the Sixth Republic. South Korea's responses to its own weakness were rational and pragmatic rather than doctrinaire – results mattered more than ideology. To make up for weak domestic savings, Korea relied on foreign loans. International export markets made up for small domestic markets. Mass-production technology provided a substitute for low productivity. Foreign technology was borrowed and adapted to Korean needs. To accomplish economic growth, Korea has relied on a mixed economy. Government provides guidance and credit, while the private sector does most of the actual investment. In 1990, for example, the government outlined a seven-year development plan to foster high technology as the foundation of growth in the 1990s. Plans were made to increase the percentage of science and technology investment in the GNP to 4 per cent by 1996 from 2.6 per cent in 1989.[6]

The plan also called for the manufacturing share of GNP to rise from 31.3 per cent (1990) to 33.3 per cent in 1996, and for an average annual economic growth of 7.0 per cent during the plan period. Exports are expected to rise an average of 9.9 per cent, and imports at 8.8 per cent.[7] There were four main objectives of the plan: industrial restructuring and technical renovation; counter-measures designed to cope with changes in international economic conditions such as the settlement of the Uruguay Round trade negotiations; relaxation of the government's restrictive measures and preparations for more local autonomy systems; and promotion of welfare services, especially in rural villages. If growth occurred at 7 per cent, then *per capita* GNP was expected to be $10,190 in 1996, South Korea thus entering the ranks of developed countries in terms of *per capita* GNP. The urbanization ratio is to be increased to 81 per cent.

Economic planning within the market system has played a key role in Korean economic development, and the organs of central direction have been subject to political changes. The Economic Planning Board (EPB) wielded great power during the Third and Fourth Republics, serving as a midwife in delivering the nation's economic policies.[8] Following the death of Park, it began losing territory to rival Ministries and agencies seeking independence. This has contributed to declining morale, according to some observers. In the Sixth Republic, the President refused to hand over full economic policy control to the EPB. Policy was sometimes criticized as the product of inter-Ministry rivalry. The EPB has a unique organizational structure, which has meant that unless it is fully backed by the President, the Board has difficulty in functioning properly on its own. Under the National Government Organization Act, other Ministries are placed under the President – only the EPB is under control of the Prime Minister.

The limits of its responsibility and authority were not well defined: 'The EPB Minister shall report to the Prime Minister concerning the planning and management of the economy and provide overall co-ordination between the Ministries and agencies concerned.' It is important for EPB success to have a strong Minister in charge. Line Ministries generally operate bureaucratically and by the book, but EPB operations have been more flexible and even ambiguous. The economic planning process of the Sixth Republic, which operated in the context of reforms, democratization and the presidential vow to end authoritarianism, led to greater competition among Ministries. Democratization meant that each organ had to find its own place in the state, so each Ministry and agency began demanding its 'independence', leaving the EPB little latitude in its previous co-ordination role.

The Sixth Republic, in order to promote its diplomacy of *Nordpolitik*, decided in August 1988 to create an exclusive office to handle economic co-operation business with communist-bloc nations and form a private economic organization (the Private Economic Co-operation Council). This triggered a leadership struggle among the EPB, the Ministry of Foreign Affairs, and the Ministry of Trade and Industry. Each organ demanded that the new office should be placed within its Ministry, but eventually it was located in the EPB. The EPB has to fight every Ministry and agency, including the party, over economic and real estate measures, counter-labour measures, price control policy, trade programmes, industrial restructuring, and investment priorities. According to its table of organization, the EPB is linked to central departments of all the economic Ministries.

Key economic policy instruments such as interest rates, monetary decisions, exchange rates, foreign exchange controls and the tax system are all under the Ministry of Finance. The EPB has the budget compiling function, but acts only once a year. In the Fifth Republic, the EPB decreed wage rate increases and autumn grain procurement prices. This generated arguments between the EPB and the Ministry of Agriculture over setting grain prices. The EPB has friends in the legislature, with as many as nine National Assemblymen formerly in its bureaucracy (all from the DLP).

The political malaise of the late Fifth Republic was paralleled and exacerbated by growing economic difficulties. Three years of double-digit wage increases contributed to a loss of competitiveness. In 1988, the Presidential Commission on Economic Restructuring submitted its report to the public on what was necessary to move to a more sophisticated economy. In June 1989, President Roh declared the economy was in a state of crisis, and in early November the government announced a package of measures to spur economic growth in general and exports in particular.

An archaic and erratic tax system contributed to higher wages. Unions claimed that much of wage rises was simply passed on to the government in the form of higher tax payments. By August 1989, the government had collected over $1 billion more than it expected in payroll taxes – mostly from low-income workers whose wages had moved upward. Lobby groups suggested that lower taxes for workers might help break the spiral of escalating wage demands. Politically, the controversy emphasized the public perception that the tax system was weighted against workers, in favour of self-employed professionals. In 1988, for example, doctors deducted 90 per cent of their income and lawyers wrote off nearly 75 per cent.[9]

Labour

At the end of the war, South Korea had few resources except land, an impoverished population, and a sympathetic segment of the international community led by the United States. With agrarian reform and population growth, a large urban work force was created. Cheap labour allowed Korean manufactures to enter international markets competitively. To maintain this competitiveness, government policy sought to keep wages low. This meant that workers were unable to enjoy the fruits of their labour. Employers argued that export success, the major source of Korean growth, was possible only with control of labour costs. They contended that the real wages of workers had quadrupled in the ten-year period before 1987, while GNP had only doubled (after adjusting for inflation). Activists said these figures ignored the rapid growth of labour productivity. In the 1980–85 period, productivity rose annually at an average of 10.8 per cent, while wages moved ahead only by 5.5 per cent per year.[10] Under the export-oriented growth strategy, government frequently intervened in labour-management negotiations. Pressures for labour reform – especially to allow union organization – were a significant contribution to the downfall of the Fifth Republic. Korean development was favoured by a large and highly motivated and well educated work force, but the perception of pro-capital favouritism increasingly alienated labour.

After the liberalization of labour, a rash of strikes broke out. Neither labour nor management was sufficiently familiar with the process of collective bargaining, and confrontation was inevitable. Korean wages rose quickly, and by 1990, were second in Asia only to Japan's. The media described wage hikes in Korea as explosive.[11] Middle-income people went on strike for higher wages, better working conditions and democratic participation in enterprise management. In order to avoid higher wages, Korean companies established plants in South and South-east Asian countries. Later, the lower wages in China and North Korea proved attractive as well. Korea's remarkable growth was based on the integration of its human resources – business, labour, and government. In Korea's pluralistic society, further integration was needed to achieve harmonization. Increasingly, labour turmoil and upward settlement of wage disputes contributed to the phenomenon of foreign businesses leaving South Korea for cheaper labour supplies elsewhere.

Managers and government were concerned about the loss of competitiveness with increasing labour costs. Improving wage conditions for workers was lessening the ability to pursue an export-oriented growth strategy – at least under conditions of stable technology. Reforms in the PRC were allowing the Chinese to compete in low-end, low-cost manufacturing, and even South Korean firms were exporting some of their fabrication and assembly lines there. South Korean businesses had at least two options. One was to further internationalize their operations, and another was to move into more complex and advanced technology. In the first, they have been following opportunities provided by the opening of markets in the communist and now former communist world – China, the Soviet Union, Eastern Europe, and Vietnam. Plant investment in a number of other developed and developing countries has been pursued – including Canada. In technology, South Korea has invested heavily in electronics. In 1990, South Korea's electronics industry produced the world's sixth largest output.[12]

Another problem facing South Korea is a possible labour shortage if growth expands beyond 7 per cent. However, in mid-1991, demand for labour still tended to be in lower-skilled areas. The jobless rate of college graduates was 4.5 per cent, 3.4 per cent for high school graduates, and 1.1 per cent for those without secondary credentials. College graduates are 25.2 per cent of total unemployed. Rural employment dropped to 19.5 per cent of the work force.[13] The higher figure for jobless university graduates may have contributed to the alienation of students and intellectuals in South Korean politics.

Despite labour turmoil and far-reaching political and social changes in 1987 and 1988, the economy performed well in 1988, with GNP growing at 12.1 per cent. Unemployment dropped from 3.1 per cent in 1987 to 2.5 per cent in 1988. However, the consumer price index rose by 7.1 per cent. The current account surplus was over $14 billion, a 40 per cent increase over the previous year. The national savings rate climbed to 38 per cent.[14]

A wage explosion followed the 1987 reforms, with a rise of 45 per cent during the 1987–89 period. GNP growth slowed to 6.5 per cent in 1989, and dollar value exports slid from 28 per cent in 1988 to 3 per cent in 1989. There has been a tendency of government to intervene to correct market distortions, especially when such moves promise to make the regime more popular. The public outcry over land prices was followed by a government programme of regulation, ordering *chaebol* to sell off property. Government wants to start using indirect instruments of control such as interest rates and tax policy, but it is difficult to accomplish in the heavily regulated economy. *Chaebol* have been the main objects of Sixth Republic regulation. The government ordered banks to grant 35 per cent of loans to small and middle-sized businesses, in part to deflect the growing public resentment against *chaebol*. But these moves may not be helpful to the economy in the long run. The *chaebol* are diversified and in competition with one another. Opening to foreign competition may be the best way of regulating them. Moreover, despite government prodding, small companies are not emerging as they are in Taiwan.

Capital – the *chaebol* and the state

Proponents of democratization in Korea demanded the dispersal of economic as well as political power. However, they face the dilemma that some part of Korea's economic success has been due to the industrial conglomerates which were able to raise capital, seek new export markets and invest in new ventures. The social cost to Korea was in terms of extended control over the economy and inability to adapt quickly. When the Roh government sought to undertake political reform, the *chaebol* provided popular targets, but when the economy faced further crisis, their utility in capital formation and tackling large projects could not be ignored.

South Korean credit policy contributed to the growth of the *chaebol*.[15] 'Economic planners kept interest rates low, using their control over bank credit to direct cheap money to those borrowers whom they thought should be favoured. These were export-oriented groups, which quickly grew into giant . . . *chaebol*.'[16] In contrast to Taiwan's small and equity-based companies, Korean enterprises were large and debt-based. The result was a combination of heavy foreign borrowing in Korea and high inflation. [17] In 1984, the top ten *chaebol* had sales equal to two-thirds of the country's GNP. Since 1981, government policy-makers have tried to reduce the power of the *chaebol* by limiting bank lending, restricting investments in affiliated companies and channelling credit to small and medium-sized industries. In the Sixth Republic, the administration perceived that their concentrated power was dangerous to the economy and a target of criticism which included the government. The *chaebol* response was to shift some of its money-raising activities to the stock markets.

There were growing political limits on loans to large business groups, and in 1987, the government initiated a policy to eliminate cross-investments by 1990. Investments in affiliated companies were limited to 40 per cent of a corporation's net assets, and the government gave companies until 1992 to phase out holdings in excess of this ceiling. These restrictions were imposed on the forty largest *chaebol*.

The Korean state has sometimes found the *chaebol* difficult to control. Start-up companies were often affiliated with a *chaebol* through personal relationships, although they remained technically independent. A common practice has been for a senior executive to 'retire' and set up a nominally independent firm that is in practice part of the executive's former company. The Lucky-Goldstar group, for example, consisted of sixty-two companies. Samsung has thirty-seven sister firms, Hyundai thirty-four and Daewoo twenty-eight. Government policy has not been successful in reducing family control of the *chaebol*. They continue to be controlled by either the founder or his son – professional managers remain the exception. Control is still exercised by personal influence, rather than through majority stock ownership.[18]

Financial reform

In the spring of 1988, the Ministry of Finance published its draft plan to reform the financial system. One of its aims was to accelerate development of the financial industry. One problem was the policy of large loans to develop key industries, which distorted the resource distribution of the financial institutions. The change of the national economy from deficits to surplus in international payments also created new needs in finance. In the past, government regarded finance as a policy tool to achieve economic development rather than as an independent industry. The Ministry planned to deregulate interest rates, establish a monetary control system through issuance of monetary stabilization bonds, expand loans to small and medium-sized firms, urge financial institutions to engage in other business areas, give the Bank of Korea more independence, ensure savers' deposits, internationalize the financial market, and privatize state-run banks.[19]

However, *won* appreciation in 1989 led to a trade deficit by the end of the year, for the first time in four years.[20] It appeared that Seoul had little alternative but to rehabilitate the *chaebol*. Widespread public distrust of them was based on the premise that their wealth was based on twenty-five years of labour repression, along with preferential treatment and cheap credit from the government. Roh Tae Woo sought to distance himself from the conglomerates in 1987 and place them under government control.[21]

As trade performance deteriorated, government found it needed the *chaebol* to pull the country out of the economic slump. By 1989, the four largest groups – Samsung, Hyundai, Lucky-Goldstar and Daewoo – were estimated to account for about half the country's GNP, and seven *chaebol* trading companies accounted for almost 40 per cent of Korea's total exports. In February the Minister of Trade and Industry said that 'policy would not be to restrict *chaebol* growth but to try to promote small and medium-sized industry so that the imbalance can be redressed'. The major reason for dropping anti-*chaebol* measures was the economic slowdown and Korea's dependence on their export prowess. Exports grew only about 2.8 per cent in 1989, and imports climbed 18.6 per cent. Annual GDP growth slumped to 6.3 per cent from an average of 12 per cent in 1986–88.[22] Seventeen major conglomerates posted deficits in 1989[23]

Government plans to control conglomerates

The financial community became anxious about announced government policy on the 'specialization of domestic business groups', which aimed to help smaller firms. The government concluded not only that domestic conglomerates did not grow to be world-wide first-class businesses but also that their international competitive power had continuously declined because they managed various kinds of diversified businesses, rather than concentrating on several major businesses representing their core activities. The government therefore sought to regulate their enterprises by identifying several specialities for each conglomerate. The business crisis of 1990 was attributed to excessive concentration. Many believed that the second generation of *chaebol* leadership was increasingly incompetent in management, and therefore less capable of leading their organizations. Also, they were perceived to spend their energy in purchasing real estate rather than in developing technology.

On 10 May 1990 the ten biggest *chaebol* announced their intention to liquidate some of their real estate holdings. This followed the semi-official disclosure of a government threat to dissolve two conglomerates and allow the owners to run only the major line of business while professional managers would run the remaining holdings. Seoul announced that future investment would be devoted to improving the competitiveness of main business lines, or to futuristic technology development, as the highest priority. The idea was to take the *chaebol* out of small and medium-size businesses. Industries would assume more public responsibility, and continue 'efforts to make their companies publicly owned and to promote management by professional businessmen, realizing that business should be publicly owned from a societal point of view'.

The resolution was developed jointly by the presidential office, the Ministry of Trade and Industry, and the Korean Federation of Businessmen, almost independently of the opinion of the financial community. Government apparently had three cases in mind as models of specialization: the Kia group, which settled down to be an automobile specialist after separating the owner from the management; the Sammi group, whose founder's second generation was successful in special steels and iron; and the Tongyang group, which was transformed into a financial specialist by the founder's son-in-law. Many believed that the 1990s were the right time to induce fair competition among industries while correcting the maldistribution of wealth to a number of conglomerates.[24]

Chaebol plans in the 1990s[25]

Chaebol reform has been a major feature of reform in South Korea. Their continued bad press as capitalist predators who control industry and important sectors of society – especially real estate – has prompted politicians to take some measures clipping their wings – at least for the sake of appearances. The major conglomerates responded to the changing political climate and economy by drawing up ambitious plans of modernization, and aiming to become leading world-class firms by 2000. Their strategies called for sizable increases in investment in high-tech industries, including semiconductors, genetic engineering, optical communications, aircraft, and chemistry. This will enable them to adjust to a fast-changing industrial order. In addition, they have expanded trade with former communist countries and sold Korean commodities on the world market. The Hyundai group cast the 1990s as a decade for high-tech development, planning to increase technological investment as a percentage of gross sales to the level of 10 per cent by the year 2000, from its current 2 per cent. The Lucky-Goldstar group planned expansion in semiconductors, electrical equipment and electronics, and petrochemicals, with the goal of acquiring a 5 per cent share of the world semiconductor market. The Samsung group aimed at ranking among the world's top ten by

2000.[26] Its strategy has been to concentrate investment in semiconductors, aircraft and space, and genetic engineering. The Daewoo group has chosen electronics, aircraft, and communications as its showpiece industries and pledges to take another leap forward in the 1990s.

Thus, the large conglomerates have tried to be more adaptable and responsive to changing markets and technology – thus enhancing their usefulness to the national economy. Like the Japanese *zaibatsu*, the Korean *chaebol* began as individual and family corporations to become major corporations in their respective nations, with government encouragement. The former were dissolved by the US occupation authorities, and re-emerged as large trading groups in modern Japan. The latter have been stimulated by political changes in modern Korea and economic shifts in the global system to move into new areas and build new strengths.

Agriculture reform

Although rapid industrialization has created a large urban population, many Koreans remain in rural areas. Fast industrialization has been accompanied by a decline in the farming population. In 1963, rural employment accounted for 63 per cent of the total, but fell to 20.7 per cent in 1988.[27] In 1980, South Korea's urban population stood at 57.3 per cent of the total, and at 65 per cent in 1986. In the United States, farmers accounted for only 3 per cent of the population, but produced 32 per cent of GNP. In Korea, the corresponding figures by 1988 were 17.3 per cent and 11.4 per cent, indicating far lower productivity. The average age of Korean farmers has also been rising – over 33 per cent of the farming population are 50 or older, and the figure has been climbing as young people migrate to the cities.[28]

Despite increasing industrialization, South Korea has had to treat the agricultural sector with special care. The Soviet model had sacrificed its peasantry to pay for industrialization, and the Chinese communists used forced agricultural savings to finance development in the cities. Other developing countries subsidize urban consumers at the expense of farmers. Through protection and agrarian programmes, South Korea has managed to feed its population while maintaining and enhancing rural livelihoods. Simultaneously, urbanization and industrialization have reduced the importance of agriculture in the total economy, but not to the point where it can be taken for granted.

Agrarian debt

A growing problem in the countryside has been the high indebtedness of farmers. According to the Ministry of Agriculture, rural household debt rose from 2.19 million *won* in 1986 to 2.4 million in 1987.[29] Despite the rising debt, the ratio of outstanding loans from the money market against the total debt showed a 19.9 per cent decrease because of policy measures replacing loans from the underground money market with loans from banking and non-banking financial institutions. Debt load was higher with more cultivated land. The growing debt was ascribed to slowing income growth rates. Earnings increased at annual rates between 3.4 per cent to 7.1 per cent during 1984–87, while those of wage-earning households in urban areas ranged from 7.1 to 15.8 per cent in the same period. Rising educational and medical costs plus large outlays on equipment were among major causes of snowballing debt.

During 1980–87 annual average farmers' spending, for example, was 18.2 per cent for education and 17.1 per cent for medical expenses. Farming household debt was 7.2 per cent of total assets in 1987, compared with 4.6 per cent in 1982. (The comparable ratio in Japan was 6.8 per cent in 1985.) The increasing farmers' debt was among the major issues in the presidential election in December 1987 and the National Assembly elections in April 1988. The government introduced a set of measures (including concessional loans) to reduce farmer debt in 1987.

Protectionist pressures

Government sought to encourage agricultural diversification away from rice cultivation. Dairy farming was stimulated as an alternative, despite a scarcity of pasturage. With increasing affluence, markets increased. Tight import restrictions excluded foreign produce, and caused considerable complaints among trading partners who saw Korea's trade surplus climb after 1986. Milk imported from New Zealand, for example, cost only one-sixth that of the Korean product.[30]

Seoul was cross-pressured from two sides in its agrarian policy. International trade partners demanded reductions and the elimination of import barriers. The Minister of Agriculture, Forestry and Fisheries, Cho Kong-sik, told US trade representatives that Seoul had to exclude fifteen food items from the Uruguay Round import liberalization list to ensure its food security and the survival of Korean farmers. He insisted that it was impossible to import rice, and that the Korean farming industry was at the level of developing countries, so it required special consideration.[31]

Domestically, the farmers opposed any concessions to GATT.[32] Officials warned that with growing militancy in the countryside and radical students trying to make common cause with the rural poor, the government could be brought down if it liberalized imports too quickly. Liberalization of tobacco imports from the United States became a symbol of resistance. Boycotts by consumer groups were organized, and the use of domestic cigarettes became a badge of national honour – even though Korea had an $8.2 million surplus in tobacco with the United States in 1987. The United States also pressured Korea to liberalize beef, and on 8–9 August 1988, the United States and Korea held the first round of trade talks devoted exclusively to agricultural issues. The cost of agricultural subsidies was growing in Korea, and the National Assembly voted itself the right to set rice prices, a signal of further politicization of agricultural policy.[33]

Another symptom of agricultural problems is that food self-sufficiency has declined from 90.8 per cent (1961) to 48.9 per cent in 1983. Arable land *per capita* in Korea (less than 0.212 acre) is even less than in Japan (0.256 acre) and the United States (6.796 acres).[34] Agricultural interests have played an important part in Korean politics, despite representing a declining portion of the economy.

Environment and pollution

Not unlike most developing countries, Korean stress on economic growth occurred at the expense of environmental concerns. A number of cases of industrial pollution of drinking water have attracted attention in the past several years. Over 13,000 industrial firms discharged about 7.4 million tons of waste water in 1991, and the Ministry of the Environment admitted that pollution control remained primitive. In spite of anti-pollution laws, most firms found it cheaper to pay fines than to treat waste water. Government equipment and personnel for detection and prosecution have been woefully inadequate. In the Ulsan branch of the Pusan District Environment Administration, for example, only eight staff cover 737 waste-emitting firms. The upper Naktong River, which provides tap water for Taegu, had sixty-eight industrial plants discharging phenol. Nationwide, no water in the twenty major water purification plants was categorized as first-class – a status which requires only simple treatment. An increasing flow of heavy metals and other contaminants has been killing off the major rivers. Prosecution of dumpers has been hampered by the law, which holds offenders subject to administrative, not criminal, penalties. Even when serious pollution has occurred, with the collusion of Environment Administration officials, penalties have been very light.[35]

The economic dimensions of social conflict

Korea's transition from developing to developed country has been accompanied by numerous conflicts – some induced or exacerbated by rapid economic change. These conflicts can also be attributed in part to the growing pains of an ethnically homogeneous society moving towards increased economic and social pluralism. Impatience has been an element in Korea's drive to development – impatience with the Japanese colonial legacy which outlawed nationalism, and impatience with a backward economy – compounded by the devastation of war. Korea's outward orientation has contrasted with mainstream development thinking outside the country, which has stressed import substitution as the remedy for underdevelopment. In the 1950s the government pursued an import substitution policy, with accompanying slow growth. From 1961, it combined protection with policies which kept domestic and international prices roughly in line – a fortunate policy in retrospect.

All sectors are not equal in Korean society. In general terms social stratification is related to economic stratification. At the top is 'big capital' – especially the *chaebol*. This class also includes the country's major corporations and financial institutions. Agriculture was the mainstay of Korean society for centuries, and remains the foundation of a decreasingly important economic and social class. The country is also witnessing the emergence of a sizable middle class, consisting of small and medium enterprise proprietors, professionals, and bureaucrats. The status of labour in Korea as a legitimate sector is a recent development. By far the most politically active segment of society has been university students – but their temporary status would exclude them from consideration as a class. Radicals lump the capitalists and government together, whereas in fact there have been increasing conflicts between them. A notable departure of the Sixth Republic has been to expand control over the *chaebol* and to pay more attention to the concerns of labour and the middle class.

Ownership of land has been a source of conflict in Korean society. Land reform was implemented after liberation to give farmers an equitable share of land, but, in the past decades, large combines have purchased property both for expansion of operations and for speculation. Over 65 per cent of all privately owned land is under the oligopolistic control of the top 5 per cent bracket of the population. As a result, a minority has become the beneficiary of capital gains and land development profits produced by the appreciation of real estate values. This phenomenon has promoted social inequity, and legislation has been introduced to set an upper limit to residential-lot ownership.

Economic development has been rapid and successful in South Korea, and the nation is moving into the ranks of the industrialized world. It will still be burdened with problems stemming from this rapid growth even when it completes development. From the standpoint of the political reforms of the Sixth Republic, perhaps the most far-reaching outcome of economic development has been the increasing activism of the middle class, working class, and farmers on behalf of their own interests – as they see government failing to confront the new challenges to the Korean economy.

5   The social context of Korean politics

Divisions and unity in South Korean society

South Korean vulnerability to northern threats and internal poverty required that defence and economic development were the major priorities of government. Overt political ideology played little role in this, and social concerns – particularly leading to a welfare state – have not been a major goal of policy-makers until recent years. It was assumed that benefits would 'trickle down' in the wake of national security and economic growth. There is also apprehension that generous welfare benefits diminish the force of the work ethic.[1] Living and wage standards among industrial workers lagged until the Sixth Republic, as holding labour costs low was part of keeping the Korean economy competitive.[2] While agricultural reforms (especially the Saemaul Undong programme of Park Chung Hee) improved conditions in the countryside, the urban–rural gap has widened.

Young Whan Kihl succinctly states the South Korean development strategy of the Park government:

> Throughout the 1960s, the government relied on the strategy of industrialization and agricultural development via resource, not technology, utilization. Only in the early seventies did it decide to follow the technology-based strategy of agricultural development . . . For this reason, the experience of South Korea since 1961 may be taken as a case of a delayed, but rather successful, response by the government to the main problems of agriculture associated with a rapidly growing economy. These are the increasing discrepancies between the industrial and agricultural sectors of the economy and the rural and urban areas in society. The role played by the central government in agricultural development, though not as domineering and pervasive as that of a centrally planned economy, was important in skilfully steering and directing the economy through the difficult period of uncertainty and imbalanced growth.[3]

Rapid economic change also required the expansion of educational institutions. University students became a significant part of the youth cohort and many expressed their dissatisfaction with political repression through public demonstrations. Student radicalism has served as a popular and unofficial conscience of the nation, dissenting from official policy, raising issues and demanding changes ignored by the government or regarded as too sensitive by the opposition parties.

The mixture of material growth, strong government institutions supported by a powerful military, emerging political pluralism, limited democracy, and a tradition of conscience and dissent has contributed to the volatility of the contemporary confrontation between state and parts of the diverse society. One missing explosive element that has exploded throughout the former communist world is ethnic rivalry – for Korea is one of the most homogeneous nation states in the modern world.[4] The relative absence of rival tribal/primordial loyalties may have enhanced the fluidity of Korean society. In theory, all individuals have an equal opportunity for upward mobility, although far fewer women are able to succeed in the male-dominated world than in many industrial societies. Progress has been made in South Korea, and by the ninth National Assembly, nearly 5 per cent of the representatives were women.[5] Despite rapid modernization, Koreans cling to many traditional mores – including the preference for sons. Unlike many developing societies, ascriptive factors (again, with the exception of sex) play much less a role in access to education – the key route upwards. The result may be that factions are strengthened and bonds of mutual loyalty intensified by the relative absence of competing ethnic identities.

Quee-Young Kim attributes the weak organization of Korean politics to 'secular personalism', which has origins in the Confucian concept of personality:

> The doctrine of the indivisibility of *persona* makes it almost impossible for Korean culture to develop a liberal democracy because the crucial distinction between public and private does not exist. Thus authority in Korean society was personified rather than institutionalized . . . Since the Confucian tradition of personalism has not provided group discipline and the habits of coordination in an organized setting in postwar Korean politics, competition and conflict among the major personalities in these groups have become endemic. Factions rose and fell in the dynamics of power. Political parties formed, disbanded and regrouped around key personalities . . . Electoral campaigns were less issue-oriented and more personality-oriented.[6]

Compromise becomes more difficult because actions provide the symbols and substance of identity. Actions which appear to weaken the explicit solidarity of the group by sending signals of conflict reduction to an opposing group may actually weaken the compromising group, since there is only a tenuous bond in the first place. Personal alliances are crucial in political struggles, and so personal ties must be reinforced repeatedly without the luxury of falling back on primordial identities.

As in traditional Confucian society, family and clan ties are important, and play a significant part in political factions. Another divisive overlay on Korean society has been regionalism. The Korean peninsula possesses geographical compactness, but regions have specific characteristics which contribute to differential roles in political life. Seoul is the national capital and megapolis, with over 25 per cent of the population. Pusan is the south-eastern anchor and major port, with a more cosmopolitan character of its own. Taegu, between the two metropolises, has produced a succession of leaders and even the local high school has achieved political importance in the formation of key personal ties. The south-west, centering on Kwangju, has remained agrarian and less industrialized – often at political loggerheads with the centre. Chollanam-do's favourite son – Kim Dae Jung – long spoke for the resentments of the region towards the centre.

Confucianism has been a powerful organizing principle in East Asia. With origins in China, it provided political, social, ethical and even aesthetic norms for over two thousand years. It provided a hierarchical concept of the cosmos and society, while fusing upward social mobility based on merit and an authoritarian social order. Its stress on education has undoubtedly benefited Korean social development, but its male–female division of labour is perceived as an obstacle to modernization and democracy. The preservation of traditional sex roles in modern Korea remains a pillar of family structure, and proponents point to the central role of the family in providing the best motivating support for education and achievement. In many Asian societies, the Western phenomena of radical individualism, gender equity, and feminism are associated with the breakdown of the family – including divorce, illegitimacy, and single-parent families – which is correlated with other pathologies such as juvenile delinquency, drugs, and crime.[7] From the conservative Korean perspective, these developments are a very high price to pay for the questionable transformation of society into a Western copy.

With the introduction of Christianity to Korea in the nineteenth century, an additional source of fragmentation was attached to society. Catholicism and the Protestant denominations made major inroads, and were far more successful in proselytization than in Japan or China. For many migrants to the cities, churches provided a focus of activity and identity, which also influenced their views on politics and economics. For women, Christianity had a certain liberating impact:

> Becoming a Christian meant a certain independence from male-determined roles for women. More importantly, 'Christian' also meant the possibility of martyrdom or of becoming an educator, physician, business woman, politician, or missionary – but all directed towards building a harmonious family and a new nation, in which men and women together would be more fully free.[8]

The present chapter will address some of the social dynamics of change and adaptation in South Korea to supply a context for the reforms of 1987. The character of the South Korean state is not only conditioned by society, but has evolved in response to the challenges of governing society. The South Korean government did not have to confront the problem of integration, for centuries of Korean history had created an integrated society. However, the destruction of the traditional state apparatus by decay and the imposition of Japanese empire meant that post-World War II government had to create a new system of governing.

A number of social issues in South Korea affect the generation of conflict and the movement towards democracy. These include education, student radicalism, the rising middle class, art and culture, agrarian reform, women, and the media. In these areas the state has been moving from a semi-repressive role to one of greater liberalization – within the limits of maintaining security, social stability, and economic development. Some movement towards an expanded welfare state is also evident. As organized labour acquires more freedom to strike, wages are pushed higher, and Korea's competitive advantage in manufacturing may decrease unless steps are taken to increase competitiveness.

Several generalizations can be stated as points of departure for understanding the impact of changes in Korean society:

1 Rapid economic and social change is transforming Korea from a predominantly rural, agricultural and ethnically homogeneous society into one which is increasingly urbanized, industrial and socially fragmented, with an increasingly complex division of labour.

2 South Korean pluralism has maintained a relatively open society, which has forced government to be accountable for its actions and policy outcomes. The notion of continuous economic improvement has become part of South Korea's operational ideology. Unequal distribution of income has pushed society towards class formation[9] and resultant frictions over inequities.

3 Emphasis on economic development has stressed education as a vital

sector of institutional development. Both the state and the private sector have attended to the needs of education. The combination of a relatively large student population, continuing (and inevitable) social and economic inequities, incomplete authoritarian control, and the rhetoric of democracy has pushed students to the forefront in dissent and activism.

4 The combination of opposition political parties, labour activism, and student dissent challenging the authoritarian state has had two major effects:

(a) A positive effect, from the perspective of democratization, has been that mutual challenges from the diverse groups in society have made it difficult for any sector to become entrenched in permanent power without responding to dissent and challenge with policy and/or personnel changes.

(b) One of the serious negative effects is the breakdown, or threat of breakdown, of civil order, which in turn has produced strong pressures on the military to intervene in politics. This intervention has been justified by the potential for North Korean opportunity for intervention and subversion.

These characteristics of contemporary Korean society will be examined below.

Factors of social change

Rapid social and economic change

Conservatism remains strong – especially in rural areas – despite the turmoil and social dislocation which accompanied the collapse of the Korean monarchy, fifty years of Japanese colonialism, the division of the country, and a devastating war. The Confucian version of conservatism remains a brake on social change – particularly in the realm of women and the family. In early 1987, thousands of Confucianist protesters gathered at the National Assembly to oppose revision of the Family Law Bill. The rewriting was supported by the Women's Union for Family Law Revision, which urged major changes in many traditional family practices and would guarantee equality for men and women within clans. Among other issues, the revised Bill permitted marriage between persons with the same surname and place of family origin. Not surprisingly, Confucian traditionalists strongly opposed the change.[10] Under the old law, marriage partners with the same ancestry could not marry – even if their common ancestor had been twenty generations ago. Their marriages could be solemnized in church, but not registered. Nor could births from these unions be legally registered, and offspring were considered illegitimate. Insurance policies were also affected and spouses could not be beneficiaries.[11] Conservatism was also evident in a social preference for sons, and widespread resistance to upward mobility in careers for women. Demographic change has also been transforming Korean society. In the period since establishment of the Republic, there has been a major migration to the cities in the search for employment and higher living standards. During 1988, for example, rural population decreased by 6.4 per cent.[12] The flow to the cities has made farms an increasingly male domain, as women and young persons go to jobs in the urban areas.

According to the 1985 (1 November) census conducted by the EPB, South Korea had a population of 40,448,486, and was the world's fourth most densely populated country, with 408 persons per square kilometre. Nearly a quarter of the population resided in the greater Seoul area – with 40.8 per cent born there. This represented an increase of 15.3 per cent for Seoul, and of 24.5 per cent for Kyonggi-do, the province surrounding Seoul, over the previous census. Pusan followed, with nearly 3.5 million (an increase of 11.2 per cent), with 43.7 per cent of the population Pusan-born.

Although the population increased by 8.1 per cent in five years, the more rural provinces showed declines. By 1989, the population growth rate had fallen to 0.93 per cent, with life expectancy at 70.8 years.[13] Chollanam-do, for example, lost 0.8 per cent and Kyongsangbuk-do lost 10.1 per cent of their respective populations since 1980. The greatest urban growth was highest in Taegu (26.4 per cent) and Inchon (28.0 per cent) The census also showed that the population was growing older, with 4.3 per cent aged 65 or above, compared with 3.9 per cent in 1980. Marriage age was increasing, from 27.3 in 1980 to 27.8 for males, and from 24.1 to 24.7 for females. The housing situation had declined, with 46.6 per cent of households without their own housing units, compared with 41.6 per cent in 1980. In the four major cities, this figure was 62.7 per cent.[14] As South Korea modernizes, the population structure changes, and living standards have improved. Two major results of change have been the expansion of the urbanized population, and the growth of an urban middle class.

In 1990, the rural population was 25.6 per cent of the total, compared with 72 per cent in 1960.[15] Because of mountainous terrain, only 21.7 per cent of the total land area is under cultivation, and the amount available for farming becomes less every year as more urban and industrial sites are created. Agricultural production doubled from 1962 to 1976, and continued to climb. Through land reform, mechanization and improved techniques, self-sufficiency in cereals increased. Small farm size contributed to high population density in rural areas, although urban migration has given some relief. Out-migration from farms affected the mix of population, with cities attracting younger people, and especially young women, who find city life more liberating than the conservative countryside.

The *Saemaul Undong*, initiated by Park Chung Hee in 1971, attempted to reduce the economic and social gap between city and country. It was a comprehensive rural development programme aimed at improving the rural environment and boosting farm income. It had funded over 14 million projects by 1984, including construction of new farm roads, bridges, waterways, new houses, and communal facilities. Electricity was supplied to nearly all farming households. Farm household income increased from 356,000 *won* in 1971 to an average of 2,227,000 by the end of the decade.[16]

Migration to urban areas has affected land prices, which skyrocketed in the wake of speculation. This caused the distortion of asset values and popular anger against windfall gains, leading to a legislative Bill in September 1989 to impose stiff controls and heavy taxes on land ownership. The outcry came loudest from lower middle-class members who saw the prices of homes rising 20 per cent and more in the cities – rises which many saw as artificially induced. Government restrictions on new house prices played a role, and helped to discourage new home builders. To solve the crisis, the government announced plans to spend $6 billion to build two new satellite towns near Seoul to provide 700,000 new housing units. With 40 per cent of the nation's population in the greater Seoul area, the housing crunch was becoming serious.[17] At the end of 1991, there were 10,580,000 family units in 7,870,000 housing units, indicating that over a quarter of Korean families were sharing their units with another family. Crowding was almost entirely an urban phenomenon.[18]

Affluence and redistribution of wealth

Economic development has resulted in the accumulation of wealth, but distribution has been a major concern. Regional disparity has been at the centre of inequity:

> President Park's and President Chun's home area of the Kyongsang provinces had a greater share of industry, infrastructure, industrialized employment, and capital, while the Cholla provinces had a falling per centage of industrial employment, a significantly higher failure rate of business, and lower *per capita* income (PCI). In 1963, *per capita* income in Seoul was 2.2 times that in Cholla and Kyongsang. By 1983, however, while the disparity between Seoul and Cholla fell to 1.8, virtual parity prevailed between Seoul and Kyongsang.[19]

While the *chaebol* have been major beneficiaries (and drivers) of economic development, a new middle class has emerged. With industrial affluence, the urban middle class is increasingly oriented to accumulation and consumption, and has become more important for growth, especially when the export-led economy lags or falters. The trend matches government efforts to defuse protectionist pressures by slowing exports. By 1988, there had been two years of wage increases of more than 15 per cent. Consumer spending rose by 19 per cent in the first half of 1988. Car sales were up 80 per cent and electronics increased by 36 per cent and consumers were expected to buy over half of estimated domestic car production. High economic growth (8.4 per cent in 1991) has allowed the *per capita* GNP to reach US$6,498 income in 1991 – double the $3,110 of 1987.[20] More than 23 per cent of the GNP was wages, due in part to an average wage increase of 17 per cent the previous year. Unemployment was at a record low. Inflation reached 9.5 per cent, as Korean consumers bought more, and travelled more.

As families become smaller, they tend to save less money for children's education – although this area of economizing may disappear as education becomes more expensive – and participate in consumer spending. Housing has become a major growth area, with increasing government involvement. The government housing budget doubled in less than five years. The Korea Housing Bank had been the country's only financial institution to offer residential mortgages, but the government began to urge commercial banks to offer mortgages as a way of stimulating house ownership.[21]

Concentration of economic resources in the *chaebol*, along with their real estate speculation, was an obstacle to housing affordability. In 1989, the thirty largest *chaebol* owned 120,000 acres of the nation's expensive private land, worth 12 trillion *won*. Their ability to expand was supported by access to loans from commercial banks at preferential rates and terms (a situation not unlike Japan's). These *chaebol* borrowed some US$72 billion from banks or other financial institutions amounting to 40 per cent of the nation's GNP for the year. They also acquired 35 trillion *won* of windfall income with the hike of their real estate values the previous year. This prompted opposition lawmakers on the National Assembly Finance Committee to call for a change in the government's financial and banking policy, which had been heavily in favour of the *chaebol*.[22]

The Korean economic miracle moved quickly into heavy industry. Some indices will indicate its success. In global terms, South Korea is second in shipbuilding, eighth in steel production, and eleventh in motor manufacturing. Over the twenty years prior to 1990, Korea's GNP increased twenty-six times, and its average growth rate was 8.6 per cent. However, personal income was fortieth in the world, despite the country having the fifteenth largest GNP in the world. It has been a contradiction breeding social conflict. Nearly one-fifth of the population holds 42.2 per cent of national income. Housing supply rates have been falling as well – from 71.2 per cent in 1980 to 70.9 per cent in 1989, far below Taiwan's 90.8 per cent. As in Japan, soaring land prices increasingly place affordable housing out of reach of workers. It takes at least twenty-eight years for a salaried person to save enough to buy a modest house. 'The disappearance of a hard-working attitude, rampant over-consumption, prevalence of runaway inflation, and shortage of workers in manufacturing are the representative negative ingredients darkening the future of the Korean economy.'[23]

The wealth of the economic elite inspired indignation and continues to be a source of friction between government and voters. The government's 1990 budget was seen by many as worsening the wealth distribution problem. The government tightened the money supply and credit to absorb the excess liquidity, but the money squeeze caught the public and small businesses in a financial pinch. For those with money, it was an opportunity to expand real estate holdings. At the lower end of society, it is estimated that over three million people live in poverty. The Economic Planning Board reported that 7.7 per cent of the entire population receive significant public assistance. The 3,315,000 welfare beneficiaries compare with Taiwan's 0.6 per cent and Japan's 1.2 per cent. Chollanam-do has the largest number of poor people (527,224), followed by Chollabuk-do with 434,310.[24]

Another area of popular resentment has been political abuse of the economic system. Elections get more expensive with genuine open competition, and candidates have looked for more cash for their campaign coffers. Election candidates also promise projects to attract voters – often with minimum regard for the feasibility and the ability of government to pay for the schemes.[25]

A rough but fluid class structure of upper, middle and lower classes has emerged in the wake of phenomenal economic growth. Continued growth and some degree of welfare disbursement have produced limited optimism and reduced misery, although many people feel their new-found prosperity remains fragile.

Pluralism and equality

Social pluralism

South Korea can be described as a plural and opening society, which has forced government to be accountable for its actions and policy outcomes. The notion of continuous economic improvement has now become institutionalized in South Korean thinking. Unequal distribution of income has led to some degree of class formation and resultant frictions over inequities. The emerging economic structure in South Korea is a source of intensified confrontation and fragmentation in an otherwise homogeneous nation. Uneven distribution of wealth certainly animates the passions of egalitarian politics, which can aggravate envy and resentment. Political egalitarianism seeks a society free from domination.[26] Development has created wealth in South Korea, and political action is seen to provide means for a more equitable distribution.

The growth of the South Korean state has been the story of the accumulation of power and material goods. As wealth increased, so did its concentration – but not to the same degree as in many other developing countries. Dissent has been fuelled by the demand for distributive justice. Counter to the idea of accumulation is distributive justice. According to Walzer, it draws the entire world of goods within the reach of philosophical reflection. Nothing can be omitted. 'Distribution is what social conflict is all about.'[27]

Material changes play a part in social diversity and political turmoil, but these economic factors are only one element among several. Two views of society's goals have produced the image of a polarized South Korea. The first was the rational-bureaucratic structures which have successfully led the country on the path of industrialization and economic growth. Requiring political order, it is a model which in practice has relied on authoritarian state mechanisms to transform and develop society. It has sought concentration of power to accumulate wealth and develop technology. It values expertise and organization, and promotes material growth as the lever to produce a more just society. The success of this model has given it considerable credibility, especially within the middle class which has been growing larger under the last four Republics.

The second view is held by dissenters, who claim that growing inequality condemns large numbers of workers and farmers to poverty. They also want to define the political community in a humane – rather than materialistic – way. This view has been influenced not only by Marxism, but by Christian ideas of justice and equality. Its roots are also in the Tong-a Rebellion of the nineteenth century, and in the Confucian tradition of resistance to illegitimate power. Patriotism and nationalism under Japanese occupation also exerted an influence on the opponents of authoritarianism. For some, the nationalism of North Korea's Kim Il Song is an inspirational alternative to what they see as consumerism and *sadae* – 'serving the Great Powers'. The contemporary *minjung* movement, which often romanticizes folk and native culture, claims to remain faithful to an authentic Korean identity.[28] To the critics of the rational-bureaucratic state, the reforms of 1987 were largely cosmetic and a grudging response to middle-class demands. In this interpretation, the Sixth Republic is merely a more mature version of bourgeois capitalist democracy, and has little relevance to the needs of justice and redistribution. Subsequent demonstrations in 1991 were more economic-oriented, and drew support from lower economic strata.[29]

Religion and Korean society

An important anchor for individuals and families in a rapidly changing society has been religious affiliation. Religious freedom was established in 1945, and churches of many denominations and Church-related educational institutions formed rapidly. Confucianism endured, with hundreds of shrines and a large number of followers. Shamanism had been neglected in the colonial past, but began a revival after the end of Japanese occupation. Popular religious sects also proliferated. Buddhism retained the largest following, and increased its strength after 1961 when the government provided more financial assistance to the church.

Protestantism has been associated with modern Western civilization and democracy and with the growing desire for a modern way of life. The number of denominations, their Churches, and other institutions grew rapidly. South Korea has the largest Protestant population in Asia, with over a dozen major Protestant denominations with over 21,000 churches and over seven million followers. A number of Korean nationalist leaders had membership in Protestant Churches.[30] Other religions, including Islam, have also attracted followers.

Christian activists have dominated South Korea's dissident movement. Their *minjung*, or 'masses', theology draws on shamanism, traditional folk tales and peasant rebellions in an attempt to create a uniquely Korean liberation theology. *Minjung* is a Korean protest myth, a moral story of bondage and liberation, as much as it is specifically Christian. Kim Dae Jung, a devout Catholic, reflects some of the *minjung* theology in the sense that the masses, in his view, are the only legitimate rulers of his country, and he claimed to be their rightful leader.[31]

This religious element of Korean social life has added a significant dimension to the pluralist complexion, providing individuals with membership in groups and associations not directly controlled by the state. This voluntary dimension of social life has increasingly found expression in non-compliance with state authoritarianism, and provided a vehicle of political protest. The case of the Korean Catholic Church offers one example.

Catholicism was introduced to Korea in the nineteenth century, and was an anti-feudal alternative to Confucianism, preaching egalitarianism. It emphasized filial piety, but placed divine authority above family. Similar to Protestantism in calling for the dignity, autonomy, and equality of men and women, it provided the spiritual correlate to democracy in Korean liberation ideas. It offered solace and hope to the lower classes, where its popularity has been strongest.[32]

The visit of Pope John Paul II to Seoul in May 1984 provided additional stimulus to Korean Catholicism. He used the occasion to canonize 103 local martyrs (ten French missionaries and ninety-three native converts) in the largest mass canonization in the history of the Roman Catholic Church and the first of its kind outside the Vatican in modern times. In this one event, the Church celebrated religion, martyrdom, and Korean national identity.

The Catholic Church contributed greatly to Korea's 'Western learning', despite the monarchy's initial persecution of native Catholics. South Korea boasts some 1.7 million Catholic converts, with over 5,000 priests and over 600 churches. The Church runs some sixty colleges and schools and seventy social and medical institutions. Both Catholicism and Protestantism are growing fast among the poor in cities as well as in the countryside. The Protestant Urban Mission was an activist group designed to protect the rights of textile workers, and the Catholic Farmers' Association was active in organizing farmers to defend their interests.[33] South Korea, remains tolerant of all faiths and beliefs, unlike North Korea, where any expression of Christianity is forbidden. Through the protests leading to the Sixth Republic and in subsequent anti-government demonstrations, the Christian Churches often provided sanctuary to dissidents. In June 1991, Myongdong (Catholic) Cathedral became embroiled in a stand-off between a student dissident and the police.[34]

Social communication – the popular media and reforms

Modern pluralism consists of a diverse group structure outside state domination, giving citizens in associations representation of their economic, cultural, and social interests. In plural societies, the media can play a crucial communication role – projecting and amplifying ideas and information within the group, among groups, and between group and government. In totalitarian systems, information channels to society are almost completely dominated by the state.

The popular media in South Korea have been both the catalyst and the beneficiaries of liberalization. While authoritarian regimes in the past imposed severe restrictions, controlled television and radio, and treated journalists as political enemies on occasion, the media had enough latitude to inform the public of a wide range of news.[35]

In August 1980 the government branded as anti-government – and purged – around 700 journalists, effectively barring them from their profession. Three months later, fourteen newspapers were forced to close, seven news agencies were merged into the Yonhap News Agency and twenty-seven privately run television stations were made part of the Korean Broadcasting System (KBS) or Munhwa Broadcasting Corporation (MBC, 70 per cent owned by KBS). Under the Basic Press Law Seoul-based newspapers were prohibited from maintaining regional bureaus, while provincial newspapers could not keep staff in Seoul. The Basic Press Law formed the primary legal basis which both established a hierarchical structure in the press and provided strong enforcement measures against any effort to alter this structure. A law was enacted to justify the legal status of KBS, which merged five television stations – a move intended to tighten control over the press.

The Basic Press Law was signed on 26 December 1980, shortly after President Chun Doo Hwan came to power, and it went into effect in January 1981. It facilitated government control of the media by giving the Ministry of Information power to license any media organization and to cancel that permission. It strictly defined the responsibility of the media, and enabled government deregistration. It stressed press responsibility at the expense of press freedom, and continued in force until 10 November 1987, when the National Assembly repealed the Basic Press Law and enacted new legislation for broadcast media. The new law established a broadcasting commission, which was founded in May 1989.

By 1987 the press was increasingly ignoring the government guidelines of the BPL, which was a major target of media pressure. In his 29 June proclamation, Roh Tae Woo pledged that the Basic Press Law 'should promptly be either extensively revised, or abolished and replaced by a different law'. An opposition group of journalists, the Council for a Democratic Press, led the fight for the liberalization of the press, arguing that it made other basic freedoms possible. In early 1987, three journalists were tried for publishing, in an underground magazine, the text of a number of secret government guidelines. The defendants were convicted, but received light suspended sentences, as the censors were losing confidence in their own work. The news media played an important part in keeping the momentum of the protests alive, serving as a 'forum for previously unheard criticism of the government – from newspapers publishing, in full, the statements of opposition leaders and groups to the television broadcasting unprecedented debates between spokesmen of the ruling and opposition parties.'[36]

Newspapers were not the only medium pressing for reform. On 15 July 1987 the Christian Broadcasting System (CBS) put aside its religious and music programming, and reported the news, with a report on constitutional talks between the opposition party and government, as well as a report on the lifting of martial law in Taiwan. The station received a warning from the Ministry of Culture and Information for violating the revised Radio Wave Regulation Law, which prohibits it from airing news or commercial advertisements. This ban on advertising had brought about a financial crisis for CBS. On 13 July, reporters of Munhwa Broadcasting Corporation issued a statement calling for independent reporting, the resignation of key government-appointed officials, and the reinstatement of the reporters and producers expelled in 1980. Reporters of KBS made the same demands two days later.

The government soon announced its intention to modify the Basic Press Law. From 1 August newspapers were allowed to set up regional bureaus[37] and a change in the press law allowed the expansion of regional newspapers. In addition, religious bodies and other corporations began broadcasting on newly available radio frequencies. There were thirty national and regional newspapers in June 1987, and by the end of 1989, the number had increased to sixty-eight. For periodicals, there were 2,241 prior to liberalization, and 3,441 by December 1988.

The media were also the locus of a struggle over union organization. Journalists had tried and failed to organize a union in 1974. In late October 1987, reporters of the *Hankook Ilbo* formed a union, and received a certificate of registration from the Jongro ward office in Seoul. It was a turning point, and was followed by other company unions. In April 1988, reporters formed the first national council of journalist unions. This was expanded in November to form a National League of Journalism Unions, with charter membership of forty-one unions. By early 1989, there were unions in forty-three media corporations.

Rigid control over the full fabric of society has not been widespread in South Korea. Economic class identification has taken place as a result of internal migration, industrialization, and economic development. Religious affiliation has been practically unobstructed, and few legal restrictions have been placed on religious organizations. The public media were a limited exception during the Fifth Republic, but even before the 1987 reforms, considerably more freedom was allowed than in communist states. Now, many of the previous restrictions have been lifted, and criticism of government is far more uninhibited than ever before. The pluralism of Korean society has been reinforced, and a strong foundation of democracy appears to be in place.

Education and Korean society

Economic development has emphasized education as a vital sector of institutional modernization.[38] The combination of a relatively large student population, continuing social and economic inequities, incomplete authoritarian control, and the rhetoric of democracy has pushed students to the forefront in dissent and activism. A pre-independence tradition of anti-Japanese activism in universities has also been a contributing factor to intellectual dissent.

The traditional notion of education involved the transmission of knowledge based on hallowed canons and orthodoxy, and examinations to recruit into government service those who had best mastered the classics. In the theory of Korean Confucianism, an educated (and aristocratic) elite was expected to provide leadership for society by setting a moral example in wisdom and virtue. In practice, political factionalism characterized the intellectual elite as often as not. Whatever unity of purpose existed under the monarchy was severely impaired during Japanese colonialism.

The collapse of traditional intellectual orthodoxy contributed to the growth of capitalism by weakening or removing the strictures against profit-making, and opening other paths of mobility. The Japanese empire also opened new scope for Korean mercantile activity, as traders and settlers moved into Manchuria, Siberia, and Japan. This diaspora, born of necessity and desperation, also established the roots of the future overseas Korean communities. When the South Korean Republic was established, a new education system was initiated. Confucian respect for learning and pragmatic recognition that education was a key to economic development focused government attention on colleges and universities as inputs to state prosperity.

An unanticipated consequence was the creation of potential centres of dissent in an otherwise authoritarian ordered state. At the local level of education, primary and secondary schools reasserted a Confucian approach to learning – with a strong dose of indoctrination. In the universities, students often experienced a major break with the old family mores, with greater freedom and a subculture at odds with local parochialism. In addition to less pressure to study – now that the major life hurdle of university admission had been cleared – extracurricular life took on a strong political element, usually directed against the government of the day.

Student protest has grown out of the pressure-cooker atmosphere of university admission preparation. Many families make great sacrifices to finance their children's higher education, with cramming schools and tutors to provide an extra edge in the competition for a university place. For four years, students engage in study, and often social dissent – opposing the government on a wide range of issues. The radical activists comprise only a minority, but peer pressures pull in many who may be apolitical. Protest has taken the form of suicide as well as violent confrontation with the police. Many policemen are of the same age as the students, and see their antagonists as pampered children throwing a tantrum. Beleaguered by stones and firebombs, they resent the combination of education and privileges they have been denied and carry a perception of irresponsible behaviour by this 'future elite'.

Education in Korea

The Korean educational system has been a contradiction. On the one hand, it has continued to produce a literate, highly skilled work force without the totalitarian regimentation that is characteristic of the north. On the other side, it also appears flawed by underfunding and the stresses caused by extreme competition for placement in universities. For millions of young people, access to university education may be the only road to a secure and prosperous future. For many, pushed to succeed by family and peers, failure exacts painful penalties. Students face intense pressures to enter the top universities in Korea. College entrance exams are highly competitive, and freshman quotas are regulated by the government. In 1988, 126 students, and 122 in 1989, in middle and high school, committed suicide, with most attributed to poor academic performance which would preclude admission to the better universities.[39] Criticism of the system finally led to a change in the Ministry of Education examination. Starting in 1994, university admission tests will include aptitude and high school grades, as well as the emphasis on memorization of the past.[40]

Even graduation does not guarantee successful employment, although the record has been improving. In June 1990, 60 per cent of job-seeking graduates had found employment, with Seoul graduates (72.2 per cent) more successful than those from provincial schools (55.4 per cent). The lowest rate of 46.8 per cent came from teachers' colleges. Men (72.9 per cent) fared much better than women (41.4 per cent) graduates.[41] Lee Won Sul, former president of Han Nam University in Taejon, reported that there were probably over 4,500 PhDs who could not find teaching positions owing to inadequate funding of higher education. In private colleges and universities, the staff–student ratio has jumped from 1 : 19.7 in 1971 to 1 : 40 at present.[42]

Korean private colleges receive very little funding from government – budgets in private institutions depend largely on tuition fees (80 per cent) for financing, compared with 38.7 per cent in the United States and 60 per cent in Japan. Private corporations have started to become involved in funding higher education, and the pattern of assistance has changed the emphasis from conventional scholarships for individual students. Some *chaebol* now extend major financial assistance to school operations, providing subsidies or building science and technology research institutions and various other facilities on campus. Seoul National University was the beneficiary of a 25 billion *won* grant from the Korea Explosives Company to mark the fortieth anniversary of its founding. The group has also been active in providing assistance to research in the natural sciences. The main objection to this trend has been the tendency to aid universities in the Seoul area, at the expense of regional schools. In another case, the Sunkyong group disposed of some of its excess land by donating it to the University of South Chungchong. It had been under pressure to reduce its holdings under the Real Estate Regulatory Measure of 10 May 1990.⁴³

Historically, Koreans have valued education as part of their Confucian legacy. With the abolition of the aristocracy and the post-war end to colonialism, economic growth and a bureaucratic meritocracy transformed educational achievement into a major avenue of upward mobility. Government has filled part of the need for mass education, along with the private sector, including religious groups, which has set up colleges and universities. The stress on private funding has led to a few school operations aimed at profit at the expense of education goals. King Sejong University began as a small women's teaching college, becoming a junior college in 1954, and a co-educational university in 1978. The founder and his wife allegedly ran the university as a 'personal kingdom', appointing relatives and followers to important administrative and academic posts. After student protests in 1988, the couple's son stepped down as dean of the graduate school of business administration. The couple had several other businesses as well. In 1990, a crisis erupted when students went on strike, closing the university. Government officials wanted the university turned over to accredited and more professional educators.⁴⁴

Educational reform

South Korea is rapidly passing from an industrial society to post-industrialism, and must nurture its knowledge and information sectors to maintain its pace. Problems had festered under previous Republics, and could not be ignored. Education had to be further modernized in order to keep up with changing markets and technology, if growth were to be maintained. The advantages of a skilled, disciplined, and low-cost work force were eroded by several factors. Political turmoil was making the economy more unpredictable, and repression of dissent only generated further alienation. Easing restrictions on labour unions had also contributed to a large number of labour disputes and strikes. The growing pains of industrialization were increasing the costs of labour. Moreover, reforms in the People's Republic of China made location in China an attractive option for foreign investors – including those from South Korea, despite the absence of formal relations. The combination of rising industrial labour costs favoured the growth of higher value-added manufacturing and also information, knowledge and service-oriented sectors. These require higher skills and greater investment in human resources and education. Under a five-year plan for educational reform, the government called for advancing the proportion of high school graduates going to college from 53 per cent to 83 per cent by 1996. It also projected training up to 50 per cent of secondary graduates in vocational education.

Plans for educational expansion faced trouble in the universities. A number of incidents at Korean institutions resulted in violence against teaching staff and officials, who decried a growing loss of respect for teachers. Other developments affecting the university reflected the shift of moral values in a changing society. These included the rebellion against authoritarianism, the prevalent parental emphasis on success, and the life of youth centered around examinations. Critics of materialism asserted that education should teach how to live, not only how to make a living.[45] With the implementation of local autonomy in 1991, local control of primary education was introduced. City and provincial assemblies began to elect board members in conformity with the new Education Law of 26 March 1991.[46]

The South Korean education system has been far from perfect, but it has been a crucial source of recruitment of personnel for rapid industrialization. Universities have been major centres of dissent against government, and demonstrators claim to be the conscience of the nation. The frustrations of education – including mismanagement, scandals and prospects of unemployment – have been part of student volatility. But the dissidents have also had an impact on the political system – arousing the conscience of the middle class, threatening civil order, pushing for democratic reforms, pressuring for contacts with North Korea, and demanding educational reform.

The emergence of the modern nation state in East Asia has been influenced much less by Western imperialism and much more by the Confucian heritage than was the case in other areas of the non-Western world – a fact not commonly recognized by social scientists. The modern success of post-Confucian, non-revolutionary societies can be attributed to traditions of social solidarity, pre-modern achievement orientation, emphasis on education, a modified feudalism which tolerated upward mobility supported by strong family ties, relatively high literacy, and a propensity to save, accumulate, and plan for extended future economic security at the clan and nuclear family level. This background and the nature of modern development in East Asia (especially the impact of war and rapid industrialization) suggest that the future content of democracy in the region will only superficially resemble its counterparts in the West. Hierarchy, family loyalty, a balance of individual and collective responsibilities, and the pursuit of competence through education are likely to resist the absorption of recent Western values such as full gender equality, multiculturalism, and self-esteem as a goal of education.

Social conflict – catalyst for democracy?

Plural society under the authoritarian state has been both a dynamic and an explosive combination in South Korea. The assortment of opposition political parties, labour activism, student dissent, and the authoritarian state has had at least two major effects:

1 A *positive* effect, from the perspective of democratization, has been that mutual challenges from the diverse groups in society have made it increasingly difficult for any sector to entrench itself in permanent power without responding to dissent and challenge with policy and/or personnel changes.
2 A serious *negative* effect is the breakdown, or frequent threat of breakdown, of civil order, which in turn has produced strong pressures on the military to intervene in politics. This intervention has been justified by the potential for North Korean opportunities of intervention and subversion. Education has been an area manifesting social disorder and the clash of traditional culture against the changes. A negative view of this clash is that it activates dysfunctional tensions which erode social solidarity and invites military intervention.

A more positive role of social ferment is that it has facilitated adaptation to the rapid economic and political changes of the nation. From the perspective of democratization, confrontation between student dissidents (who may not always understand the issues they are protesting about – such as north–south talks) and the military (who desire order and security – the survival of the state – above all) has a beneficial role in forcing government to address public issues. The broad popular demonstrations of 1960 overthrew the Rhee oligarchy, and each step towards civilian constitutional government has been provoked by the threat of collapsing order. In a sense, South Korean civil order has been a hostage of society.

The ubiquity of violence

Violence and confrontation have long been part of the South Korean political process. With elections often manipulated by the government party or subjected to the excessive influence of money, citizens become cynical, as evidenced in the local voting in June 1991. Frustrated in the balloting, a broad spectrum of groups saw confrontation or withdrawal as the rational response to corrupted politics. With the reforms initiated by the Sixth Republic, confrontations have become less violent, and the political process is more embedded in elections.

The most violent uprising and suppression occurred in 1980, when residents of the southern city of Kwangju (the provincial capital of Chollanam-do) seized weapons from the local arsenal. The affair undermined the legitimacy of the Fifth Republic, and haunted the Sixth Republic. The affair was debated in the press and legislature. After over ten years, the government decided to pay compensation upon request for the 200 civilians killed and 1,100 injured when martial law troops opened fire on civilians protesting against the declaration of martial law in May 1980.[47] Nevertheless, the incident has continued to haunt state–society relations since then.

From violent confrontation to political manoeuvres

A common feature of modern Korean politics has been the fragmentation and squabbling of political parties within a context of often violent confrontation in the streets. The increasing consultation of opposition parties in government was a tentative contribution to normalization of politics at the beginning of the Sixth Republic, and helped carry out the reforms. After the 1987 election, Roh Tae Woo promised to maintain consultation with the opposition parties, but frustrations and instability led to the formation of the new DLP on 22 January 1990. This set off a new wave of demonstrations during the remainder of the year. The Party for Peace and Democracy (PPD) mounted an intensified street struggle against the government. It started with a national campaign to collect signatures from 10 million people by 26 March, to be followed by outdoor rallies.[48] However, the opposition groups failed to mobilize sufficient support for their spring drive. In August they sought to combine street demonstrations with their own organizational restructuring. Most significantly, the PPD and the Democratic Party (DP) could not agree on the nomination of a leader for the prospective unified opposition party or on sharing party posts. The PPD negotiators demanded unification before anything, while the DP side called for a solution before unification.[49]

The government claimed that many of the demonstrations were either North Korea-directed or preludes to armed uprisings – invoking the spectre of further Kwangju-type turmoil. In August 1990, military and civilian police arrested twenty-seven people on charges of plotting an uprising to overthrow the government. The arrests were conducted by the defence security command under the authority of the Natioional Security Law. All 'were in their 20s and college students on temporary absence from school or suspended'. The accused were charged with 'forming an alliance of revolutionary workers' class struggle' in March 1987 and planning to topple the government in an armed uprising and set up a socialist state.[50] The National Police Headquarters claimed that the group master-minded anti-government rallies and demonstrations, and that the 'group attempted to organize a revolutionary army by attacking a munitions area where weapons are kept for reserve Army troops.'[51]

After Roh took office on 25 February 1988, the number of people arrested for political offences doubled, according to the PPD. The party said that between that date and 30 November 1990, an average of four people a day were arrested for anti-government activities, or a total of 4,020. The arrest rate for the so-called public security offenders soared from 2.6 a day in March–December 1988 to 4.2 a day in 1989 and 5.2 a day for the first eleven months of 1990, according to data compiled in co-operation with social and religious groups, colleges and universities. Many of the arrestees were charged with violating more than one law. Charges brought under the National Security Law took up the biggest share at 537, followed by the law on assemblies and demonstrations at 246, on firebombs at 271 and on violence at 219. The law on firebombs was enacted on 1 July 1989 in a bid to control frequent and violent demonstrations. Under the law, anyone who causes injury or property damage with a firebomb can be sentenced to seven years in jail and fined up to 3 million *won* (US$4,195).[52]

Labour unrest

Another area of social conflict has been labour relations. The Roh reforms were accelerated by the growing participation of labour in the opposition to government. A major concern in the waning days of the Fifth Republic was the convergence of student and labour opposition, with growing evidence of middle-class sympathy and support. The tactics to prevent this included isolating the student movement and labelling it as subversive, while managing labour unrest by compromise. As for the middle class, the 29 June reforms were an important concession that satisfied a large number of citizens.

In the two months after the reform declaration, there were more than 650 labour disputes – more than the total for 1985 and 1986 combined. Workers won settlements in more than half the cases. Several Hyundai enterprises closed down when management refused to negotiate with workers demanding wage hikes of 30 to 40 per cent. By 13 August 1987 strikes were estimated to have cost the economy over US$220 million. (The wave of strikes was attributed to expanding profits and slow wage increases – in the first half of 1987, profits were up 69 per cent at 250 of the 262 firms listed on the Korea Stock Exchange, while wage increases, from an average of $1.84 per hour, averaged less than 8 per cent in spring wage negotiations.) After June, the government used riot police sparingly, and pledged to remain neutral in disputes. Before the 1987 strike wave, the country had been relatively strike-free – a mere half-day per 100 workers lost to strikes from 1979 to 1983 while in the United States the rate was nearly 100 times as great. There was a decline in strike activity by the autumn, with fewer than 100 unsettled strikes in early September – compared with up to 700 in July and August.

After years of repression, workers demanded more rights. Low wages and rigid labour policy helped deliver two decades of remarkable economic growth, but the workers had one of the longest working weeks in the world and job safety was appalling. In 1986, 1,660 workers were killed out of a work force of over 16.1 million, and there were 141,809 reported job-related accidents.[53]

Union membership was among the lowest in the industrializing world. With reform, workers took advantage of political liberalization to press demands for freer trade unions, higher wages and better working conditions. Strikes had been illegal under existing laws, and the military used labour disorder as a pretext for imposing martial law in 1961 and 1980. The Labour Minister warned that government would act if the disputes affected the national economy and security. Prolonged strikes were also being politicized as radical elements joined with workers in protests against a government allied with capital.

The labour movement had been repressed throughout the Park and Chun regimes. Productivity had grown twice as fast as wages, and workers resented that they had not shared in the benefits of economic growth. The Christian Churches developed links with labour, and opposition political parties pledged to guarantee labour the right to organize freely as they prepared for the presidential elections in late 1987. The constitution of the Fifth Republic guaranteed workers' right of free association, to bargain collectively and to collective action 'within the scope of the law'. In practice, restrictive laws had made almost every labour dispute since 1980 illegal. Management tried to meet labour demands in many cases, but worker suspicion remained high, and both sides lacked experience in collective bargaining. This almost always ensured confrontation. Organized labour also wanted to take advantage of opportunities presented by the reforms and presidential election, fearing that the political thaw could end quickly. The government-sanctioned labour organization, the Korean Federation of Trade Unions, faced attacks from the emerging activists who felt it had been too pliable and accommodating. The Federation lost credibility with workers when it endorsed Chun's suspension of constitutional debate on 13 April 1987 – which had led to weeks of rioting and the subsequent reversal of the decision.

The government had prohibited the KFTU from aiding local unions until December 1986, which meant that workers were on their own in local negotiations. This generated demands for strong, independent, and autonomous unions. Although some unionists and religious workers hoped to form a new political party representing social democratic or Christian democratic interests, years of government efforts to neutralize the labour movement reduced the likelihood of success.

By the mid-1980s, Korea was no longer a low-wage country. This was recognized by the passage of the first comprehensive minimum-wage law, which went into effect in January 1988. Wages made up less than 10 per cent of the manufacturing bill, and studies showed that Korean workers were only about half as productive as their Japanese counterparts. For factory owners, this meant that the unskilled and semi-skilled work force could be reduced without major damage to profits. Gender differences further characterized wages: the 6.5 million working women earned an average of $1.07 per hour, while men made an hourly $2.00.[54] There was a growing shortage of skilled manufacturing workers which was having a negative effect on productivity improvement. Many university students faced increasing problems in finding work, and in 1986 around 124,000 graduates were unemployed and a worse situation was expected – the prospects of economic downturn fuelled the growing dissent against government and capital.

Kim Dae Jung was pro-labour, although not a socialist – but still presented an image which may have weakened his middle-class support.[55] The governing DJP was willing to help unions with economic gains, but wanted unions to remain politically powerless. The party promised that government would no longer meddle in unions' internal affairs, in contrast to central ability to blackball union officials and reverse internal policies. Workers in government enterprises, except those in defence industries, were also allowed to form unions, but most government workers were prohibited from union activity.

The future of South Korean labour as a political force was one of the thorniest issues the National Assembly faced when it convened in September 1987. A general consensus existed among members of the ruling DJP and the major opposition that labour had the right to organize, strike and bargain collectively. Organized labour further wanted an end to restrictions on political activity. The unions demanded the right to support political candidates and address political issues. Management complained that workers were factionalized, making it impossible to negotiate an agreement that would stick, and some of the most bitter labour disputes were prolonged by factional struggles among workers.[56]

Quantitative changes have also occurred. In June 1987, there were 1,267,457 members of 2,742 unions. By the end of 1990 there were nearly three times as many organizations, with 1,887,884 workers in 7,698 unions, accounting for 21.7 per cent of the labour force.[57] Young Rae Kim sees significant progress by the labour movement, but the standard of labour's participation in politics is still at a low, with the entire scroll of the government, labour and employers to be blamed for the lacklustre performance.[58]

The role of the state

The posture of the state towards society under the Park and Chun regimes was heavily influenced – if not dominated – by priorities of economic growth and national security. The former furnished employment for an increasingly urbanized population and foreign capital for modernization and industrialization. The export-oriented growth relied in part on low-cost labour which was ensured by rigid controls on unions, while national security was threatened by civil disobedience. The breakdown of civil order was dangerous in the fragile environment of a divided Korea, in which the north could take advantage of government distraction to intervene with subversion or outright provocation. Seoul's discovery of over a dozen tunnels under the Demilitarized Zone, constructed by North Korea over a number of years and considered to be preparation for subversion and aggression, exacerbated fears of the communist threat. However, the credibility of military concern for national security had been eroded by the willingness of commanders to withdraw units from the northern frontier at the time of the Chun coup in 1980 – leaving the country vulnerable to a northern attack at the time.

A major task of political reform under the Sixth Republic has been to overcome popular perceptions of the government as a military-dominated regime and to create a higher order of political harmony. Roh distanced himself from his former military backers – including President Chun Doo Hwan – and moved to create a state more responsive to social demands with his reform declaration. Democratic reforms have defused some of the suspicions, and the announcement of Kim Young Sam as the DLP presidential candidate in 1992 indicated a move towards full civilian government, culminating in his election in December.

South Korea has also been moving towards a more extended welfare state. Responding to political pressures, the government revised its development plans to expand social 'safety nets'. Key points in 1988 were a national pension plan, a national medical insurance system and the construction of more rental housing units. Officially, it was stated that delays would worsen the unbalanced distribution of wealth, which would lead to new rounds of instability and further hamper sustained economic growth.

The government began financing 50 per cent of the insurance plan from July 1989. Businesses with over five employees became entitled to benefits from a national pension plan in the early 1990s and from an industrial accident insurance system in 1991. To improve the living environment, the government began grants of 3 million *won* in concessional loans to low-income people to help them repair or reconstruct old housing units. From 1988 to 1992 the government planned to build 2 million housing units to provide homes for urban workers and low salary earners. In the 1983–87 period, 1.2 million low-cost units were built. By 1993, the government intended to designate 350 areas as agro-industrial sites to increase farming households' annual incomes to 13 million *won* (from 6.5 million in 1987). The revised development plan called for equalization of the tax burden, prevention of real estate speculation and liberalization of financial markets.[59]

Conclusion

The government of the Sixth Republic has been responding cautiously to dissent and social pressures. It recognizes the middle-class stake in democracy, social order, and economic growth, while initiating policies to broaden participation and well-being. While the broad moves towards liberalization make sense in adapting the successful state and economy to a changing environment and the emerging middle class, one wonders whether the pace of change would have been as rapid if not for the constant prodding from the student and labour dissidents. Often a nuisance, and sometimes a threat to social order, the demonstrators have been a voice of idealism in the Korean nation. The martyrs and protesters were constantly reminding society and the world of the hidden costs of economic growth and authoritarianism. Perhaps, without their courage and obstinacy, the Korean economic miracle might have stagnated in the machinery of authoritarian order. Now, the country is making steps towards fuller democracy and a more just state. A strong presidency, aided by a cohesive bureaucracy and army, has led the country into the ranks of modernity. The dissidents – including writers, students, and workers – have also played a major role in humanizing this progress.

Kent Calder, in his study of policy formulation in Japan,[60] demonstrates that there has been a cycle of crisis and compensation – that policy has evolved in response to pressures from organized groups. The opposition parties have played a role in formulating responses, and the LDP has often adopted these as its own, thus maintaining its longevity in power. The same phenomenon may be evolving in South Korea, as pressure groups articulate interests and see them finding expression in legislation and policy. So far, the political parties of opposition have not been very successful in this articulation – except as regional protesters. Their main task has been survival and winning seats in elections. Now that local autonomy has been introduced, a new layer of political activism has been opened, and the articulation–implementation linkage may be improved. Nevertheless, the South Korean state is still a fragile construct, and a series of major crises – economic, military, or political – could undo the advances thus far.

6 State reform in a comparative context

The political reforms in South Korea were part of a larger phenomenon of state reform that swept the world in the 1980s. Francis Fukuyama interpreted in a much broader sweep:

> And yet, despite the powerful reasons for pessimism given us by our experience in the first half of this century, events in its second half have been pointing in a very different and unexpected direction. As we reach the 1990s, the world as a whole has not revealed new evils, but has gotten *better* in certain distinct ways. Chief among the surprises that have occurred in the recent past was the totally unexpected collapse of communism throughout much of the world in the late 1980s. But this development, striking as it was, was only part of a larger pattern of events that had been taking shape since World War II. Authoritarian dictatorships of all kinds, both on the Right and on the Left, have been collapsing. In some cases, the collapse has led to the establishment of prosperous and stable liberal democracies. In others, authoritarianism has been followed by instability, or by yet another form of dictatorship. But whether successful democracy eventually emerged, authoritarians of all stripes have been undergoing a severe crisis in virtually every part of the globe. If the early twentieth century's major political innovation was the invention of the strong states of totalitarian Germany or Russia, then the past few decades have revealed a tremendous weakness at their core. And this weakness, so massive and unexpected, suggests that the pessimistic lessons about history that our century supposedly taught us need to be rethought from the beginning.[1]

This upheaval has sometimes resulted in democratization or fragmentation (as in the Soviet Union) in the non-Western world. The Chinese market reforms which began in late 1979 demonstrated that modification of socialist, centrally planned economies was not only possible, but necessary. However, Deng Xiaoping has consistently stopped short of political reform, for fear of setting off a loss of party control. In the USSR, Gorbachev initiated reforms a few years later, but from the political direction rather than the economic – with disastrous results for him and the Communist Party of the Soviet Union (CPSU). Most other communist states – except Cuba and North Korea – followed suit. The common feature of nearly all the non-Western reforms – including those in South Korea – is that they were launched from and by the central government/party apparatus. Unlike classical revolutions, they did not originate in immediate social dysfunction or class contradictions.[2] The state was still strong enough to take the lead in reforms.

This chapter will examine several other cases of state reform and their relation to economic development in order to provide comparisons with South Korea. Taiwan is the most relevant, with parallels of national division between communist and non-communist, an authoritarian ruling party, a Japanese colonial heritage, high export-led growth, and simultaneous political liberalization. Nevertheless, there are sufficient differences between the two that Cheng Tun-jen has warned: 'Indeed the divergence between Taiwan and Korea has been so significant that treating them as *the* East Asian model obscures rather than clarifies.'[3] North Korea has remained stagnant under 'the world's first socialist monarchy', faithful to Kim Il Song and his Stalinist model. Despite a common cultural background and ample natural resources, North Korea has fallen increasingly behind the south, while maintaining one of the most repressive state apparatuses in the world.

China and the Soviet Union watched the rapid economic progress of the NICs and could not avoid the economic lessons they demonstrated. Prior to the 4 June 1989 massacre in Beijing's Tiananmen Square, Chinese reformers were advocating changes in the direction of the South Korea and Taiwan patterns. Deng Xiaoping's formula of major economic reform with minimal political change broke down in the spring of 1989, and resumed in early 1992, with encouraging signs at the Fourteenth Party Congress. In contrast, Gorbachev's reforms in the late 1980s emphasized political rather than economic change, and were threatened by a conservative backlash in the surge of growing ethnic nationalism. His reforms emancipated new forces – freedom and nationalism – and proved to be more than he could control, and he stepped down after a 1991 coup by the old guard.

State building and social engineering in South Korea

While South Korea was emerging from desperate poverty over the past several decades, scores of other societies sought to achieve the same ends, with less success. South Korea remains *sui generis* in many respects, but certain broad patterns can be identified.

The development of the South Korean state has exhibited no single pattern, except progress from extreme scarcity to relative well-being in less than a half-century. Parallel to this, and probably reinforcing economic growth, has been the evolution of increasingly effective government and bureaucracy. Since the demise of Park's Fourth Republic, there has also been a shift towards constitutionally-responsible government under Chun Doo Hwan, and intense democratic institution-building since 1987.

The lurches and discontinuities which characterized these developments cannot be attributed to a consistent ideology or plan or vision – except one of conquering adversity, for the South Koreans have engaged in a vigorous experiment in social, economic and political engineering. The goals have always been clear – survival, then prosperity, of society in the face of a powerful and aggressive neighbour, and the means may have changed from one Republic to the next, and as well as within each regime. Each experiment partially failed to achieve its purpose, but the Koreans have learned from their mistakes and incorporated the experience into the next experiment.

The Korean process of state-building has incorporated a rough scientific method as much as social engineering will allow. According to Karl Popper: 'The game of science is, in principle, without end. He who decides one day that scientific statements do not call for any further test, and that they can be regarded as finally verified, retires from the game.'[4] In science, all statements are tentative, and subject to verification. In politics, verification is generally impossible and impractical. Politics requires actions without a clear idea of consequences – yet some political systems have been founded on a claim of infallibility, or at least the claim of superiority over the past or others. Modern communism replaced the tentativeness of science with ideological certitude. Stalin was consistent – if ideology and science conflict, the latter must conform. The dogmatism of past religions has been secularized in modern – especially communist – states, with the result of totalitarianism. Now their key claim to under- standing history has been invalidated – capitalist societies did not weaken and collapse. Rather, those systems which adopted Marxism as their organizing principles were left behind by those which adopted market-oriented economies and less disciplined polities.

Dogmatic ideology is erroneous in science and politics. Popper distinguished piecemeal from holistic science and engineering:

> Piecemeal social engineering resembles physical engineering in regarding the ends as beyond the province of technology . . . In this it differs from historicism, which regards the ends of human activities as dependent on historical forces and so within its province.

. . . The piecemeal technologist or engineer recognizes that only a minority of social institutions are consciously designed while the majority have just 'grown', as the undesigned results of human actions.[5]

Although written nearly half a century ago, Popper's distinction has application to understanding how South Korea (and Taiwan, to a lesser extent) differs from the holistic pattern of communist development. Unlike many Third World states, South Korea did not adopt a holistic approach to socio-political engineering (or 'institution-building'). Division, war, poverty, and threats of social chaos were the immediate stimuli to reform. No leader in South Korea emerged at the time of independence to grasp charismatic power and impose his vision of order and progress on society. The naive attraction of Kim Il Song to dissident students may reflect a universal longing for a strong leader in a time of political turmoil. The only leader to approach the power of Kim Il Song in South Korea was Park Chung Hee. His vision for his country was based on nationalism and the economic achievements of non-communist industrialized societies. The implementation of economic growth was left to the planners and the private sector (although the *chaebol* were guided by government). With the military and police, and a political party subordinated to the needs of winning votes, he maintained a firm hand on the helm until mutiny by a subordinate destroyed him. His dictatorship proved effective in economic growth, but stunted political progress towards democracy.

With the end of the Park regime, old wounds were reopened, and the prospect of civil war was laid bare in the Kwangju uprising. The Fourth Republic experiment in high economic growth/low democratic growth nearly collapsed, and the military were again enticed to action. Chun's experiment modified the Park presidency by limiting the term to seven years. The strong state/high growth pattern had led to serious tensions in society, and needed a more broadly representative government.

The project of socio-political engineering in the Fifth Republic succeeded in restoring order and economic growth, but was only a temporary solution. Dissent and demonstrations have been messages of protest, alienation and refusal to the government. From the standpoint of socio-political engineering, they have also been a crucial and sensitive flow of raw information to government – elections were manipulated, and the media were controlled, but street violence was feedback that could not be repressed or ignored. Its momentum was fed by middle-class frustrations in 1986 and 1987, forcing the Fifth Republic government to re-evaluate its socio-political experiment. In this light, Roh's 1987 reforms began a new series of social experiments in the Popperian sense. If South Korea was merely *sui generis*, its vitality and approach would be a footnote in world political history. However, it illustrates the points Karl Popper made over five decades ago concerning piecemeal *v.* holistic experiments in social engineering.

I propose that we view political reform as a version of social engineering. 'Government' is the top-down 'engineer', and must be in charge to conduct the experiment. In an open society, the subjects of the experiment are acutely sensitive to manipulation by the state and will continue to question, criticize, oppose or co-operate and even reject the experiment – making the idea of a 'controlled experiment' impossible. Closure refers to the degree to which citizens (subjects) are excluded from participating in and affecting the planning, process, and evaluation of government actions. The greater the openness, the higher the participation.

If we think of the typology of political systems as a spectrum from totalitarianism to democracy, varying in the degree of individual freedom and sovereignty and societal autonomy (openness), the special characteristic of authoritarian societies is that they are about midway between liberal democracies and totalitarianism in their degree of openness. Channels of protest exist to report responses to policy experiments (and aren't all policies experimental?). Organs of coercion are also effective in maintaining strict limits on protest. This means that authoritarian regimes have normal bureaucratic sources of information and feedback, as well as some limited response of raw protest.

Totalitarian regimes (a declining phenomenon at the end of the twentieth century) are near the closed end of the spectrum. Channels of protest and independent information flows are severely constricted. The holistic engineering taking place in totalitarian society derives inspiration from ideology, and usually has an explicit master plan – formulated in five-year plans. Stalin and Mao Zedong were perhaps the most egregious master planners in this century, but their disciples have included Ho Chi Minh, Kim Il Song, Enver Hoxha, and Pol Pot, to name a few. Their holistic experiments in socio-political engineering have included massive population transfers, re-education on a massive scale, radical social and economic restructuring aimed at eliminating vestiges of the free market, the subordination of science, art, and culture to ideology, and even genocide. The claim that the end justified the means was falsified by the evidence that the means were making the announced goal of human justice and equity impossible to attain.

In economic growth, the lessons of the decade 1980–89 point to the superiority of relatively free markets. The collapse of socialist/communist systems in Eastern Europe and the continued problems of the decline of the Soviet Union serve to underline this. Democratic societies have tended to be market-oriented – a disposition which places a high value on the free flow of information, and unrestricted trial and error in the exchange of commodities as prices move to levels acceptable to buyers and sellers. The correlation of high scientific achievement – in both pure and applied research – with democratic societies is also related to the free flow of information and ideas. There is relatively little ideological impediment to paradigm shifts, and the post-war era has been a series of technological innovations and breakthroughs. Totalitarianism and authoritarianism do not preclude progress in science and technology, but these types of states usually claim the prerogative of directing where research resources will be allocated – usually in the name of national security.

To illustrate this important distinction in societies with medium to maximum closure, we can arrange five less than democratic societies along an axis (Figure 1).

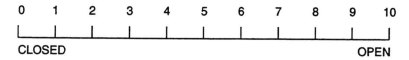

Figure 1 Scale – closed *v.* open societies

The South Korean movement towards openness can be graphed as in Figure 2. Two major trends are evident: the first is that South Korea has managed to establish a strong state out of the shaky beginnings of the post war period, and the second is that the move towards openness of the political system. In both trends, consolidation of the state took place with constitution-making for each new Republic.

On this axis, 10 represents maximum openness, with 0 as maximum closure. To move to an even higher degree of openness, right of 10, a society dissolves. Social bonds, civic obligations, and all sorts of contracts

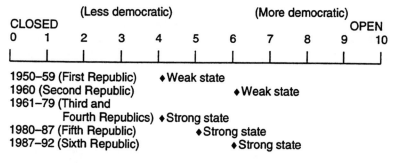

Figure 2 Scale: South Korea's movement towards openness

are restrictive, and enforce some closure. However, they also are necessary for the existence and continuity of civil society. Democracies tend to be in the zone towards 10, while totalitarian states approach 0. Authoritarians spread along the middle. No system remains stationary, and is moving one way or another at any given time, or different parts may be moving in opposite directions.

I would argue that South Korea and Taiwan occupy the relative position 4–6, with a strong tendency in recent years towards 10. The People's Republic of China was at the 0–2 zone under Mao, moved towards 10 (openness) during the 1980s reforms, and moved sharply back towards 0 in the wake of Tiananmen (June 1989), and has started again to move towards 6 – which may be the limit of openness the regime may want to tolerate. The USSR hovered in the left zone under Brezhnev, after some limited experiments in reform during Khrushchev's period. Under Gorbachev, the Soviet state dissolved, and now the Russian state has moved close to 6 in relative openness. On the extreme left is the maximally closed state. It is not perfectly closed, as a prison camp within a totalitarian state might be. Some degree of voluntarism is required to maintain society, while prison camps such as those set up by Stalin and Hitler made little pretence of voluntarism. For the present, perhaps the North Korean state remains the most closed model.

As much as possible, this spectrum should be objectively determined. The permeability of information into and out of the system is an important criterion. Monopoly of information is another standard – the greater the closure, the tighter the monopoly. Social diversity, expressed in pluralism which actively participates in affecting public policy, is a sign of openness. Genuinely competing political parties in the contest for state power are a key indicator of openness. A free press and media, tolerance of religious belief, liberty of property, freedom of association – these are all indicators of an open society. System openness for states may be more important than rigidity in adaptability to environmental change. It is this openness, rather than a particular strategy of economic development or theory of industrial management, which contributes to the long-run improvement of economic and social well-being, as well as political stability. In the rush of events and upheavals in Eurasia, it is vital to extract lessons to move into the future.

What is state reform?

The Sixth Republic has been significant for its shift from economic growth as the primary goal of the state to a broader set of aims in which the aspirations and demands of society are incorporated. Democracy means more than expansion of narrowly defined political rights. The various authoritarian regimes in South Korea were not so repressive as to stifle all protest and dissent. Past governments significantly raised the cost of public dissent, and the Roh administration has not refrained from suppressing more radical opposition. The dilemma of genuine political reform is to expand democracy without dismantling the power of the state. Power rested on an alliance between the *chaebol* and the military from the Third Republic through to the Fifth, and has assumed a more civilian character under Roh Tae Woo.

In locating the South Korean reforms in a comparative context, a number of variables must be addressed, including ideology, party structure, government, social structure, and economic planning. The five societies of North East Asia (South Korea, North Korea, Taiwan, Russia, and mainland China) have all had considerable interaction with one other, have been outside the Western legacy of democracy and individualism until the nineteenth century, and have been successful modernizers in some period of their twentieth-century history.

Reforming the state is similar to constitutional revision in the way both redefine the relationship between state and society. It is what Popper called 'piecemeal social engineering' in the political context. It consists of trial and error, it is public and non-holistic, and generally it has visible results. Constitutional revision has been a major vehicle of political reform in South Korea. It occurred when previous legal relationships of authority and submission were no longer adequate or acceptable to important parties in the state. More generally, constitutional revision may require a reformulation of federalism, a restructuring of government, a major revision of the constitution, electoral reform, the legalization of previously disenfranchised groups, and the addition or detachment of certain territories. Constitutional revision is political reform which takes place within well-defined limits of law and custom.

Another type of reform is non-constitutional political reform. Here, written constitutions are less relevant, in part because of the absence or weakness of the rule of law. In general, a resultant constitution is a legalistic statement of changes and reforms brought about by extra-legal or non-legal means. Beyond political reform is revolution – which occurs when political reforms do not proceed far enough or sufficiently fast to satisfy citizens and groups, who seek redress through violent and non-legal means. The threat of revolution or anarchy has been a major incentive to state reform in South Korea.

Constitutional reform is customarily addressed in state constitutions, so the procedure is fairly predictable, although the outcome is not. Enfranchisement, multi-party systems, representative government, and arguments about the rule of law, often trigger the legal mechanisms to set constitutional revision in motion. Where constitutional government is weak, or not supported by a citizen culture, the legal mechanisms to initiate reform are absent or inadequately developed. It may require crisis and breakdown to inspire the leadership to embark on state reform.

Taiwan – another 'piecemeal experiment'

It is no coincidence that other piecemeal experiments (including Taiwan, Singapore, and Hongkong) have relied so heavily on market economies. Free markets are experiments based on trial and error, but accurate feedback is quickly available. They are often frustrating and costly to participants, but they are also open-ended and can produce efficiency in the longer run.

In contrast, major communist systems have moved into the dustbin of history, although many of the old apparatchiks are managing to return to power through democratic elections (in Romania, for example) – indicating that a degree of separation between communist systems and their personnel is possible. Mongolia, the oldest of the Soviet satellites, saw a new election law drafted, an opposition party established, and elections.[6] New opposition organizations emerged in the former Soviet Union and Eastern Europe. On the anti-*perestroika* side, China tried to breathe new life into its moribund united front CPPCC (the Chinese People's Political Consultative Conference) as a substitute for multi-party competition, and Vietnam rejected any hint of a democratic system. Communist parties have failed to elicit legitimacy and must deal with political reform in a way that acknowledges alternatives to single-party dictatorship before major liberalization can occur.

The emergence of true opposition parties is a crucial ingredient for liberalization in modern authoritarian countries – now including the former Soviet Union and the People's Republic of China. Ethnic opposition in the former Soviet Union was essentially anti-state, desiring new institutions, to be dictated by national identities. It differs from the partisan opposition familiar in South Korea, Japan, and other relatively democratic polities where the boundaries and membership of the state are generally accepted. Two antagonistic visions of the state confronted each other – Gorbachev's was the Leninist–Stalinist, cosmopolitan pan-nation whose citizens were an artificial nationality, the 'Soviet people'. Yeltsin has been more the Russian patriot, whose idea of the state conforms to the nineteenth-century nationalisms that have been unleashed in Eastern Europe and the corners of the USSR. To him, ideology is an artifice and cannot create a new sense of loyalty to supersede the centuries of language, art, religion, culture and other ingredients of national consciousness. In the PRC, there is still no place for political opposition – in contrast to Taiwan, where a healthy opposition flourished for years in the *dangwai* (non-Guomindang) and, more recently, the Democratic Progressive Party (DPP). With the lifting of Taiwan's martial law in 1987, there has been a slight decline in social order, and some members of the DPP have participated in demonstrations, which were once forbidden. Should violent opposition agitate effectively for independence, the PRC has reserved the right to intervene and restore order.

Mainlanders remain a ruling minority on the island, and this numerical factor has played some part in inducing the Guomindang to make accommodations to the majority of Taiwanese, who tended to support the opposition. Had the Guomindang defeated the communists in 1949, it is likely that some sort of opposition parties would be flourishing on the mainland today. Although the party is loosely based on Leninist principles,[7] adherence to the ideas of Sun Yat-sen has a moderating influence on a totalitarian ancestry.

Taiwan has been the society most comparable to South Korea in terms of rapid development and political character. Like South Korea, it is a semi-state, although its international status has not included United Nations membership since the 1970s. Taiwan's international weakness is due to the great inequality between mainland China and the island-province of Taiwan. Both societies have achieved high rates of economic growth, albeit with different strategies. Korea has relied on large industrial conglomerates, and Taiwan has succeeded with reliance on small and medium-size enterprises.

In the realm of differences, Taiwan has watched interest and investment shift to its protagonist on the mainland[8] – especially with the more enlightened reform policies of Deng Xiaoping. In contrast, South Korea's adversary, North Korea, has lost much of its status as a rival for international recognition. South Korea has surpassed Kim Il Song totalitarianism as its economy has soared ahead, and with Russian and Beijing recognition of South Korea, North Korea has become increasingly irrelevant – except perhaps as a spoiler with a capacity for nuclear weapons. Taiwan saw its fortunes fade in the 1980s, with the reforms of Deng Xiaoping, and then revive with the Tiananmen massacre, which dampened the ardour of the West. Slowly, the PRC rebuilt its bridges externally and domestically, capping the triumph of the reformers in the Fourteenth Party Congress in late 1992.

Background

The Guomindang faced a number of challenges when it arrived on Taiwan after World War II. With defeat on the mainland, it had to change the former Japanese model colony into a bastion against the apparent communist juggernaut. Mainlander–Taiwanese relations remained tense, and a major task of the Republic of China on Taiwan was to overcome local suspicion against the mainlanders, and to integrate Taiwanese into the party and government structure. The Guomindang successfully rebuilt the state structure which had collapsed on the mainland.[9] Because of this institutional baggage, they were spared the numerous trials and errors the South Koreans faced in their succession of Republics as they tried to create a state apparatus out of a former Japanese colony and split peninsula. On Taiwan, many of the officials who had staffed government, party, and military organs quickly re-established political order. The semi-socialist ideology of Sun Yat-sen provided a usable programme for the reborn Republic of China on Taiwan. Sun's ideas were sufficiently diffuse that they did not impose a holistic plan on his followers. Moreover, the China he envisaged had passed through wars and revolutions, and then transplantation to the island fortress of Taiwan, so pragmatism took precedence over conformity to the canons of Sun Yat-sen.

Initially the mainlanders distrusted the Taiwanese because they had been outside the mainstream of Chinese experience during 1895–1945 while under Japanese control. The suspicion was mutual against the defeated and beleaguered remnants of the old Chinese Republic. Gradually, the natives prospered and demanded a greater voice in Taiwan affairs. Active in local and provincial politics, the Taiwanese did not share the mainlanders' hope of retaking China from the communists. Many overseas Taiwanese supported an independence movement.

Two priorities dominated Guomindang domestic policy. The first was social and political stability as authoritarian measures were used to prevent the outbreak of dissidence. Outspoken critics of the regime were imprisoned or forced into exile, and Chinese nationalism (in contrast to Taiwanese nationalism) was stressed at all levels of education. Slowly, native Taiwanese rose in the ranks of government and party. The second priority was economic growth. From 1953 to 1984, GNP rose by an annual average of nearly 9 per cent. Income equalization was pursued and the ratio between the highest 20 per cent and the lowest declined from 20.47 in 1953 to 4.4 in 1984.[10] This outstanding performance helped to legitimize the regime at home, especially when contrasted with the uneven performance and instability on the mainland.

With US support, the ROC was able to retain its seat in the United Nations until 1971. In the 1970s, a large number of countries transferred diplomatic recognition from Taiwan to the PRC. When the United States normalized relations with Beijing at the end of 1978, the fiction of the ROC as a government in temporary exile could no longer be maintained. Despite the loss of broad international recognition, Taiwan has maintained its economic growth and broad international economic relationships.

Crisis of legitimacy and political reforms

The US transfer of diplomatic relations to Beijing created a crisis of legitimacy for the ROC, which stimulated a number of rapid reforms, including the recognition of opposition parties. These reforms have increased liberalization, although falling far short of democratization. In a process he terms 'political amortization', Wu Yu-shan notes that there has been a shift of:

> major legitimacy principle from traditional reciprocity to modern political contract. The ability of the government to continuously deliver material benefits can no longer guarantee regime legitimacy; this has to be supplemented by contractual approval in regularized elections.[11]

Opposition parties were legalized in 1986, although the *dangwai* groups had an electoral following approaching one-third of the electorate by 1977. Wu attributes the 'marketization' of politics to pressures from below, and to the 'international demonstration effect of the Philippine revolution and the South Korean turbulence, Chiang [Ching-kuo]'s desire to be remembered as a great reformer in history, and the Guomindang's plan to preempt the emerging political market by introducing sweeping reforms'.[12]

The reforms had begun several years earlier, when the Guomindang launched plans for the democratization of Taiwan. It was a case of seeking to prevent Taiwan from backsliding into irrelevance and eventual abandonment by its major ally, the United States. Electoral reforms and plans for broader participation were introduced. The reforms partly responded to the modernization occurring on the mainland. A major portion of the ROC's legitimacy was that it was 'Free China' and had higher claims to loyalty than the totalitarianism of the PRC. Taiwan's land reforms in the 1950s stressed private ownership, in contrast to the collectivization of the mainland, and provided a base for Taiwan's industrialization. With the turn to pragmatism and economic reform in mainland China, it was important for Taiwan to maintain its viability and credibility. The old generation of diehards was passing away, and greater mobility for the Taiwanese would give them an increased stake in the regime.

Contrast with South Korea

Both regimes were established as responses to communist challenges. A major difference was that the Guomindang transplanted the state structures which had started to take root to new territory, while the ROK began with a wide array of individuals, factions, and approaches which may have dissipated collective energies. The Guomindang was a quasi-Leninist organization which could impose unity within its own ranks, while no similar organizational structure existed in South Korea. From 1949 until Chiang Ching-kuo's death on 13 January 1988, father (Chiang Kai-shek) and son had ruled the ROC with the Guomindang. South Korea had no parallel continuity and fell into instability on several occasions. Both regimes launched political reform as the result of domestic and international pressures, and a failure to respond with some meaningful measures could have resulted in collapse.

A major shock occurred to Taiwan with the transfer of US diplomatic recognition from Taiwan to the PRC in 1979. The multi-party system was introduced, and the process of further liberalization which continues to unfold today – including the democratic election of the legislature in December 1992. A stimulus to Taiwan's democratization has been the improvement of conditions on the mainland. As if to illustrate its claim to superiority over communist China, Taiwan responded to mainland moves towards liberalization with democratic reforms of its own – including legalization of opposition parties and constitutional revision. As long as Taiwan is able to maintain its greater economic and political attraction, it will be an attractive alternative for the loyalties and support of overseas Chinese.

The People's Republic of China

The state-building experiences of the PRC have been a mixture of piecemeal and holistic engineering. The various mass campaigns initiated during Mao's reign were a series of trials and errors, followed by retrenchments and return to a more piecemeal approach. Even the mass campaigns, such as the Great Leap Forward and the Cultural Revolution, began as relatively small-scale programmes and later ballooned into mass political movements to reconstruct society. In this light, Deng's reforms since 1979 have been part of a holistic programme – with the NICs as an implicit model – to reconstruct China, but the method has been more trial and error than Mao's dogmas. The virtue of a holistic approach is that it provides a vision to be communicated to the citizens who are the objects of change, and encourages them to participate in various degrees of activism, transforming their passivity into voluntarism. The holistic idea is communicated through slogans and images – Mao's command 'Serve the people' has become Deng's celebration of wealth-creation.[13]

Comparing South Korea and the PRC contrasts the piecemeal, with implied messages of necessary sacrifices and deferred consumption, to the holistic ability to generate collective energy. At least one generation of young Chinese was sacrificed in the Great Leap Forward, and many of those who survived were devoured by the Cultural Revolution. The holistic mobilization of hundreds of millions of Chinese was physical and psychological coercion, but there was also present an element of patriotic voluntarism. After Mao, and with the return of Deng Xiaoping to power, the PRC embarked on a series of reforms in late 1978 which lasted slightly more than a decade. Limited liberalization in politics accompanied gradual shifts to a more open and international market economy. Domestically, political and constitutional reforms were introduced. The reforms moved the economy from the centrally planned model of the Soviet Union and enabled rapid growth in many sectors, but Deng demurred dismantling the state-owned economy. The reforms since 1979 have been pursued under the holistic myth of a Chinese road to socialism, while learning from capitalism. The Special Economic Zones (SEZs) have been both laboratories for more advanced experiments and conduits for the transmission of foreign capital and technology into China. Some marketization of agriculture has been accomplished, but state domination of industry has maintained the holistic approach of socialism.

Unlike Soviet *perestroika*, which concentrated on political reforms, the Chinese have focused on economic change. The reluctance of the leadership to engage in any liberalization of the polity contributed to the explosion of popular dissent in June 1989, when hundreds were massacred by the People's Liberation Army (PLA). The hard-line leadership subsequently sought to reimpose centralized planning, but much of the economic progress has been brought about by the private and co-operative sector.

Comparing South Korea, Taiwan, and the PRC, a common thread has been the harshness of state-building after World War II. The impact of Japanese imperialism has also played a role in provoking popular nationalism. The repressiveness of all three (and even more so in North Korea) was directly related to building the monopoly of state force. All three faced enemies which would undermine them if anarchy provided an opportunity for subversion or easy invasion: South Korea by North Korea, Taiwan by the PRC, and the PRC by Taiwan. This does not justify harsh state dictatorship, but should provide some perspective. Only when the state apparatus (the complex of administrative and party and military organs) occupied the 'commanding heights' could the process of trial and error, piecemeal or holistic (or both) social engineering begin.

Taiwan and the PRC had advantages of previous government/state development. The Guomindang state dated back to the late 1920s, when the nationalist republic was established in Nanjing. Through the 1930s, under Chiang Kai-shek's leadership, the republic fought warlords and Japanese, and created a sovereign China. The communist revolution inherited the unity imposed under the nationalists, and moved the People's Republic into the camp of Soviet socialism. We can contrast the relatively unencumbered sovereignty of the two Chinas with the triple burden of South Korea: ex-colony, half a nation, and almost destroyed by the Korean War. The war made South Korea a ward of the United States and the United Nations, but also helped to build the military into the strongest and most cohesive organization in the modern state.

Economic reforms

A Soviet sinologist described the Chinese approach to holism succinctly:

> Today the Chinese note that one of the major errors committed in the 1950s and 1960s was the substitution of a long process by one with an ultimate and tenacious goal that was considered to be easily accessible in a short span of time. The leftists renounced the need for protracted development, and ignored the challenges to the building of socialism in an economically backward country. They did not understand that it was impossible to socialize instantly a heterogeneous economy, institute egalitarian distribution, and introduce centralized planning for the entire economy. . . . Only after the third plenary session of the CCP Central Committee in December 1978 did the Chinese begin to see that the building of socialism in a backward country is a long, complicated, and difficult process.[14]

It was a process best described as 'holism in a hurry'. The Russian author further condemned the principle of sweeping egalitarianism. Now

> the idea that some individuals, groups, and collectives may become rich earlier than others has been given a legal status and accepted as an instrument to boost the productivity of the people.[15] (This) new approach has yielded positive results . . . The annual income of peasants grew from 133.5 yuan in 1978 to 463 yuan in 1987. In 1980 the maximum annual income of more than 60 percent of the rural population was 200 yuan. In 1987 the number of peasants with such an income had declined to 8.2 percent. The system of contracts and leasing of enterprises also has helped intensify economic efficiency in industry and commerce. . . . By late 1987 about 75 percent of industrial enterprises had begun to work on a contractual basis. . . . In criticizing the Maoist slogan that poverty is the optimal condition for the transition to

communism, the Chinese experts reasonably note the baneful influence of eulogizing poverty in an economically backward country in which the overcoming of backwardness, poverty, and ignorance constitutes the main problem.[16]

Deliusin favours piecemeal, decentralized experimentation over centralized, holistic planning and engineering:

> The reduction of the sphere of centralized directive planning is accompanied by the granting of greater autonomy to provincial and urban organs of authority. This, to a certain extent, has liberated local authorities from excessive guidance from Beijing, which has served to promote the creation of a more flexible system of management over industrial enterprises.[17]

A major strength of reform as restructuring is that it can prevent another Cultural Revolution. It circumscribes the powers and functions of the state and party, empowers local organs, and reduces the bureaucracy. This should help in the democratization of Chinese society, and so far the PRC has not moved to follow Gorbachev's *perestroika* of major political reform.

Democracy is linked to decentralization in that the number of participants in making vital decisions is expanded. An additional connection is that the regional and local decision-makers are closer to the conditions where policy is made and implemented, and are more directly accountable to those affected by policy. This is not synonymous with democracy, but is an important precondition. It is a condition which makes holistic engineering and totalitarian dictatorship more difficult to implement.

Loyal opposition

Taiwan and South Korea, in their initial phases of state-building, viewed political opposition with hostility and suspicion. Dissent was treated with repression, which was reinforced by control of the media. Some of the harshness was ameliorated because of US sponsorship of the security of the two regimes. Moreover, there never was total prohibition of opposition, as has been the case in communist countries. The Hundred Flowers movement in mainland China cautiously tolerated limited dissent, but came to an abrupt and violent halt when the criticism began to undermine the party dictatorship. The reforms in the 1980s also saw the emergence of cautious discussion of social and political issues, especially among state intellectuals. This was halted in June 1989 by state violence.

To the Chinese communists (and in traditional Confucian politics), the idea of a loyal opposition is an oxymoron. How can an individual or a group be loyal to the party or the government or a principle (which is what the party claims to represent), and still oppose its authority? Fang Lizhi personified the anti-party opposition type so abhorred by Beijing. His critiques of the Communist Party and Maoism were devastating and played no small part in inspiring the democratic dissidents in the spring of 1989. From Beijing's standpoint, seeking sanctuary in the US embassy (where he remained until late June 1990) symbolized his enthralment to foreign ideas and provided further evidence that he was an alien intellectual who had betrayed his country. Similarly, the Chinese authorities have treated dissidents as criminals – anti-social and anti-socialist deviants who are either punished and allowed to repent, or are driven abroad – 'proving' that their true loyalties are not to China, but to 'international bourgeois capitalism'. Savage reprisal has also been visited upon the Tibetans, who seek some autonomy from the Chinese suffocation of native culture. They are not merely opposition, but 'rebels' and traitors to socialism.

North Korean politics – the Kim Il Song dictatorship

The DPRK has remained one of the most closed societies in the modern world. Political power is highly centralized, and the media are tightly controlled to ensure that only the government version of events is possible in public. In contrast to the changes in all the socialist countries, North Korea has sought to maintain its centrally planned, totalitarian system in the economy and politics, with the result of growing isolation and economic stagnation. North Korea has remained on the far left, at around 1 or 2 on the previous scale. The system has maintained a holistic approach to its social engineering vision, placing high priority on excluding foreign influences, except for some selected Chinese and Soviet influences. In September of 1948, for example, Pyongyang initiated a language reform, officially banning the use of Chinese characters (*hancha*). This inaugurated a nationalistic and exclusive use of the Korean alphabet (*hangul*).

North Korea's holistic vision is expressed in the ideology of *Chuch'e*, which is translated as independence or autonomy. It is hostile to pragmatic thinking in practice, although in theory it could take a piecemeal approach to social engineering. Kim Il Song has defined *Chuch'e* as 'holding fast to the principle of solving for oneself all the problems of the revolution and construction in conformity with the actual conditions at home, and mainly by one's own effort'.[18]

As the official ideology of North Korea, *Chuch'e* is based on the conviction that the management of the domestic and international affairs of the country should be handled by North Koreans alone, independent of any foreign interference, through the policy of self-reliance. Kim Il Song has combined into the notion elements of Korea's nationalistic heritage with Marxist–Leninist ideas. In building the state, Kim and the Korean Workers' Party (KWP) followed the models of Stalinist and Maoist cults and totalitarianism to the extent that the state has become the extension of the 'great Leader'. In becoming hard, however, the polity has become brittle. It may have avoided the collisions and stresses of South Korea, but it cannot change without major surgery on its key institutions.

Facing mounting pressures from economic and international conditions, leaders and people in North Korea probably realize that their concept of self-reliance is an antiquity in the modern world, but the problem remains the 'personalist state' of North Korea. Opening society to outside influences will create serious problems of discontinuity in North Korea's political culture, as well as questions of its validity. If China is the model for North Korean pragmatism, it must be noted that Mao's death was the turning point for China. Few observers believe that Kim's son and designated successor, Kim Chong Il, could continue his father's legacy intact for long.

As in other communist states, the party is the ultimate wielder of state power. In North Korea the central role of the Communist Party is justified on the basis of the dictatorship of the proletariat. Complete concentration of power in one man echoes Stalin, Mao Zedong, Castro, and Hoxha. Purges of followers eradicated potential threats, and Kim assumed all important positions in party and state. He became general secretary of the party, President of the state, first-ranking member of the Central People's Committee (CPC), Supreme Commander of the People's Army, chairman of the CPC defence committee and chairman of the party military committee.

There have been a few periods of apparent relative opening which have helped the North Korean system to adapt to changing conditions. In 1984 Pyongyang initiated a resumption of 'direct dialogue' with South Korea to improve its militant image and bolster its new open-door policy in dealing with other countries. South Korea accepted North Korea's offer of flood relief, and the transfer led to more discussions but no substantive results. There was an agreement to form a North–South Joint Committee for Economic Co-operation headed by deputy premiers of both governments (20 June 1985). In the south, this was seen as significant progress in north–south dialogue because it indicated tacit acceptance by each government of the legitimacy of the other. In retrospect, it was more a temporary adjustment to maintain the viability of North Korea, which has faced economic stagnation for a decade. There was further evidence of pragmatism. On 26 January 1984, Kim Il Song declared that the time had come to expand the scope of foreign economic relations, as Pyongyang was seeking to revive a sagging economy. In September 1984, North Korea adopted a Joint Venture Law to attract overseas money and technology. In December 1991 the two Koreas signed a non-agression pact, and raised new hopes for the reunification progress. A major stumbling block has been suspicion over the North Korean nuclear weapons programme.

The USSR and its successor, Russia

In the years Gorbachev was in power, changes in the Soviet Union occurred at a dizzying rate. The presumed communist monolith showed deep fissures, and shed its Eastern European satellites far more quickly than was ever anticipated. The implosion of the Lenin–Stalin–Brezhnev empire ushered in a new era of world politics. Unlike Deng Xiaoping, who initiated economic reforms with relatively little tinkering with the state, Gorbachev attempted to reform the political system before tackling the economy. His strategy was to change the relations between the state and the economy, seeing the party, the military, the KGB, and the bureaucracy as the most formidable obstacle to reforms. Once they were isolated, changes in the economic system could be implemented.

The CPSU had become a privileged elite since the Russian revolution, and was a major owner of economic assets. The military consumed a huge share of the national budget, and precluded the capital investment and improved productivity required for further modernization. Ronald Reagan's 'Strategic Defence Initiative' would certainly have provoked massive military spending in the Soviet Union to keep up with the United States.

To emulate reforms in the PRC, Gorbachev needed maximum control of the state–party apparatus. He sought this by opening up the political system to some hitherto excluded groups. A major difference between China and the Soviet Union was that the former had gone through the ruinous Cultural Revolution, which dramatically weakened the major groups which could resist modernization – the party, bureaucracy, and the military. Radical egalitarianism and central planning had been weakened and partially discredited in China. Earlier attempts to expand Chinese agriculture by tightening the command economy had contributed to past disasters. Also, the Chinese revolution was only a generation old when the Deng reforms began, so communism had driven individual incentive underground, but it had not wiped out several generations of rural entrepreneurs and the work ethic, as had happened in the Soviet Union. Finally, many overseas Chinese were responsive with capital and a little patriotic idealism to participate in the reconstruction of post-Mao China.

The Chinese mainland was welcomed by the United States and Japan as a market for investment and a customer for goods and services. Furthermore, from the US perspective, a market-oriented China would be a useful strategic counterweight to the USSR. The PRC had never been a military superpower, and did not generate the same suspicion as did the Soviets within the US defence posture. Until 1989, the Soviet system of satellites and buffers in Eastern Europe was testimony to Moscow's desire to remain protected from Western Europe by maintaining its own sphere of influence with the Warsaw Pact and COMECON – the guarantors of Soviet hegemony in the region. When the Soviet Union failed to interfere against the overthrow of communist regimes in Eastern Europe in 1989 and 1990, it became fully apparent that the old order was collapsing. Acceptance of German reunification by Moscow further indicated benign Soviet intentions – or fatalistic acquiescence. Once begun, the process of the dissolution of the USSR could not stop. The former Soviet republics declared their independence, with resulting fragmentation of the old empire proceeding to completion. Gorbachev may have had a strategy but he had no programme. In retrospect, he was either naive or cynical to believe that weakening the seven-decade dictatorship of the CPSU would leave the state intact. He knew what the problems were, but he lacked the will and power to make economic reforms, and so he played off the state apparatus against dormant social forces, decimating the remainder of unified Soviet power. The failed coup in 1991 only reinforced the perception of a failing empire.

The maximum closure was attained by the Soviet state during the Stalinist period. Some opening occurred under Nikita Khrushchev, but control was re-established under Brezhnev. Gorbachev resumed where Khrushchev left off, and opened the state to foreign ideas and investment. Yeltsin has continued the liberalization process in the Russian sovereign republic, and has moved to the conversion of the centrally planned economy into a more market-oriented system. By the spring of 1993, conflict between the legislature and executive in Russia threatened a breakdown of the political system.

The comparison of the USSR and PRC raises the question of whether the Deng strategy of economic reform would have been appropriate for Gorbachev as well. One advantage of economic reform was that the benefits were evident in a short time to a large proportion of people, and so had immediate consequences. By introducing limited markets, profits, and access to consumer products, Beijing was in effect transferring material rewards to the population at rather small cost. It also helped to reduce the power of the planners and bureaucrats who could have blocked Deng. Chinese communist power remained intact, and the state system was threatened only from the periphery. Genuine democratization was also avoided and dissidents were suppressed by a coercive infrastructure, backed by the military. Deng held out the prospect of future political reform, and a few moves were actually made in the direction of the 'rule of law', a lesser role for ideology in the spirit of new pragmatism, and election law reforms. None of these had any significant impact on the communist monopoly of power. Except for Tibet, the Chinese did not have the problem of preserving a multinational empire as did the Soviets. Chinese control of the non-Han minorities has been accomplished by repression, colonization and assimilation of peripheral areas. The Russians, in contrast, were only a slim majority of total Soviet population, and faced cultural rivalry from the Ukrainians. Islam has been a centripetal force in Central Asia, and is threatening to remove vast areas from the former Soviet state.

Implications

These five modernizing systems of North East Asia are defined by their mutual propinquity and historical interaction. Wars, diplomatic competition, influence from Japan, and the struggle to develop their economies have been a common focus of the East Asian experience. The responses have varied broadly, but the single goal for each has been to build a strong state – one that enjoys sovereignty at home (as the supremacy of government in law and practice over defined territory) and security from threats abroad (in the sense of ability to resist foreign intervention). Without a sovereign state, neither holistic nor piecemeal socio-political engineering can be effectively accomplished and consolidated. The five cases of reform offer a sampling of societies that have established states with strong apparatuses in order to seek specific political and economic goals. During the last decade each has been forced to modify its respective programmes and approaches. Relative closure/openness is displayed in Table 1.

Ideology is the explicit belief system projected by the political system as its legitimacy formula. It also summarizes the premises of its programme

Table 1 Tendencies of current political systems*

Political system	Close/open	Tendency (1992)
South Korea	3	→ open
Taiwan	4	→ open
PRC	6	→ open
Russia	5	→ open
North Korea	9	Unchanging

*See Figure 1, page 125

of socio-political engineering, including plans for labour and capital, attitudes towards private and public ownership, the role of government, and the system of education.

South Korea

Alone of the five cases examined, South Korean politics has almost completely lacked an explicit ideology. The government has continually appealed to economic self-interest, anti-communism and nationalist pride as the tenets of its programme. The formulas of economic growth have worked well, although unevenly, and democratic reform has temporarily reduced some of the popular pressures on government. Pragmatism has dominated the thinking of leaders and much of the opposition – to the extent that the public cynically equates politics and opportunism. The exception has been radical splinters, which adhere to the Chuch'e of Kim Il Song, or the home-grown *minjung* nativism.

Taiwan

The ideological format of state-building in Taiwan remains the thought of Sun Yat-sen, updated by Chiang Kai-shek and Chiang Ching-kuo. The Three People's Principles and Confucianism are taught in all levels of schools, and expounded regularly. Another element of the Taiwan-based Kuomintang ideology has been the claim that the party represented the only legitimate government of China, and that eventually it would retake the mainland. In recent years, the government has modified this position and its no-contact policy in the face of significant Taiwanese investment on the mainland.

The People's Republic of China

Chinese communist ideology claimed to derive its legitimacy and principles from Marxist–Leninist thought. Revolutionary experience and the adaptation of ideology to the specific conditions of China produced 'the thoughts of Mao Zedong'. Adaptation of the Soviet model of state, party and society stressed Marxism–Leninism in the period 1949–56, but the Great Leap Forward marked the upsurge in Mao thought and the blossoming of his cult of personality. The Cultural Revolution was the heyday of ideological politics in China, followed by the pragmatism of Deng Xiaoping.

Chinese communist ideology has provided a formula for the disposition of power. Although Mao's 'New Democracy' claimed to be a multi-class alliance under the leadership of the Communist Party of China, in reality it was a full party dictatorship. Its major difference from the Soviet Union at the time of the Chinese revolution was a greater collective leadership, in contrast to Stalin's iron grip on power. Mao remained the *primus inter pares* and never enjoyed the extended hegemony of Stalin. Despite – or because of – claims to be scientific and historical, Chinese communist support for social justice was belied by the actions of a party and government which sacrificed millions of their own people. The Chinese communist government's claims to nationalism were compromised by ideological subordination to the Soviet Union during the 1950s. Only when the Marxist ideological dogmas were put aside did greater economic prosperity begin to appear in China – but this was interrupted in June 1989, when the party and army attacked the proponents of greater democracy.

Traditional China was defined by Confucianism, which provided a unifying myth and operating ethics for roughly two millennia, until its abandonment at the beginning of this century. The Chinese communists have been searching for some equivalent of classical Confucianism. Ideological pragmatism allowed them to re-examine some aspects of Confucianism, as social chaos seemed to accompany the reforms. To the Chinese communists, political and economic unification seems to require a single world outlook as well.

Russia

Soviet communism had its roots in pre-revolutionary culture. The Orthodox Church in tsarist times provided a high degree of social cohesion, despite great inequalities. With the 1917 revolution, the Church was outlawed, and a new secular hagiography and eschatology were put in its place. Lenin and Stalin became the new tsars, and orthodoxy was replaced with Soviet communism. After the death of Stalin and a period of struggle for succession, Nikita Khrushchev initiated a period of political and economic reforms, and was ousted from power. A long period of economic and political expansion under Brezhnev proved to have been expensive to the point of exhausting the country. From 1985 to 1991, numerous concessions were made to domestic forces, and international rivals, while the economy declined at a precipitous rate. Marxist–Leninist ideology had little relation to the deepening reality of stagnation, and has been abandoned in the modern homeland of revolution.

The Democratic People's Republic of Korea

In North Korea, the personality and family cult of Kim Il Song tried to disguise itself as state ideology of Chuch'e. Kim tried to play off the Soviet Union and China, and was successful until mid-1990, when rapprochement between Seoul and Moscow occurred. In the past, attempts at reform in North Korea were cut off by stubborn refusal to alter the ideology of Kim Il Song. Its near-thorough totalitarian penetration of society makes it difficult to modify without eliminating much of the edifice erected during the post-war years.

Conclusions

The five cases of authoritarian regimes owe their origins to revolution and war which dramatically altered nearly all aspects of polity, economy and society. The Soviet revolution was the forerunner of the Chinese revolution, and was also responsible for the installation of the North Korean regime. South Korea and Taiwan represent the survivors of the revolutions, and transformed their merely survivalist continuation into strength and prosperity. South Korea endured the division of the Korean peninsula, the Korean War, and the Cold War. The regime in Taiwan is based on republican remnants and loyalists who survived and fled the communist revolution.

Holistic vision of remaking society has been a feature of communist states. As a secular religion, communism claimed to have formulated the strategy of creating a new order – just, equal, and superior to capitalism. The two anti-communist states were more concerned with survival than creating a new society with new citizens. The supreme criterion has been effectiveness, tried in experiment after experiment, with far more evidence in favour of the piecemeal 'survivors'. This is not to characterize the communist states as entirely holistic in approach. The strong ideological content of their political constitution has made experiments in free markets and private property, for example, most difficult to embrace unless disguised as temporary expedients.

Building a strong state structure has appeared to be a solution to a number of development problems around the world. The modern state provides an apparatus for resolving difficulties of conflict and co-ordination, and for mobilizing economic resources for growth. But in the 1980s, new strong states have reached an impasse. In communist systems, economic stagnation and increasing popular pressures for democracy have resulted in thorough reforms – with dissolution of the regimes in numerous cases. In several East Asian non-communist countries, authoritarian governments have responded to stagnation and popular opposition – or the prospect of these – with measured portions of democratization.

The two regimes on the Korean peninsula represent nearly polar extremes in their approaches to state-building. North Korea has maintained its closed, holistic programme based on the Chuch'e ideology. Some reforms have been tolerated, but only to the extent that they serve to prop up the totalitarian rule of the Kim dynasty. South Korea, on the other hand, has been far more open and experimental. The road to modernization has been filled with obstacles and detours. Most important, the South Koreans learned from errors – their own and those they observed in other systems. This learning – and the absence of a holistic predisposition to select only approaches conforming to a specific world-view – have been vital in a broad range of social, political, and economic progress.

Taiwan, the PRC, and the former USSR fill in the continuum between the two poles. In Taiwan, the continuity of the Chiang family provided stability in the republic's authoritarianism. The vague holism of Sun Yat-sen's Three People's Principles provided a blueprint for government, a definition of Chinese nationalism, and an active economic role for the state. It has endowed the republic with an integrative vision, which is also implemented in education and party (Guomindang) organization.

The PRC has moved from holistic revolutionary mobilization under Mao through the Dengist semi-piecemeal reforms to the present. These reforms were interrupted in June 1989 with the leftist counter-attack, but have been resumed in 1992. The problem for Deng and his successors will be to preserve the holistic vision of Chinese socialism while moving ahead with non-socialist experiments to advance economic development. Finally, the USSR experienced an implosion with effects as yet undetermined. Marxist–Leninist ideology had been institutionalized by Stalin and his successors in the centralized, totalitarian state, and has now been discarded. After over seven decades under communism, a new identity and successor state system have yet to emerge completely to replace the old.

7 South Korea's international environment and foreign policy

The South Korean state has not only established its presence on the Korean peninsula, but now projects it into a contentious international environment as well. During the years of the Cold War, Seoul depended primarily upon the United States for supplementing its defence, and on the United Nations for legitimizing its sovereignty. The end of the Cold War could have created a crisis of identity and survival for South Korea if the country had only passively accepted a role of 'forward fortress' for the United States and the West. Clearly, the Koreans now envisage far more active participation in their region and in the world.

Hosting the 1988 Summer Olympics was a major hinge of this participation. For several years prior to the event, the government made preparations, not only by building elabourate physical facilities, but also with an aggressive diplomatic outreach not seen in the history of the games. The project was more than hosting an athletic competition – it was to announce to the world that South Korea had modernized and to demonstrate its economic and social achievements. The government used the preparations as a vehicle for broadening contacts with countries of the East European and Soviet blocs, as well as China. The diplomacy associated with the games had the effect of outflanking North Korea by establishing relations with Pyongyang's ideological allies where possible. The stagnating socialist economies looked to trade with South Korea for help. Diplomatic recognition proceeded with expanded cultural and economic exchanges.

Because the games were vital to South Korean prestige and the regime's credibility, political interference or the collapse of the government and subsequent failure to host them would have been a major embarrassment. The student dissidents and the increasingly disaffected middle class possessed a powerful hostage in the Olympics. Without considerable concessions to democratic reform, the government would possibly have lost the privilege of holding the games in the face of potential massive disorder. The games were a watershed in reorienting South Korean foreign policy to new realities – the decline of communist solidarity under Gorbachev, and the dominance of the Pacific region by the United States From being a primarily dependent and relatively compliant small power, Seoul embarked on a more assertive policy to engage the allies of North Korea simultaneously with the Olympics preparations. It was a policy Seoul termed '*Nordpolitik*' to take advantage of the momentous changes in the communist world and to facilitate dialogue with North Korea.

South Korea as a rising middle power

The Gorbachev years produced epochal changes in international politics – not the least of which were the decline and break-up of the Soviet Union and the emergence of genuinely sovereign states in Eastern Europe. In China, the promise of continued modernization was replaced with a revival of quasi-military dictatorship and the repression of democratic forces in mid-1989. In 1992, there was movement towards moderation as reformers pressured the ageing leadership to restrain their hard line. The Gulf War (1991) underlined that the United States remained not only a superpower – but the *only* superpower, albeit an increasingly reluctant one. Soviet efforts to play a part in the war were frustrated as the union's power and military credibility rapidly eroded with near economic collapse.

Two developments have supported and reinforced South Korean diplomatic success: rapid economic progress in world markets, and the demise of international communism. The south has been strengthened by the success of the economic development initiated under President Park Chung Hee in the 1960s and 1970s. As the gap with North Korea has widened,[1] South Koreans have been able to translate their economic status into a significant diplomatic presence in the international system.

The decline of international communism in the 1980s severely weakened the ability of North Korea to challenge Seoul – except as a military threat. Both China and the former Soviet Union underwent extensive reforms which distracted their leaders from maintaining support for communist allies. The Soviet Union's and subsequently Russia's economic troubles also forced major reductions in subsidies to even their most loyal clients – Vietnam, Cuba, and North Korea. The South Korean response has been to grasp the opportunities and translate them into diplomatic instruments. Thus the 1988 Olympics provided a platform of international recognition for South Korean achievements, and forced Pyongyang to respond with an ineptness which eroded support for its demands to boycott the games.

On the goals of South Korean foreign policy

A historical perspective illustrates the Korean geopolitical dilemma of location at the convergence of Russian, Chinese, and Japanese frontiers. The Korean peninsula has been at the centre of international turmoil for over a century. It was a battlefield between China and Japan in the first Sino-Japanese War (1894–95), and a prize in the Russo-Japanese War (1904–5). It became a battleground again in the Korean War of 1950–3, and remains the site of delicate stalemate. This environment affects nearly all aspects of the South Korean state today.

Korean potential has been circumscribed by the modern international system. Division at the end of World War II deprived Korea of a wide range of possibilities of sovereign nationhood. National division performed a political lobotomy on South Korea – removing millions of people, many with close relatives in the south, and excluding resources in the north. In both north and south, the two populations were transformed into mutual enemies. Modern Korean nationalism consists of paradoxical emotions – a longing for national reunification on one hand, and deep suspicion towards the political system on the opposite side of the Demilitarized Zone, on the other. Both Seoul and Pyongyang have long claimed that each is the only legitimate government on the peninsula, and that the other is a fascist military dictatorship, or a nepotistic despotism.

Effects of detente

In the earlier moves towards US–Soviet detente, there was relatively little effect in the area of North Korea's relations with the Republic of Korea. Some tentative moves towards dialogue occurred with Gorbachev's *perestroika*, but Pyongyang's central objective remained to undermine the South Korean government and unite the entire peninsula under its control. According to Norman D. Levin, writing in mid-1990,

> Pyongyang continues to adhere to its four-legged posture: strong opposition to 'cross-recognition' or other steps which, from the north's perspective, would 'solidify' the division of the peninsula; insistence on a 'tripartite' conference involving the United States and the two Koreas to discuss arms reduction, non-aggression and peace agreements; a demand for the total withdrawal of U.S. military forces from South Korea; and a call for a 'confederation' between Seoul and Pyongyang, which would 'respect' the existing systems. With the possible exception of North Korean willingness to allow a phased, rather than immediate, withdrawal of U.S. forces, there is little indication of North Korean flexibility on any of these positions.

Finally, the effect of detente is minimal regarding North Korean methods. Although in deference perhaps to Soviet and Chinese interests Pyongyang may have somewhat downgraded its emphasis on naked force, it continues to build up its offensive military capabilities. It also continues to emphasize approaches designed to subvert the authority of the ROK government and to foster instability in South Korea.[2]

South Korean foreign policy: *Nordpolitik*

Since the early 1960s, South Korea has competed with North Korea for international recognition. In the context of the Cold War, the lines were clearly drawn, with communist states supporting North Korea, while the United States and its allies endorsed South Korea. Some Third World countries indicated sympathy with Pyongyang's nationalist rhetoric and often received military aid. In recent years, the South Korean economic miracle has bolstered its viability as a model for other developing nations. United States–Soviet Union detente provided a crucial window of opportunity for Seoul. With the defection of the Eastern European countries from Soviet domination, most established diplomatic relations with Seoul. This was partly due to expectations that economic investment and aid would be forthcoming, and also to the realization that the North Korean system was a political and economic liability in a world increasingly oriented to market systems.

Nordpolitik

The South Korean government first referred to *Nordpolitik* in a speech given by Foreign Minister Lee Bum-Suk in 1983. The policy's purpose was 'to prevent a recurrence of war on the Korean peninsula'. Its task was to normalize relations with the Soviet Union and China.'[3] Gorbachev's Vladivostok speech in August 1986 and the subsequent collapse of communist hegemony in Eastern Europe gave new impetus to *Nordpolitik*.[4] One by one, the former satellites of Moscow opened trade, then diplomatic relations with Seoul – ignoring protests of betrayal from Pyongyang.

One area where Moscow diplomacy had some notable effect was the Korean peninsula. By shifting support from Pyongyang to Seoul, it forced Pyongyang to think the unthinkable – dialogue with South Korea. This could have strengthened the Soviet hand in the Far East, if the Gorbachev regime had not collapsed. While the present government in Russia grapples with challenges to its existence, the former Soviet Far East remains an area of some concern. At the very least, no government in Moscow can allow the area to fall into the sphere of Japanese influence.[5]

However, the effect of this apparent Russian achievement has been to maintain a level of control, rather than a net increase in influence. Moscow shifted a significant portion of support from North Korea to South Korea and has become more even-handed towards the two regimes, even though this has undercut Pyongyang support for Moscow. While the Republic of Korea may claim this development as a victory for its *Nordpolitik* policy, it also marks a renewed and pragmatic presence for the Russians in Korea. The former USSR has reassessed its interests in North East Asia and has acted to reduce tensions.

Perestroika, combined with Gorbachev's anxiety to secure Western support for reforms and modernization, opened new opportunities for *Nordpolitik*. Seoul cultivated relations with communist countries for several reasons. First, the ROK has been in conflict and competition with North Korea for diplomatic advantage. Each communist country that recognized South Korea was testimony that Pyongyang is not the only legitimate government on the Korean peninsula. This process helped to isolate the North Korean government.

Second, the breakdown of the Cold War system possibly aids in pacification of the region by reducing tensions and the possibility of renewed war. The end of the Soviet–US confrontation has reduced the strategic value of North Korea for Russian security.[6] Third, the emerging republics in Eastern Europe and the new order in the former Soviet Union (and also the PRC) represent a new market for South Korean products and investment. Development of these markets could help South Korea reduce dependence on the United States and Japan, while creating a major niche for itself. Another advantage of the relationship is that it will provide an alternative source of technology for South Korean industry. Improvement of trade relations also plays a role in further economic development of the south-western region of South Korea, which has traditionally lagged behind other areas. A massive programme of 126 projects was planned to transform this less developed area into a bridgehead for trade with China and the former Soviet Union. The programme would boost the *per capita* gross regional product from 77 per cent of the national average to par by 2001.[7]

Fourth, cultivation of ties with Moscow can help in moderating the stalemate with North Korea. In October 1989, the Soviet Union dropped its opposition to South Korean entry into the United Nations, and called on North Korea to do the same, so that the two governments could be represented.[8] In doing this, Moscow denied Pyongyang's position that such a move would perpetuate division of the Korean peninsula. From the official Russian standpoint, South Korea is a completely sovereign state.[9] The Director of the Russian Institute of the World Economy, Vladimir

Martynov, stated that 'South Korea is an independent and objective entity regardless of whether we like its ideals and policies or not.'[10] The Russians were moving to a position which would have enabled them to act as broker in reconciling the two regimes of Korea. Martynov (with Georgiy Kudnadze) stated in another article that the two regimes 'should recognize each other as totally sovereign states based on the principle of international law. Reunification will be achieved only through extended reconciliation, and both sides will have to make major changes to their domestic systems.'[11]

Pyongyang responded to the Soviet acceptance of two states on the Korean peninsula, asking: 'Why does the Soviet Union, which wants to keep union republics from breaking away, intend to hamper the North and South . . . from being reunified and to help those who want to create two states?'[12] Subsequent fragmentation of the Commonwealth of Independent States (CIS) must have given Pyongyang a sense of poetic justice. Soviet recognition of the South Korean government further undermined the influence of North Korea, with its personality cult of Kim Il Song. The move place immense pressure on the north to reform, but this must await solution of the succession question.

Finally, Soviet recognition of Seoul significantly reduced Pyongyang's diplomatic leverage between the USSR (CIS) and China. Now North Korean diplomacy is almost reduced to a single track in the communist world – relations with China. The Russian Soviets have been using the linkage with Seoul as a stepping-stone to increase their influence in East Asia. Economic and military aid to North Korea remains an important lever of power. If Moscow could expedite dialogue between north and south – succeeding where the United States has failed – its prestige would certainly rise significantly.

For Gorbachev, the opening to South Korea had few risks and several potential gains. Despite North Korean indignation over the rapprochement, they have few options. Near stagnation of the North Korean economy meant that Kim Il Song had to continue to depend on Soviet aid. Following the Roh–Gorbachev meeting in June 1990, South Korea experienced 'Soviet fever', with high expectations of trade and investment opportunities.[13] Obstacles include the inconvertibility of the rouble, vast Russian Soviet foreign debt, and socialist economic systemic idiosyncrasies. By June 1990, the Soviet Union had failed to pay nearly $2 billion owed for goods shipped by Western countries.[14] It was in default of over $30 million owed to South Korea. Much trade was in the nature of barter.

Another advantage of the link for South Korea was that it could obtain industrial technologies from the Soviet Union that were denied by Japan.[15]

Although South Korea is not a member of the seventeen-member Co-ordinating Committee for Exports to Communist Areas (COCOM), it has a system of export controls of strategic items which is in compliance with COCOM.[16] Economic development of Siberia can become an important element in restoring growth to the former Soviet Union. Moscow has tried to attract Japanese capital and technology there, but the weak economy makes the repayment of loans questionable. Moreover, without a settlement of the Northern Territories problem, Tokyo has not looked favourably at aid to Russia. The ROK government hoped that changes in Eastern Europe – such as the overthrow of Ceaucescu and the reunification of Germany – would force Kim Il Song to read the writing on the wall and modify his stubborn policy opposing any change. South Korea's public pursuit of relations with the USSR and PRC confirmed the desire of the South Korean government to make an impact on the North Korean outlook.

South Korean *Nordpolitik* diplomacy has been hugely successful in its links with the former USSR. The Gorbachev–Roh meeting produced a major defeat for Kim Il Song. Subsequently, the USSR and South Korea normalized diplomatic relations. Japan expressed approval of establishing diplomatic ties between South Korea and the Soviet Union, hoping that it would hasten detente in the region.[17] From the Soviet side, there were ample reasons to pursue friendly relations with Seoul. The Soviets were interested in reducing the influence of the United States over South Korea. From their perspective, the purpose of US forces in South Korea is not to defend it from North Korea, but to block Russian and Chinese expansion further into North East Asia. The South Korean connection may also increase Russian leverage over Japan. The Russians see Seoul as an enthusiastic trade partner, and a source of technology and investment. Revelations about the Soviet shootdown of flight KAL 007 on 1 September 1983, however, clouded the euphoria over Russian–South Korean relations.[18]

Russian policy toward the Korea peninsula remains essentially a single complex, with emphasis on security interests in North Korea, and economic interests in South Korea. By maintaining relations with Pyongyang, Russia has one advantage absent in Japan and the United States. Access to North Korean ports and overflight rights give the Russian military a broader presence in the Asia–Pacific region than would otherwise be possible. The CIS military has signed an agreement with North Korea strengthening relations between the Russian Far Eastern and Transbaikal military districts and North Korea – apparently without the knowledge of the Russian Foreign Ministry.[19]

China

China and South Korea were linked historically through trade, religion, politics and culture. Today there is economic complementarity, with China's labour abundance and low wages.

> The great potential trade between the two economies is labour intensive manufactures exported by China in return for capital intensive and high technology products from South Korea. The key stumbling block concerns China's ability to pay, which ultimately depends upon China's ability to increase its manufactured exports.[20]

Improvement of relations with the PRC has been an important goal of South Korean diplomacy. Despite the collapse of communism in Eastern Europe and the Soviet Union, China has sought to maintain its own version of socialism. The government had preferred to sacrifice economic growth and its international reputation rather than liberalize its political system from mid-1989 until 1992. The key conflict had been between the hard-line conservatives who want to preserve the centrally planned socialist state and those who see 'peaceful evolution' towards a market system. Beijing has kept its channels open to Pyongyang, but simultaneously expanded trade and other non-governmental links with Seoul. During the first eight months of 1989, South Korea registered a trade deficit of US$125 million. During the period, imports from China climbed 33.2 per cent to US$1.14 billion, while exports rose 12.2 per cent to $1.01 billion. In 1988, Sino-Korean trade was $3.1 billion which represented 84 per cent of Seoul's trade with communist states.[21] South Korea first sought to open limited diplomatic ties. The basis for optimism in late 1989 was past agreements to open trade offices in each other's capital and give consular functions to the office.[22]

In early November 1989, Kim Il Song made a 'secret trip' to Beijing, at which time Deng Xiaoping reportedly advised Kim to deal flexibly with north–south dialogue 'for stability and relaxation of tension on the Korean peninsula'. Kim reportedly requested Chinese support in improving US–North Korea relations.[23] At the time, Beijing refused to establish official relations with Seoul – a position that was welcomed in North Korea.[24] This resistance eroded in August 1992, when normalization was concluded. A South Korean vision of a regional bloc including Korea, China and Japan was asserted by DLP representative and key adviser Pak Chun-kyu. He portrayed China's role as enhancing security, supplying resources, providing markets and taking over labour-intensive industries. Japan would promote liquidity, supplying technology and providing markets, while Korea would contribute to 'security, liquidity and markets'. China is also in a position to restrain North Korean adventurism.[25]

The Asian Games in Beijing provided further opportunity for back-door diplomacy. A Ministry of Foreign Affairs diplomat was stationed in Beijing as the Korean Olympic Adviser. In addition, direct charter flights between Seoul and Beijing were agreed to.[26] Seoul's *Tong-A Ilbo* complained that South Korea's efforts were one-sided, with little reciprocity from China – especially at the Asian games.[27] Taiwan was apprehensive (correctly, in retrospect) that success of the South Korea feelers would result in normalization at the expense of Taipei–Seoul relations. The Taiwan ambassador indicated that Beijing was unwilling to offend Pyongyang, and diplomatic relations with South Korea were 'far away' in 1990.[28] Seoul–Beijing normalization came as a shock for Taipei.

Seoul explained that

the reasons why the government is stepping up its efforts to improve relations with China and the Soviet Union are to deal actively with the change expected in the 1990s in inter-Korean relations, and to study the question concerning the submission of an application for admission to the United Nations at this year's General Assembly.[29]

China and the Soviet Union concluded an agreement on 24 April 1990 to reduce their armed forces deployed in their border areas. Seoul welcomed the move as it would reduce tensions on the Korean peninsula as well.[30]

Japan

Japan's relations with South Korea have been intimately involved with domestic politics. For years, the Japan Socialist Party (JSP, and now renamed the 'Democratic Socialist Party of Japan') maintained pro-north policies. In October 1988, Masashi Ishibashi, ex-chairman of the party, led a delegation to Seoul as a signal indicating acknowledgement of the South Korean government, but ambiguity remained.[31] In late 1989, the JSP presented a memorandum to the South Korean embassy in Tokyo, in which the party virtually recognized the treaty regulating relations between South Korea and Japan. This was a major modification of its earlier hostility towards South Korea and disapproval of the 1965 treaty.[32]

In 1982 Japan set up a US$1.85 billion aid package, to be provided over a seven-year term. In 1989 Tokyo discontinued further loans to South Korea because the country was on the verge of joining the ranks of developed nations, and could not be viewed as eligible for economic assistance. This perception was reinforced when South Korea set up a governmental fund in 1987 to provide economic aid to other countries.[33]

Despite close security links with the United States, there were few signs of defence co-operation between Japan and South Korea. The Japanese

Self-defence Agency announced plans to set up language training programmes so that its officers could study at South Korean service academies. Japan decided to promote the exchanges to cope with the projected closure of US bases in South Korea and the scheduled reduction of US troops in Japan. This has been a reversal of earlier Japanese reluctance to engage in exchanges with South Korea.[34]

Many Koreans continue to distrust Japan. With the report that Japan planned to spend 23 trillion yen on defence over the next five years, the *Choson Ilbo* noted that Japan ranks sixth in the world in defence expenditure. The paper stated distrust of Japanese intentions: 'Reduction or weakening of the US Forces in Korea will surely invite Japan to play a military role in place of the United States.'[35] The Defence Ministry in Seoul released its 1990 white paper, and expressed reservations over the Japanese build-up. The document called Japan's apparent defence expansion a 'negative factor' affecting South Korea's national security. It is also a factor which could affect the military policies of North Korea, China and Russia.[36] In 1992, the Japanese establishment of Peacekeeping Operations in Cambodia, which allowed the overseas dispatch of Self-defence Force (SDF) personnel for the first time, was greeted with suspicion by South Korea.

To alleviate suspicions, President Roh Tae Woo made a three-day visit to Tokyo in May 1990. Critics warned that his career was on the line unless there was a major concession from Japan – in particular an apology for Japanese imperialism prior to 1945 and a change in the policy of fingerprinting resident Koreans in Japan. There were memories of the storm of anti-government feeling in 1965 over normalization with Tokyo.[37] In Tokyo, Roh heard Prime Minister Kaifu express apologies for the sufferings inflicted by Japan on Korea during the period of Japanese colonial rule. Emperor Akihito was more reserved, in part because the constitution excludes him from politics, and expressed 'deepest regret'.[38] The South Korean President indicated that this removed a major stumbling block in closer bilateral ties.[39] Takako Doi, leader of the Japan Socialist Party, met briefly on Roh's visit, and became the first JSP leader to meet a South Korean leader.[40]

In economics, South Korea continues to rely on Japan. According to the Korea Institute of Economy and Technology, the dependent trading structure results in Japan reaping much of the profit generated by production and exports. In fields such as chemistry, steel and machinery, South Korean dependence on Japan was at 10 per cent.[41] The Japanese government banned the transfer of 200 ultra-modern technological items to South Korea until 1995 – a move bound to aggravate this situation. Tokyo also decided not to join in forming the ROK–Japan Committee for

Industrial and Technological Co-operation, which Roh Tae Woo had proposed on his May visit. This reversal, which implied 'technological protectionism' to South Koreans, and Tokyo's diplomatic opening to North Korea, may have signalled a change of attitude in Japan, as Seoul was looming more as a potential rival than as a junior partner.

Dialogue with North Korea

A serious obstacle to north–south dialogue has been the deep mistrust born of years of hostility and the large military deployment on both sides of the Demilitarized Zone. A short summary of halting steps towards dialogue illustrates some of the difficulties. On 11 January 1986, North Korea announced a unilateral halt to large-scale military exercises, but nine days later suspended all negotiations in response to the South Korean announcement that the annual Team Spirit military exercises with the United States would occur as usual on 10 February. In November the US Defence Department and US Eighth Army command in South Korea announced that a battery of Lance missiles would be deployed in the area of the US Second Division near the Demilitarized Zone. The missiles were capable of carrying nuclear warheads, but the US military declined to confirm whether they had such armament.

Possibly in response, the Soviet Union reportedly (29 January 1987) agreed to provide North Korea with SS-21 missiles – a rough equivalent to the Lances. On 3 March Pyongyang proposed military and political talks with the south – a significant change from previous demands of the north that any military discussion must include the United States. Seoul rejected the offer and suggested a meeting at the Prime Ministerial, rather than Presidential, level, provided there was a reopening of existing channels of communication and that there was prior discussion of the Kumgang dam, but no agreement was reached at the time. Seoul remained suspicious of the overtures, since little had changed in the north – except a declining economy. Pyongyang may have seen the political turmoil in the south as an opportunity to further divide a society already pushing hard against the Chun government. On 23 July 1987 North Korea tabled a bilateral disarmament plan to lower armed forces levels below 100,000 men on each side by 1992 and for the gradual withdrawal of US forces. Details of the plan would be worked out through tripartite talks in Geneva the following March. The north followed this up with an announcement that 100,000 North Korean troops would be disbanded by the end of 1987 as a unilateral gesture of goodwill.[42] The south rejected the plan, stating that the so-called troop reductions were actually a redeployment of troops from military to construction duties. Seoul suggested a meeting between the Foreign

Ministers of both sides to discuss all aspects of inter-Korean relations. The north rejected the suggestion on 6 August, repeating the previous offer of tripartite talks.

In a New Year statement, President Kim Il Song indicated that representatives of North Korea were willing at any time and at any level to meet their counterparts from the south. In mid-January 1988 the north offered to take up the south's earlier offer and convene a north–south conference to consider all aspects of inter-Korean relations. This offer was made while the south and the United States were preparing for the 1988 Team Spirit military exercises. Pyongyang also denied involvement in the bombing of a South Korean airliner. The south rejected the offer of a joint conference and said talks could not be held until the north apologized for the sabotage. President-elect Roh refused to cancel Team Spirit. Over the years, the joint US–ROK military exercise has been both the issue and the symbol of tensions on the peninsula.

On 18 October 1988 Roh addressed the UN General Assembly and called for an international conference to end the division of the Korean peninsula. His speech was a reply to an earlier announcement by Gorbachev in September, who had called for the reduction of tension between the two Koreas. Roh said the conference would lay a solid foundation for durable peace and prosperity in North East Asia. He offered to meet Kim Il Song for a summit meeting. The North Korean representative welcomed the discussions, but said that implementation would require cancellation of Team Spirit and repeal of the National Security Law.

Preparations for summit talks between the Prime Ministers broke down in February 1989 over Team Spirit – military exercises symbolizing US commitment to South Korean security. On 17 October 1989, President Bush said that US forces would stay in Korea 'as long as there is a threat from the North', although he did not promise to maintain the current level of 43,000. Roh assured the United States that South Korea would take on a greater share of the defence burden and make more progress to open its markets. On 24 May 1990 the North Korean President called for the signing of a peace treaty between the north and the United States and the negotiation of a non-aggression pact between the north and south.

By July 1990, the growing detente between Seoul and Moscow prompted Pyongyang to modify earlier reluctance. Negotiators agreed that the Prime Ministers would meet in Seoul in early September, with further sessions in Pyongyang the following month. When they met in Seoul, the South Korean Prime Minister, Kang Young Hoon, suggested an exchange of military personnel and information, including notification of significant troop movements, and the establishment of a hot-line telecommunications link between the respective Defence Ministers. The DPRK focused on lowering military and political confrontation. North Korea's Premier, Yon Hyong Muk, suggested an arms control agreement between the two countries, involving a three-phase troop decrease based upon reducing the standing army of both sides by 10,000 men, within a time frame of three to four years. The agreement would also require the withdrawal of US forces and the removal of nuclear weapons from the Korean peninsula. He also suggested establishing a communications link between the respective military commands and the creation of a joint military group to discuss border disputes and the provision of on-site inspections to ensure that the arms agreement was observed.

Willingness to accept a gradual US withdrawal was a departure from previous demands for immediate troop withdrawal, but it was accompanied by a parallel demand for negotiations with the United States alone to replace the present armistice agreement with a full peace treaty. This was conditional upon the north agreeing to a non-aggression declaration with the south. North Korea also specified three more conditions for the pursuit of inter-Korean dialogue: release of southern dissidents who had been jailed for visiting the north, the end of Team Spirit exercises, and the termination of Seoul's unilateral attempt to join the United Nations.

The second round of talks took place in Pyongyang on 16–19 October 1990, with little progress. The South insisted on agreement on inter-Korean reconciliation measures such as telephone and mail links, freer travel, and economic exchanges. The DPRK demanded a joint non-aggression declaration and a commitment to disarm. Membership in the United Nations was also an issue – South Korea's Prime Minister proposed separate seats until reunification was achieved, while North Korea wanted a single seat to be shared by the two governments.

When the two sides met again in Seoul (12–13 December 1990), there was evidence of a reduction in the difference between their positions. Pyongyang proposed a ten-point Declaration of Non-aggression and Reconciliation, and the south demanded confidence-building measures such as freedom to travel between the two Koreas, the restoration of communications, and co-operation in economic and technical matters. DPRK Prime Minister Yon reiterated the demand for the ending of Team Spirit exercises, the release of dissidents who had been jailed for visiting the north, and a stop to the south's attempt to join the United Nations. Prime Minister Kang rejected Yon's proposal and offered a ten-point Basic Agreement on inter-Korean Relations, which focused on the achievement of basic confidence-building measures as a precondition to the negotiation of a non-aggression agreement. The atmosphere was adversely affected by Roh's scheduled trip to the USSR. The North Koreans cancelled the next round of talks over Team Spirit.

Since 1991 there has been growing concern over the North Korean nuclear capability. On 20 April 1991 Gorbachev and Roh called upon North Korea to open its nuclear facilities to inspection by international agencies. Previously the South Korean Defence Minister, Lee Jong Koo, had suggested that a commando-style attack on the facilities might be necessary to remove the threat of an atomic bomb developed there. His comments were later officially retracted. With Gorbachev's support for Seoul's seat in the United Nations, Pyongyang felt isolated as never before. The rapid expansion of trade and investment between the Soviet Union and the Republic of Korea further worried Kim Il Song.[43]

In September President Bush announced that the United States would remove all tactical nuclear bombs from South Korea as part of a disarmament initiative including Europe and Asia. The removal applied to ground-based tactical nuclear weapons only and not air-delivered bombs. The United States was believed to have about sixty such bombs stockpiled in South Korea for use on F-16 aircraft.

Parallel with the dialogue between the two Koreas, the nuclear problem was addressed. Roh agreed to multilateral talks following press reports that North Korea was close to developing atomic weapons within two years. In November 1991, the Defence Secretary, Richard Cheney, announced that the United States was halting proposed troop withdrawals from South Korea. These were scheduled in February as part of US defence budget reductions. The possible North Korean nuclear threat was given as the reason for halting withdrawal, which could not continue 'until the dangers and uncertainties of the North Korean nuclear program have been thoroughly addressed'. The United States had already reduced its presence to 39,000 troops from 43,000. Cheney said the withdrawal of 3,000 more troops would continue as scheduled by the end of 1992, but a later withdrawal phase concerning the removal of an additional 6,000 in 1993 was now on hold.

The two Premiers signed a comprehensive agreement (13 December 1991) governing non-aggression, reconciliation and other issues in the fifth round of talks since September 1990. Entitled 'Agreement on Reconciliation, Non-aggression, Exchange and Co-operation', the pact aimed at the eventual negotiation of a formal peace treaty. Some in South Korea have criticized the agreement for not dealing with the issue of North Korean atomic weapons, but some compromises were necessary to even conclude a pact of any kind. The north had previously required that all treaty negotiations should be conducted with the United States, but dropped that requirement in an important and implicit recognition of the south's sovereignty. The south had previously said an agreement on the nuclear issue was a precondition for all other agreements. Other provisions in the declaration said that both sides would issue a joint declaration of non-aggression, they would give advance notice of troop movements and exercises, and they would install a hot line between top military commanders. They also agreed to ban terrorist activity and attempts to overthrow each other's government. The north agreed for the first time to call for efforts to reunite families and dropped the demand that the south should repeal laws restricting contact with the north.

Soon after the declaration, President Roh stated that all US nuclear weapons had been withdrawn, so North Korea had no reason to develop nuclear arms or to reject international inspections of nuclear installations. The south suggested that both countries should permit mutual inspections of nuclear facilities to permit North Korean representatives to visit US bases in the south and confirm the removal of US nuclear devices. In return, the southern inspectors would be permitted to visit northern installations believed to be developing atomic weapons. By year-end, both sides had agreed not to 'test, produce, receive, possess, deploy or use nuclear weapons'. The 'Joint Declaration of a Non-nuclear Korean Peninsula' pledged both countries to use nuclear energy for peaceful purposes only and never to reprocess nuclear fuel. The pact called for 'inspections of objects chosen by the other side and agreed to by both parties', but did not set out specific procedures for inspections. A joint nuclear control committee was to be created for deciding on procedures. Western intelligence continues to believe the north could produce atomic weapons in the near future.

On 30 January 1992, North Korea signed a nuclear safeguards accord which would allow international inspection of its facilities, following the US and South Korean decision to cancel Team Spirit. The terms of two earlier accords[44] went into effect when the Premiers met in Pyongyang for the sixth round of talks on 19–30 February. A delay was that North Korea had not yet ratified the nuclear safeguard agreement – waiting for ratification by the Supreme People's Assembly in April. The agreement required North Korea to declare all its nuclear sites to the International Atomic Energy Agency (IAEA) and submit a precise inventory of the fissionable material they contained. The accord was ratified as scheduled, but mutual suspicions increased over the nuclear inspections, including setting a timetable for inspections.

By September 1992 two more rounds of Premier-level talks had taken place, but there was no progress on the nuclear inspection issue. Pyongyang had permitted inspectors from the IAEA to visit sites, but the United States, Japan and South Korea considered this inadequate. The agency had missed evidence of Iraq's secret nuclear projects before the Gulf War, and was not fully trusted by South Korea and its allies.[45] By early 1993, the issue had not been resolved, despite significant international pressure, and in March, Pyongyang declared it was withdrawing from the Nuclear Proliferation Treaty.[46]

Briefly, the North Koreans have been increasingly nervous over their likely survival and may hope to have a nuclear guarantee in the perilous future. They have lost their main allies – Russia and China – after normalization with the Republic of Korea. Their economy is stagnant and approaching bankruptcy, and a leadership crisis is certain to occur with the death of Kim Il Song. Kim Chong Il will be the immediate successor, but his long-term fortunes are open to doubt. With the collapse of communism in most of the world, North Korea is isolated from most power centres. Its only ensurance for sovereignty, and its main bargaining chip, may be the nuclear capability Pyongyang seems to be developing.

An assessment of *Nordpolitik*

State-building in the Korean context cannot be separated from diplomacy and adaptation to the international environment. Sovereignty cannot be detached from security. *Nordpolitik* has been a strategy to bring about a setting in which South Korea does not depend on the United States for trade and defence, or on Japan for its well-being. The dilemma of the policy has been that its very success in enhancing sovereignty makes it an obstacle to peninsular reunification.

The original *Nordpolitik* goal of threat reduction on the Korean peninsula has been served, but is far from having been achieved. It would be difficult to establish that South Korean diplomacy alone can take credit for its success – one cannot discount the good fortune of communist collapse in the trade and political gains. The benefits of threat reduction are obvious, and include the diversion of economic resources from military expenditure to peaceful development. Equally important is that there should be a reduction of opportunities for major powers to interfere in Korean affairs. Much of Korean nationalism on both sides of the Demilitar- ized Zone has been directed against the proclivities of the four powers to treat Korea as a zone of strategic interface – with wars fought there as a matter of course. A divided Korea can only protract this unhappy condition.

The method of *Nordpolitik* has been to proceed with diplomatic links in tandem with commercial intercourse, while pursuing a specific agenda in each of four target regions. Each region has had its own function to perform in South Korean strategy: Eastern Europe was the most accessible – especially the liberalizing or reforming countries where Soviet dominance was most resented and opposed – Poland, Hungary, Yugoslavia, and Czechoslovakia. Once links were established in these states, other Eastern

European states were less likely to resist Seoul's overtures. The acceleration of Soviet reforms enabled the Republic of Korea to move its schedule ahead much faster than anticipated as one communist regime after another fell or pursued policies independent of Moscow. By late 1989, it was apparent that the Soviet Union was ripe for further pressure and enticement. In March 1990, a Democratic Liberal Party delegation, led by Kim Young Sam, visited Moscow and discussed normalization. The meeting between Roh Tae Woo and Gorbachev in June culminated in diplomatic exchange in September. With this, a major prop of support for Pyongyang had fallen.

China remains the major foreign support for the DPRK, but even here there has been serious erosion. Having competed with Moscow for influence in Pyongyang so often in the past, Beijing was not in a hurry to follow the Gorbachev road of rapid normalization with South Korea. First, the Chinese communist leadership enjoyed political leverage over North Korea and economic benefits from South Korea, so there was little incentive to disturb this *status quo*. The Chinese communists clearly distinguish between economics and politics at home and abroad. Trade is flourishing, and the periphery of the Yellow Sea is becoming an important regional trade basin.

Second, the Chinese hard-liners were reluctant to endorse a policy that reinforces the changes made in the past several years that have benefited the capitalist powers or weakened socialism – whether it is *perestroika* or the 'new world order' or *Nordpolitik*. As reformers increased in influence in Beijing, however, this position softened. Third, acceptance of 'two Koreas' has too close a parallel with the notion of 'two Chinas', which remains anathema to Beijing. Consistency alone dictated that China should insist on non-recognition of the ROK – i.e. a second Korea. For unclear reasons, however, Beijing has suspended this concern in normalization with South Korea. Finally, the Soviet abandonment of North Korea as an ally created an opportunity for China to enhance its influence with Pyongyang, and perhaps exert leverage over a strategic state in North East Asia. While Sino-Soviet relations have lost much of their previous hostility, Russia and China are likely to remain competitors over the long run.

The Chinese delay in normalization until August 1992 demonstrated the major limitation of *Nordpolitik*: it is a complex strategy that requires appropriate strokes of luck as well as persistence. The relatively sudden isolation of North Korea has created an opportunity not only for China, but Japan as well. Negotiations between Tokyo and Pyongyang could have resulted in a lifeline for North Korea, and continuation of the *status quo* of division in the region. Thus, *Nordpolitik* may have indirectly created obstacles to the realization of peninsular reunification.[47]

There is an inescapable dilemma in Korea's *Nordpolitik*: the more the policy has succeeded in reducing security threats by enhancing the sovereignty and legitimacy of the South Korean state, the greater the possibility of the stability and intractability of the *status quo*. *Nordpolitik* has been successful because it has altered the terms of involvement of the major external participants on the Korean peninsula. The former USSR has balanced its involvement in both north and south. The United States has been slowly developing contacts with North Korea. China provides political and military support for Pyongyang, and treats Seoul as a favourable trading partner. Japan maintains occasionally prickly relations with South Korea, but has pursued negotiations with the north.

These trends and events undoubtedly contribute to peace and stability on the Korean peninsula, but they also fortify the two existing states. The four major powers of North East Asia now, or may in the not-too-distant future, have sizable interests in both North and South Korea. This will certainly complicate attempts at reunification. The policy of *Nordpolitik* has internationalized support for and acceptance of both Korean regimes. While not complete cross-recognition, it does approach the concept in its impact and implications: to strengthen the division of the country.

There may be a fundamental contradiction between *Nordpolitik* and peninsular reunification for Korea. The former has served to strengthen the South Korean state, while the latter requires some surrender of sovereignty by one or both parties. *Nordpolitik* was framed in the context of reinforcing the state security of South Korea, and has fulfilled this purpose – but perhaps at the expense of making reunification much more difficult to accomplish.

If *Nordpolitik* is such a good idea for South Korea, why didn't North Korea pursue *Sudpolitik*? It might be argued that Pyongyang takes reunification much more seriously than does Seoul – even to the extent of risking war to accomplish it. It also helps to explain why student radicals in the south give a higher rating to the nationalist credentials of Kim Il Song than to the Seoul leadership – because it appears that Seoul is willing to consolidate its own sovereignty at the cost of postponing national reunification. When *Nordpolitik* was conceived in the early 1980s, few could imagine the sequence of events leading to USSR–ROK normalization. Conventional expectations were a continuation of the Soviet–American stand-off, and of tensions on the Korean peninsula. The policy of expanding relations with Moscow to reduce strains in a divided country was first pursued in Germany as *Ostpolitik*, using prosperity and trade as levers to open the USSR, and, in the process, build some indirect bridges to East Germany.

The success of German reunification in the wake of Bonn's *Ostpolitik* suggests that *Nordpolitik* should be able to facilitate, rather than hinder, Korean unity. There was no devastating war between East and West Germany to fortify mutual antipathy as there was in Korea. Furthermore, the two Germanies were integrated into two defence alliances – the Warsaw Pact and NATO, which provided both with considerable international stability as long as the treaty systems remained intact. Shifting alliances and uncertainty about the future role of the United States in the region require that the two Koreas should maximize their diplomatic independence. This combination of peninsular polarization and multi-polar involvement suggests further obstacles to reunification than those faced by Germany. In addition, North Korea has proved to be far more hermitic than East Germany. The abolition of the German Democratic Republic with reunification has certainly stiffened North Korean resolve to resist absorption. In this respect, the combination of successful *Ostpolitik* and German reunification has made one part of *Nordpolitik* more difficult, since the most probable outcome is the ultimate extinction of the DPRK.

To summarize the gains of *Nordpolitik*:

1 Normalization with former Soviet bloc countries has proceeded much faster than anticipated – after the initial breakthroughs in Eastern Europe. This has provided additional international legitimacy for the Republic of Korea, strengthened it in a wide range of diplomatic dealings, and isolated North Korea.

2 Trade with socialist countries has expanded in a major way, although their weak economies will impair the ability to repay loans and to provide profits to Korean companies. China's economy continues to expand with the impetus of the reforms of the 1980s – despite the pro-planning preferences of the Beijing leadership. South Korea moved into this market despite the absence of formal diplomatic links before 1992.

3 North Korea has become more pliable as it has fewer and fewer options. Resistance to double entry into the United Nations weakened in the face of Chinese and Soviet refusal to veto South Korea's admission.

4 Perhaps at no time since World War II has the threat of war been so distant. The issue of North Korean nuclear development remains, and conventional forces remain enormous, but neither of Pyongyang's patrons would be willing to underwrite a second attempt to unite the peninsula by force.

5 *Nordpolitik* may indirectly enhance domestic political stability in the long run with the government's proof of diplomatic skill to strengthen national sovereignty in the international system. Despite the telegenic demonstrations in Seoul that dominate Western images of the country,

violent radicalism appears to be declining. There seems little evidence that the Korean middle classes are sympathetic to dissidents.

Nordpolitik can be characterized as a policy of high risk, high gain. The gains have been significant, but several risks remain:

1 It could endanger relations with South Korea's major ally, the United States, if not synchronized. There remains a low potential for conflict in the American relationship with North Korea. The United States and Japan are more likely to favour *status quo* division of the peninsula, and inertia could hamper reunification in the future. Unlike Germany, which has been part of a regional security organization in the post-war years, the Republic of Korea's security has been tied to the alliance with the United States and the guarantees of the United Nations. This means that any break with the United States could weaken South Korea's national security, since no regional or multilateral alliance exists to replace it.

2 South Korea's success in normalizing relations with the PRC has damaged relations with Taiwan, a long-standing ally and trading partner. While Taiwan and South Korea have been commercial competitors in many sectors, with several parallels in development strategy, they have also had numerous common interests. The decline of anti-communism has reduced these interests, but Seoul may have been too hasty in abandoning an old ally in the euphoria of success in dealing with major powers – whose predatory habits could easily resurface.

3 To push North Korea into a corner could also be dangerous, especially as ROK–China normalization broadens to greater co-operation. The north's conventional military power and potential nuclear capacity, and ability to engage in subversion in South Korea, should not be minimized. So far, its closed society has been able to avoid the wholesale demoralization which took place in Eastern Europe. Jeopardy to DPRK survival could arouse an unpleasant reaction.

4 Japan's major attention remains focused on relations with the United States. However, if the relationship between South Korea and the former Soviet Union becomes too close, Tokyo might be provoked to take counter-action. The timing of discussions with North Korea certainly allows Tokyo additional leverage over South Korea to discourage too much co-operation between Seoul and Moscow. It is also unlikely that Japan would welcome a strong, united Korea as a competitor in the region.

5 Russian fragmentation and decline have been an economic liability to South Korea, with its considerable investment there. Material circumstances in the former USSR are worsening, and market prosperity remains a faraway vision. The prospects of political chaos do not augur

well for *Nordpolitik* as well, since another set of leaders in Moscow may not be as friendly to Seoul as Gorbachev and Yeltsin have been.

Conclusions

South Korean foreign policy during the presidency of Roh Tae Woo proceeded on the foundations established by the Chun Doo Hwan regime. Seoul seized the initiative provided by the breakdown of Soviet hegemony and established relations with former Soviet clients with breathtaking diplomacy. South Korean strategy has been to offer some of the economic advantages held by the Japanese – albeit on a smaller scale – and gain footholds in what could develop into important markets. Geopolitically, Korea remains the key area in North East Asia where major powers will barter and manoeuvre for advantage. Russia has indicated that it wants to remain a player, thereby making concessions to Seoul at the expense of Pyongyang. Japan has countered by opening its negotiations with North Korea although little progress was made. Pyongyang's refusal to open nuclear installations to international inspection and a nearly bankrupt economy have been major obstacles to rapprochement.

Still, *Nordpolitik* has been an outstanding success. Even tempered with the recognition that victory has been due as much to historical accident as to careful planning, it has been impressive. Opportunities have occurred and Seoul was prepared to take advantage of them with personnel and resources. However, this success will make reunification more difficult, as argued above. With dual entry of North and South Korean into the United Nations, the sovereignty of the two halves has become part of the international *status quo*. In its diplomatic offensive, South Korea may continue to achieve its agenda in dealing with socialist (and formerly socialist) countries. This depends upon a modicum of stability in the economy, government, and society. Equally important is the tacit acceptance of this new order by the major powers of the region, as well as acquiescence from North Korea.

The six Republics of South Korea represent a series of experiments in state-building. Four goals have dominated these efforts: security, stability, prosperity, and democracy. In Table 2 there is a rough scorecard of the

Table 2 Comparison of the Six Republics of South Korea

Republic	Democracy	Security	Stability	Prosperity
First	+	+	0	–
Second	0	0	0	+
Third	+	+	+	–
Fourth	+	+	+	–
Fifth	+	+	+	0
Sixth	0	0	+	+

Source: + Primary goal. 0 Secondary goal. – Tertiary goal.

importance of the four goals for each Republic. A plus sign approximates high emphasis, a zero denotes medium emphasis, and a negative indicates relatively lower importance.

Each of these goals was vitally affected by perceptions of, and responses to, the international environment. The anomaly of the shortlived Second Republic paying less attention to security and stability may have been a factor in the military coup that toppled it. With the end of the Cold War the isolation of North Korea, and the success of *Nordpolitik*, the Sixth Republic could afford to reduce the stress on defence and civil order.

This mix of state goals also suggests that there is a certain incompatibility between the 'soft' option of democracy, and the 'hard' objectives of security and stability. Security is 'hard' because it requires military resources and the paramountcy of preparedness against an enemy. It requires the organization of force, maintaining discipline, and preventing subversion. Alliances can also make contributions to state security, but are no substitutes for the 'hard' elements of military preparedness. Where there are no threats, the state has much less need to maintain military security. Stability may also require instruments of force, such as the police. A preferable form of stability is voluntary civil order, in a well integrated society, and under a government of laws. In times of rapid change this may not be possible, as has been the experience of South Korea. A major shift has occurred with the increasing importance of political parties as the arena of political conflict – in contrast to the battles in the streets. The nation is far from solving the fissures in society, but there is a government, a constitution, and a political system which is increasingly capable of minimizing the destabilizing influence of military intrusions and student demonstrators.

Prosperity is the goal of economic development. It can further enhance security and stability by allowing the nation to maintain a standing armed force, afford necessary weapon systems, divide a larger national income and lower resentments over inequalities, and provide employment and opportunities for otherwise alienated young people. It was only in South Korea's authoritarian Third Republic that economic development took on a consistent character of steady growth, albeit at the expense of democracy. Democracy has been the most fragile of goals for developing states, and the Second Republic sought to implement democratic institutions almost at the expense of the other goals – prematurely as it turned out. However, the present Sixth Republic is building on more solid political institutions and economic achievements, and shows the beginnings of genuine democracy.

It is premature to generalize that the South Korean trials and errors in socio-political engineering have a general application to the developing nations of the contemporary world. However, the case does demonstrate that its approach of trial and error appears to be far more efficacious than the holistic strategies of the communist countries. As the Koreans learned from their own and others' mistakes, and tortuously moved from poverty and authoritarianism, so too must other societies find their own way.

The Republic of Korea faces a time of historic opportunity. Backsliding to authoritarianism is still possible, but it is increasingly unlikely if responsible opposition becomes institutionalized. Military intrusion is also increasingly unlikely as the threat from the north and domestic disruption subside. A democratic political culture is emerging, albeit with specific and authentic Korean characteristics. The strong presidency can trace its lineage from the principle of the monarchy in the past. Regionalism and opposition leadership based on claims to virtue also have historical precedents. The populism which found expression in the mass demonstrations of 1960 and 1985–7 can probably trace their roots to Tong Haks, peasant uprisings, and the 1919 independence movement. Even the divided peninsula echoes earlier times when rival kingdoms faced each other.

This does not condemn the future to resemble the past, but it does provide a set of parameters for Koreans to understand themselves and their society. It also suggests that Korean democracy will resemble Western democracy in but a few dimensions. Korean politicians, intellectuals, and citizens now face the task of defining this democracy, and building its institutions, while maintaining the economic growth which has facilitated the expansion of liberty.

Appendix
Roh Tae Woo's declaration of 29 June 1987

(1) The constitution should be expeditiously amended, through agreement between the government party and the opposition, to adopt a direct presidential system, and presidential elections should be held under a new constitution to realize a peaceful change of government in February 1988.

(2) In addition to switching to a direct presidential election system through constitutional revision, I think that, to carry out elections democratically, it is necessary also to revise the Presidential Election Law so that freedom of candidacy and fair competition are guaranteed and so that the genuine verdict of the people can be given. A revised election law should ensure maximum fairness and justness in election management, from the campaigns to the casting, opening and counting of ballots.

(3) Antagonisms and confrontations must be resolutely eradicated not only from our political community but also from all other sectors to achieve grand national reconciliation and unity. In this connection, I believe that Mr Kim Dae Jung should be amnestied and his civil rights restored, no matter what he has done in the past. At the same time, all those who are being detained in connection with the political situation should also be set free, except for those who have committed treason by repudiating the basic free and democratic order on which our survival and posterity hinge and a small number of people who have shaken the national foundations by committing homicide, bodily injury, arson or vandalism.

(4) Human dignity must be respected even more greatly and the basic rights of citizens should be promoted and protected to the maximum. I hope that the forthcoming constitutional amendments will include all the strengthened basic rights clauses being proposed by the Democratic Justice Party, including a drastic extension of Habeas Corpus.

(5) To promote the freedom of the press, the relevant systems and practices must be drastically improved. The Basic Press Law, which may have been well meant but has nonetheless been criticized by most

journalists, should promptly be either extensively revised or abolished and replaced by a different law.

(6) Freedom and self-regulation must be guaranteed to the maximum in all other sectors also, because private initiative is the driving force behind diverse and balanced social development, which in turn fuels national progress. In spite of the forthcoming processes of amending the constitution, local councils should be elected and organized without any hitch according to schedule .... Colleges and universities – the institutions of higher learning – must be made self-governing and educational autonomy in general must be expeditiously put into practice.

(7) A political climate conducive to dialogue and compromise must be created expeditiously, with healthy activities of political parties guaranteed. A political party should be a democratic organization that presents responsible demands and policies to mould and crystallize the political opinion of the people. The state should exert its utmost efforts to protect and nurture political parties, so long as they engage in sound activities and do not contravene such objectives.

(8) Bold social reforms must be carried out to build a clean and honest society. In order that all citizens can lead a secure and happy life, crimes against life and property, such as hooliganism, robbery and theft, must be stamped out, and deep-seated irrationalities and improprieties that still linger in our society must be eradicated. Groundless rumours, along with regional autonomism [*sic*; parochialism] and black- and white-attitudes, should be banished for ever to build a society in which mutual trust and love prevail ....

Notes

1 State reform in South Korea

1 Robert Tucker, *The Inequality of Nations*, New York: Basic Books, 1977, p. 3.
2 See Paul Kennedy, *The Rise and Fall of the Great Powers*, New York: Random House, 1987; and Henry Bienen, ed., *Power, Economics and Security: The United States and Japan in Focus*, Boulder: Westview, 1992.
3 'Piecemeal Social Engineering', in David Miller, ed., *Popper Selections*, Princeton: Princeton University Press, 1985, pp. 304–318.
4 Regarding these, see Frederic C. Deyo, ed., *The Political Economy of the New Asian Industrialism*, Ithaca: Cornell University Press, 1987.
5 Yang Sung Chul, 'The Evolution of Korean Nationalism – A Historical Survey', *Korea and World Affairs*, 1987, vol. 11, no. 3, pp. 424–425.
6 Ibid., p. 435.
7 See 'The Standard of "Civilization" and the Entry of Japan into International Society', in Gerrit W. Gong, *The Standard of 'Civilization' in International Society*, Oxford: Clarendon Press, 1984, pp. 164–200.
8 Ibid.
9 On US policy on Korea, see Robert L. Messer, 'American Perspectives on the Origins of the Cold War in East Asia, 1945–1949', in Akira Iriye and Warren Cohen, eds, *American, Chinese, and Japanese Perspectives on Wartime Asia*, Wilmington: Scholarly Resources, 1990, pp. 254–255.
10 'Although sometimes regarded as an expression of uninterest, which gave the green light for a North Korean attack, Acheson's speech was in fact an exercise in ambiguity, designed to restrain both sides. In this respect, it was a faithful reflection of American policy.' Callum A. MacDonald, *Korea: The War before Vietnam*, New York: Free Press, 1986, p. 17.
11 The Third and Fourth Republics were the exception in leadership change, since both were under the presidency of Park Chung Hee.
12 On definitions of revolution, see Chalmers Johnson, *Revolutionary Change*, Stanford: Stanford University Press, 1982.
13 These and other factors are explored in greater detail in 'The Determinants of Military Power', by Klaus Knorr, in Henry Bienen, ed., *Power, Economics and Security: The United States and Japan in Focus*, Boulder: Westview, 1992, pp. 69–133.
14 K.C. Roy distinguishes between economic growth and economic development:

172 *Notes*

'The former refers to a rise in national or per capita income and product, while the latter implies certain fundamental changes in the structure of the economy, such as a rise in the share of national product originating in the industrial sector, and the participation by nationals in the process by which these changes occur.' 'Development, Income Inequality, and Poverty in LDCs Revisited', *International Studies Notes*, 1991, vol. 16, no. 2, p. 55.

15 *Economic resources* consist of material and financial assets which can be accumulated, bartered, squandered, exchanged for other assets or services, and generally quantified. These resources can be increased or decreased, produced or destroyed by physical acts.

16 *Political resources* refer to power relationships in state and society. In contrast to economic resources, they cannot be quantified or produced mechanically. Essentially, political resources in a state are distributed among government, social groups, and individuals. Totalitarianism is a system which aims to concentrate all political resources in the state. Anarchism seeks the reverse – the elimination of all state power.

17 See Yang Sung Chul, *Korea and Two Regimes: Kim Il Song and Park Chung Hee*, Cambridge, Mass.: Schenkman, 1981.

18 See Han Soongjoo, *The Failure of Democracy in South Korea*, Berkeley: University of California Press, 1974.

19 Young Whan Kihl, *Politics and Policies in Divided Korea: Regimes in Contest*. Boulder: Westview Press, 1984, p. 61.

2 The institutions of government

1 Even the armed forces network (AFKN) broadcasts in English helped to inform Koreans of foreign affairs simultaneously while many sought to improve their language facility through listening.

2 Larry Diamond, Juan J. Linz and Seymour Martin Lipset, *Politics in Developing Countries: Comparing Experiences with Democracy*, Boulder: Lynne Rienner, 1990, p. 273.

3 We can define the state as a 'set of organizations invested with the authority to make binding decisions for people and organizations juridically located in a particular territory and to implement these decisions using, if necessary, force'. Dietrich Rueschemeyer and Peter B. Evans, 'The State and Economic Transformation: towards an Analysis of the Conditions Underlying Effective Intervention', in Peter Evans, Dietrich Rueschemeyer and Theda Skocpol, eds, *Bringing the State Back In*, Cambridge: Cambridge University Press, 1985, pp. 6–47.

4 Ibid.

5 'Despite the existence of the apparatus of absolute despotism, the centralized structure of government masked the limitations on royal authority by the yangban aristocracy. The most important reason for these limitations was that the sources of power, wealth, and prestige were not controlled by the crown; they were also based on inheritance of status and landownership.' James B. Palais, *Politics and Policy in Traditional Korea*, Cambridge, Mass.: Harvard University Press, 1991, p. 10.

6 J.S. Migdal, 'Strong States, Weak States: Power and Accommodation,' in Myron Weiner and Samuel P. Huntington, eds, *Understanding Political Development*, Boston: Little Brown, 1987, p. 397.

7 *Yonhap*, 6 October 1989, in *Daily Report: East Asia* (hereinafter, *DR: EA*), 6 October 1989, p. 28.
8 *Yonhap*, 19 October 1989, in *DR: EA*, 19 October 1989, p. 36.
9 Chong himself resisted resignation, saying he had had no part in the Kwangju military operation. Assembly hearings on the incident also failed to clarify Chong's role. His supporters said that if he had done wrong, then he should be dealt with by legal – not political – procedures. *The Korea Times*, 14 October 1989, p. 6, in *DR: EA*, 19 October 1989, p. 37.
10 *The Korea Herald*, 16 December 1989, p. 1, in *DR: EA*, 19 December 1989, pp. 14–15.
11 *The Korea Times*, 28 December 1989, p. 2, in *DR: EA*, 28 December 1989, p. 17.
12 The viewing rate was over 70 per cent when it began in the morning, but around 40 per cent in the afternoon after he was interrupted several times by shouting matches between government and opposition assemblymen. *The Korea Herald*, 1 January 1990, p. 2, in *DR: EA*, 4 January 1990, p. 23.
13 Chun Doo Hwan's younger brother, Chun Kyong-hwan, was sentenced to seven years in prison in May 1989 for embezzlement and corruption. He had been head of Saemaul headquarters during the Fifth Republic. He was released on parole in June 1991, after serving more than half his prison term. *The Korea Times*, 25 June 1991, p. 3, in *DR: EA*, 25 June 1991, pp. 32–33.
14 *Choson Ilbo*, 10 December 1990, p. 3, in *DR: EA*, 11 December 1990, p. 27.
15 *Iryo Sinmun*, 13 August 1989, p. 3, in *DR: EA*, 2 November 1989, p. 23.
16 *Sindong-A*, November 1989, pp. 310–325, in *DR: EA*, 28 November 1989, p. 27. The activities of Park Chul-un, Kim Pok-tong, and another somewhat distant relative were closely watched by the press. See *Tong-A Ilbo*, 24 June 1990, p. 2, in *DR: EA*, 8 August 1990, pp. 24–26.
17 *Far Eastern Economic Review*, 25 January 1990, p. 24.
18 *The Korea Herald*, 24 February 1989, p. 2.
19 See Appendix.
20 An excellent background to the question is provided by Kang, Chi-Won. 'The Pros and Cons of the Political Choice between the Presidential System and the Cabinet System for Korea's Political Development.' *Korea and World Affairs*. vol. 16, No. 4 (Winter 1992) pp. 695–713.
21 *Far Eastern Economic Review*, 15 November 1990, p. 12.
22 *Yonhap*, 23 January 1990, in *DR: EA*, 25 January 1990, pp. 21–22.
23 *Wolgan Chungang*, June 1990, pp. 154–173, in *DR: EA*, 5 September 1990, p. 37.
24 *Wolgan Chungang*, June 1990, pp. 154–173, in *DR: EA*, 5 September 1990, pp. 31–42.
25 25 January 1990, p. 6, in *DR: EA*, 26 January 1990, p. 28.
26 9 May 1990, p. 6, in *DR: EA*, 11 May 1990, p. 32.
27 *Yonhap*, 20 June 1990, in *DR: EA*, 20 June 1990, p. 39.
28 *Yonhap*, 25 June 1990, in *DR: EA*, 25 June 1990, p. 25.
29 *The Korea Herald*, 26 October 1990, p. 2, in *DR: EA*, 26 October 1990, p. 30.
30 *Chugang Ilbo*, 13 November 1990, in *DR: EA*, 21 December 1990, pp. 41–42.
31 *Yonhap*, 1 April 1991, in *DR: EA*, 1 April 1991, pp. 24–25.
32 The seventy-member PPD caucus had earlier resigned in protest against the DLP unilateral passage of certain Bills in the last session. *Yonhap*, 30 July 1990, in *DR: EA*, 1 August 1990, p. 33.

33 *Far Eastern Economic Review*, 1 March 1990, pp. 8–9.
34 *Far Eastern Economic Review*, 10 August 1989, p. 24.
35 These are various Cabinet-level officials in charge of national security, foreign and domestic policies, and other state affairs.
36 Chapter Six of the 1988 constitution.
37 Harold C. Hinton, *Korea under New Leadership: the Fifth Republic*, New York: Praeger, 1983, p. 24
38 *The Korea Herald*, 24 January 1990, p. 3, in *DR: EA*, 25 January 1990, p. 24.
39 *Chugang Ilbo*, 30 November 1989, p. 3, in *DR: EA*, 2 February 1990, p. 29.
40 *The Korea Times*, 2 August 1990, p. 2, in *DR: EA*, 2 August 1990, p. 34.
41 *The Korea Herald*, 21 December 1989, p. 8, in *DR: EA*, 28 December 1989, p. 25.
42 *Tong-A Ilbo*, 8 August 1990, p. 3, in *DR: EA*, 19 October 1990, pp. 33–35.
43 *Tong-A Ilbo*, 18 September 1990, p. 19, in *DR: EA*, 30 September 1990, p. 33.
44 They also agreed to reform the Defence Security Command, which was held responsible for undercover operations against dissidents. Other issues were also to be discussed in a joint committee. *Yonhap*, 19 November 1990, in *DR: EA*, 20 November 1990, p. 39.
45 *Chugang Ilbo*, 20 December 1989, p. 3, in *DR: EA*, 6 March 1990, p. 31.
46 *Chugang Ilbo*, 18 December 1990, p. 12, in *DR: EA*, 28 February 1990, p. 39.
47 *Yonhap*, 5 March 1991, in *DR: EA*, 5 March 1991, p. 22.
48 *Iryo Sinmun*, 9 September 1990, p. 11, in *DR: EA*, 19 November 1990, pp. 31–32.
49 *Chugang Ilbo*, 20 December 1989, p. 3, in *DR: EA*, 6 March 1990, p. 32.
50 *Choson Ilbo*, 21 February 1990, p. 1, in *DR: EA*, 2 May 1990, p. 19.
51 *The Korea Herald*, 14 March 1991, p. 1, in *DR: EA*, 14 March 1991, p. 30.
52 *Yonhap*, 28 March 1991, in *DR: EA*, 1 April 1991, p. 23.
53 Cheju had the highest turn-out with 74.7 per cent, while Seoul had the lowest, with 52.4 per cent.
54 *Yonhap*, 21 June 1991, in *DR: EA*, 21 June 1991, p. 17.
55 Seoul KBS-1 Television Network, 22 June 1991, in *DR: EA*, 24 June 1991, p. 34.

3 Political parties and South Korean politics

1 'Personalism played an important role in propagating meaningful orientations towards the world and in regulating personal feelings and contributed directly and indirectly to individual stability and social solidarity. Questions such as to whom or to what to be loyal, after whom to model one's self, which patterns of behaviour to adopt or adjust, all had their obvious answers in the ethical principles of Confucianism.' Quee-Young Kim, 'Korea's Confucian Heritage and Social Change', *Journal of Developing Societies* vol. 4, no. 2, p. 257.
2 Andrew C. Nahm, *Korea: Tradition and Transformation*, Seoul: Hollym, 1988, pp. 261, 276–277.
3 Ibid., p. 341.
4 Han, Soong Joo. *The Failure of Democracy in South Korea*, Berkeley: University of California Press, 1974, p. 4.
5 'An Analysis of Military Expansion in South Korea, 1945–1980' *Asian Perspective*, vol. 11, no. 2, 1987 p. 269.
6 *Choson Ilbo*, 15 November 1992, p. 18, in *DR: EA*, 5 January 1993, pp. 28–29.

7 Samuel Huntington, quoted in Ahn Byong-man, 'Korean Political Parties and Political Development: Crucial Elections and the Process of Institutionalization of the Political Party System', *Korea Journal*, 1978, p. 31.

8 He divides institutionalization into two periods, the first from liberation until 1961 and the second from May 1961 to 1972. He shows that political party development goes through a series of stages: factionalism, then a dominant party system forms, followed by a two-party system brought on by a 'crucial election' and finally the two-party system itself collapses and another process of institutionalization begins. The renewal of this process was seen in 1961 with the military coup followed by a brief period when political parties were banned until the return to civilian government in 1963 and was shown again in 1972 when the Yushin constitution was enacted and the National Assembly disbanded.

9 Leon D. Epstein, *Political Parties In Western Democracies*, New York: Praeger, 1967, p. 9. Quoted in Michael G. Roskin, Robert L. Cord, James A Medeiros and Walter S. Jones, *Countries and Concepts: An Introduction to Comparative Politics*, Englewood Cliffs: Prentice Hall, 1989, p. 214

10 Roskin *et al.*, op. cit., pp. 215–218.

11 Gregory Henderson, *Korea: The Politics of the Vortex*, Cambridge, Mass.: Harvard University Press, 1968, p. 271.

12 Henderson, op. cit., pp. 277 ff.

13 National Association for the Rapid Realization of Korean Independence (NARRKI): 'It was the incarnation of Rhee's ideal of a patriotic society, mystically united, with which he could manipulate a mass society without the interference of interest groups.' Henderson, op. cit., p. 282.

14 Around 5 per cent voted on the basis of party or affiliation in the 1948 and 1950 elections. Nearly half of the first National Assembly were independent. Henderson, op. cit.,. 287.

15 Nahm, op. cit., p. 425.

16 Han, Soong Joo, op. cit., p. 13. His 'lack of enthusiasm for building a political party is understandable if one realizes his aspiration to pose as leader of the whole nation rather than a group, his apprehension over the possibility that a powerful competitor might arise from under his wing, and the willingness of the bureaucracy, police, and intelligence personnel to serve him without a political party' (p. 14).

17 Han, op. cit., p. 35.

18 Han, op. cit., pp. 35–36.

19 Henderson, op. cit., p. 293–294.

20 Han, op. cit., p. 21.

21 Henderson, op. cit., p. 295.

22 Henderson, op. cit., p. 302–303.

23 Han, op. cit., p. 46.

24 Han, op. cit., p. 31.

25 Nahm, op. cit., p. 440.

26 Han, op. cit., p. 47.

27 Han, op. cit., p. 51.

28 David I. Steinberg, *South Korea: Economic Transformation and Social Change*, Boulder: Westview, 1989, p. 56.

29 Peter R. Moody, *Political Opposition in Post-Confucian Society*, New York: Praeger, 1988, p. 128.

30 Moody, op. cit., pp. 128–136.
31 Moody, op. cit., p. 129.
32 Moody, op. cit., p. 131.
33 Moody, op. cit., p. 131.
34 *The Christian Science Monitor* (hereinafter *CSM*), 25 January 1985, p. 13.
35 Steinberg, op. cit., p. 61.
36 *CSM*, 5 April 1985, p. 12.
37 *The Korea Herald*, 2 March 1984, p. 1.
38 *CSM*, 14 March 1986, p. 14.
39 *Korea Report* (Embassy of the Republic of Korea, Ottawa, Canada), 13 April 1987, p. 1.
40 *CSM*, 6 June 1986, p. 10.
41 *Far Eastern Economic Review*. 16 April 1987, p. 24.
42 'From Authoritarianism to Democracy in South Korea', *Political Studies* vol. 37, no. 2, 1989, p. 252.
43 An official half joked to this writer in late 1986 that his country seemed to face two choices – either a military republic or a student republic.
44 *Asiaweek*, 12 July 1987, p. 15.
45 *Asiaweek*, 13 September 1987, p. 24
46 *Far Eastern Economic Review*, 24 September 1987, p. 12.
47 Steinberg, op. cit., p. 64.
48 Kim Hong Nack, 'The 1988 Parliamentary Election in South Korea', *Asian Survey*, 1989, vol. XXIX, no. 5, pp. 480–495.
49 Ibid., p. 482.
50 Ibid., p. 486.
51 One member of the Hangyore party was elected but switched to the PPD. Ibid.
52 Ibid., p. 490.
53 'The 1988 National Assembly Election in South Korea: The Ruling Party's Loss of Legislative Majority', *Journal of North East Asian Studies*, 1988, vol. 7, no. 3, p. 67.
54 *Sindong-A*, September 1989, pp. 182–191, in *DR: EA*, 30 October 1989, p. 28.
55 *Yonhap*, 28 December 1989, in *DR: EA*, 3 January 1990, pp. 26–27.
56 *The Korea Times*, 7 January 1990, p. 1, in *DR: EA*, 9 January 1990, p. 32.
57 *Chinsanggwa Naemak*, October 1989, pp. 18–23, in *DR: EA*, 12 January 1990, p. 26.
58 *Policy Series*, No. 1990–2, 22 January 1990.
59 *Backgrounder*, vol. 60, 6 March 1991.
60 Liberalization became even more pronounced in the elections to the Legislative Yuan in December 1992.

4 The economic context of reform

1 Park, Ungsuh Kenneth, 'A Bird's Eye View of Korean Economic Development', *Korea and World Affairs*, 1987, vol. 11, no. 1, p. 138.
2 Ibid., p. 139.
3 Ibid., p. 137.
4 Nevertheless, this has not prevented some radical elements in Korea from embracing a romanticized version of traditional rural life – expressed in the idea of *minjung*. On the concept and the role of the dissenting Church, see Donald N. Clark, *Christianity in Modern Korea*, New York: The Asia Society, 1986, pp. 39–45.

5 Alice H. Amsden, *Asia's Next Giant: South Korea and Late Industrialization*, New York and Oxford: Oxford University Press, 1989, pp. 63–64.
6 Seoul *Choson Ilbo*, 3 February 1990, p. 1, in *DR: EA*, 2 May 1990, p. 32.
7 Seoul *The Korea Economic Journal*, 5 November 1990, p. 1, in *DR: EA*, 8 November 1990, pp. 25–26.
8 Seoul *Sindong-A*, May 1990, in *DR: EA*, 9 August 1990, p. 23.
9 *Far Eastern Economic Review*, 23 November 1989, p. 74.
10 *Asiaweek*, 25 January 1987, p. 67.
11 Seoul *The Korea Herald*, 4 February 1990, p. 8, in *DR: EA*, 7 February 1990, pp. 40–41.
12 *Far Eastern Economic Review*, 31 October 1991, p. 66.
13 *The Korea Herald*, 24 May 1991, p. 6.
14 Ro Sung-Tae. 'The Korean Economy: Performance and Prospects', *Area Studies*, 1989, vol. 10, no. 1, p. 43.
15 Dennis McNamara finds the origins of the *chaebol* in the colonial period: 'I find postcolonial continuities most striking in patterns of concentration, continued prominence of the family in large-scale enterprise, and persistence of close business–state ties. Bureaucratic control of critical economic resources by a state with at least the ambitions for comprehensive direction remained a part of economic life in postcolonial capitalism on the peninsula.' Dennis L. McNamara, *The Colonial Origins of Korean Enterprise, 1910–1945*, New York: Cambridge University Press, 1990, p. 127.
16 *The Economist*, 14 July 1990, p. 20.
17 Ibid.
18 *Far Eastern Economic Review*, 29 September 1988, p. 103.
19 *The Korea Herald*, 21 May 1988, p. 6.
20 The economic slowdown affected the *chaebol* in 1989. Seventeen of the fifty major *chaebol* posted deficits, and their average profit-to-sales margin was a mere 0.76 per cent. *The Korea Times*, 31 October 1990, p. 10, in *DR: EA*, 1 November 1990, p. 27.
21 *Far Eastern Economic Review*. 1 March 1990, p. 46.
22 Ibid.
23 Seoul *The Korea Times*. 31 October 1990, p. 10, in *DR: EA*, 1 November 1990, pp. 27–28.
24 'Government Plans to Control Conglomerates', from Seoul *Hanguk Ilbo*, 28 June 1990, p. 9, in *DR: EA*, 20 August 1990, pp. 26–27.
25 Seoul *Tong-A Ilbo*, 15 January 1990, p. 17, in *DR: EA*, 30 March 1990, pp. 38–39.
26 In the *Fortune* ranking list it ranked twenty-fourth in 1989.
27 *A Handbook of Korea*, Seoul: Korean Overseas Information Service, 1990, p. 463.
28 *The Korea Herald*, 12 March 1989, p. 8.
29 *The Korea Herald*, 10 June 1988, p. 6.
30 *Far Eastern Economic Review*, 12 January 1989, pp. 53–54.
31 Seoul *Yonhap*, 30 October 1990, in *DR: EA*, 1 November 1990, p. 27.
32 In August 1990, thousands of farmers hissed the Agriculture Minister's speech to a rally, denouncing the Uruguay Round negotiations. About 4,000 farmers and fishermen staged a sit-in protest. *The Korea Times*, 22 August 1990, p. 3, in *DR: EA*, 22 August 1990, p. 29.
33 *Far Eastern Economic Review*, 25 August 1988, p. 66.

34 Park, op. cit., pp. 138–139.
35 *The Korea Herald*, 26–28 March 1991, p. 3, in *DR: EA*, 4 April 1991, pp. 25–28.

5 The social context of Korean politics

1 Not an unrealistic or over-harsh judgement, according to some studies showing how government-provided transfer payments generate disincentive effects with respect to the job market behaviour of the unemployed and creates greater dependence status. Arthur J. Mann, and Robert Smith, 'Public Transfers, Family Socioeconomic Traits, and the Job Search Behaviour of the Unemployed: Evidence from Puerto Rico' *World Development*, 1987, vol. 15, no. 6, pp. 831–840.
2 This was more true of the period after the coup by Park Chung Hee: 'The limiting of labour demands was, it seems, viewed as an integral component of the new industrial course (in the mid-sixties) . . . Labour had been weakened before the turn to outward-looking growth . . . The initial controls on labour under military rule resembled those on other social groups and had no distinctive economic rationale.' Stephan Haggard, *Pathways from the Periphery: The Politics of Growth in the Newly Industrializing Countries*, Ithaca: Cornell University Press, 1990, p. 63.
3 'Politics and Agrarian Change in South Korea: Rural modernization by "Induced" Mobilization', in Raymond Hopkins, Donald Puchala and Ross Talbot (eds.), *Food, Politics and Agricultural Development: Case Studies in the Public Policy of Rural Modernization*, Boulder: Westview, 1979, p. 134.
4 Regional differences have been a source of friction. The small Chinese minority has not been a target of xenophobia in Korea.
5 R. Darcy and Sunhee Song 'Men and Women in the South Korean National Assembly: Social Barriers to Representational Roles', *Asian Survey*, vol. 26, no. 6, 1986, p. 681.
6 'Korea's Confucian Heritage and Social Change,' pp. 260–261.
7 Some of this argument is summarized by Barbara Dafoe Whitehead, 'Dan Quayle was Right', *The Atlantic*, 1993, vol. 271, no. 4, pp. 47–84.
8 Donam Hahn Wakefield, 'Religious and Cultural Wellsprings of Korean Women', *Korea Journal*, 1980, vol. 20, no. 5, p. 15.
9 The idea of much permanent class membership must be tempered with the recognition that outlooks are significantly altered by rapid mobility and the fluidity of development. There is the phenomenon of some class solidarity among workers as a tactical stand for economic bargaining which must be balanced against steady improvement – individually and collectively – for workers.
10 *Asiaweek*, 26 April 1987, p. 76.
11 *Far Eastern Economic Review*, 26 February 1987, pp. 38–39.
12 *The Korea Herald*, 9 March 1989, p. 6.
13 *Korea Annual 1992*, pp. 121–122.
14 *The Korea Herald*, 10 November 1987, p. 6.
15 *Korea Annual 1992*, p. 122.
16 Ruth Grayson, 'Rural Population in Decline', *Business Korea*, September 1984, p. 93.
17 *The Economist*, 18 September 1989, p. 36.

18 *Korea Annual 1992*, p. 225–226.
19 David I. Steinberg, 'Sociopolitical Factors and Korea's Future Economic Policies', *World Development*, 1988, vol. 16, no. 1, p. 25.
20 *Korea Annual 1992*, p. 224.
21 *Far Eastern Economic Review*, 1 December 1988, pp. 76–77.
22 *The Korea Herald*, 10 October 1989, p. 2, in *DR: EA*, 10 October 1989, pp. 33–34.
23 *The Korea Times*, 18 June 1991, p. 8.
24 *The Korea Herald*, 5 July 1990, p. 3.
25 *The Korea Times*, 11 October 1989, p. 9, in *DR: EA*, 11 October 1989, pp. 26–27.
26 Michael Walzer, *Spheres of Justice: A Defence of Pluralism and Equality*, New York: Basic Books, 1986, p. xiii.
27 Ibid., p. 3.
28 On the reformist potential of the folk tradition, see Lim Jae-Hae, 'Tradition in Korean Society: Continuity and Change', in *Korea Journal*, 1991, vol. 31, no. 3, pp. 13–30.
29 *The Korea Herald*, 31 May 1991, p. 5.
30 Nahm, op. cit., pp. 500–502
31 *Far Eastern Economic Review*, 1 October 1987, p. 42.
32 *The Korea Herald*, 24 February 1984, p. 4.
33 *CSM*, 3 May 1984, p. 13.
34 *The Korea Times*, 16 June 1991, p. 3; 18 June 1991, p. 3.
35 See Youm Kyu Ho and Michael B. Salwen, 'A Free Press in South Korea: Temporary Phenomenon or Permanent Fixture?', *Asian Survey*, 1990, vol. 30, no. 3, pp. 312–325.
36 *CSM*, 1 July 1987, pp. 9–10.
37 *Asiaweek*, 9 August 1987, p. 60.
38 'The countries of East Asia, excluding Japan and China, spend an average of 16.9 per cent of government money on education, compared with just 4.5 per cent in the West.' *The Economist*, 30 January 1993, p. 34. Money alone will not produce a more literate and better trained work force, but the proportions are significant indicators of East Asian priorities. Moreover, if Korean education is anything like as effective as Taiwan, China and Japan, the results will certainly help to propel society into the competence in high technology demanded by the post-industrial society. See Harold W. Stevenson, 'Learning from Asian Schools', *Scientific American*, December 1992, pp. 70–76.
39 *The Korea Herald*, 6 July 1990, p. 2.
40 *The Korea Herald*, 29 April 1990, p. 3.
41 *The Korea Herald*, 5 June 1990, p. 3.
42 'Higher Education in Crisis', *Korea Newsreview*, 13 February 1993, p. 33.
43 *The Korea Herald*, 19 July 1990, p. 3.
44 *The Korea Herald*, 13 July 1990, p. 3.
45 *The Korea Times*, 21 June 1991, p. 6.
46 *The Korea Times*, 23 June 1991, p. 3.
47 *The Korea Times*, 31 July 1990, p. 2, in *DR: EA*, 1 August 1990, p. 35. Seoul *Yonhap*, 8 August 1990, in *DR: EA*, 8 August 1990, p. 24.
48 *The Korea Times*, 20 March 1990, p. 2, in *DR: EA*, 21 March 1990, p. 20.
49 Seoul *Yonhap*, 8 August 1990, in *DR: EA*, 8 August 1990, p. 23.
50 Seoul *Yonhap*, 22 August 1990, in *DR: EA*, 22 August 1990, p. 23.

51 *The Korea Times*, 23 August 1989, p. 3, in *DR: EA*, 23 August 1990, p. 21.
52 Seoul *Yonhap*, 20 December 1990, in *DR: EA*, 20 December 1990, p.16.
53 This means more than 4.5 lives lost daily. By 1991, the rate had increased to six lives per day. *The Korea Times*, 16 June 1991, p. 3.
54 *Far Eastern Economic Review*, 27 August 1987, pp. 14–19.
55 *CSM*, 21 September 1987, p. 10.
56 *Far Eastern Economic Review*, 10 September 1987, p. 22.
57 Yong Rae Kim. 'Korean Labour Movement and Political Participation', *Korea Observer*, vol. 23, no. 1, 1992, p. 6.
58 Ibid., p. 14.
59 *The Korea Herald*, 30 July 1988, p. 11.
60 *Crisis and Compensation: Public Policy and Political Stability in Japan*, Princeton: Princeton University Press, 1988.

6 State reform in a comparative context

1 *The End of History and the Last Man*, New York: The Free Press, 1992, p. 12.
2 See, for example, Chalmers Johnson, *Revolutionary Change*, Stanford: Stanford University Press, 1982.
3 'Distinctions between the Taiwanese and Korean Approaches to Economic Development', *Journal of East Asian Affairs*, vol. 7, no. 1, 1993, p. 117.
4 'Scientific Method', in David Miller, ed., *Popper Selections*, Princeton: Princeton University, 1985, p. 140.
5 'Piecemeal Social Engineering', in ibid., p. 308.
6 In the election of June 1992, the old ruling party, the Mongolian People's Revolutionary Party, won seventy-one of the seventy-six seats in the legislature, effectively returning to single-party rule. The party had renounced its Marxist–Leninist ideology and reportedly received assistance from the PRC. Tsedendambyn Batbayar, 'Mongolia in 1992: Back to One-party Rule', *Asian Survey*, vol. XXXIII, no. 1, 1993, pp. 61–66.
7 See Cheng Tun-jen, 'Democratizing the Quasi-Leninist Regime in Taiwan', *World Politics*, vol. 41, no. 4, 1989, pp. 471–499.
8 Taiwan investors and traders have also been eager participants in the burgeoning China market as restrictions have eased. See 'Taiwan–Mainland Trade Still Booming', *Free China Journal*, vol. 9, no. 80, 1992, p. 3.
9 See Wu Yu-shan, 'Marketization of Politics: The Taiwan Experience', *Asian Survey*, 1989, vol. 29, no. 4, pp. 382–400.
10 Ibid., p. 384.
11 Ibid., p. 386.
12 Ibid.
13 During the Maoist period, a common slogan was 'Wei renmin fuwu' ('Serve the people'). This was slightly modified with the re-introduction of the profit motive to 'Wei *nin* fuwu,' or loosely, 'Serve *you*' (the customer).
14 Lev P. Deliusin, 'Reforms in China: Problems and Prospects', *Asian Survey*, 1988, vol. 28, no. 11, pp. 1101–1102.
15 Ibid., pp. 1101–1102.
16 Ibid., p. 1103.
17 Ibid., p. 1114.
18 Rhee Kang Suk, 'North Korea's Pragmatism: A Turning Point?', *Asian Survey*, 1987, vol. 27, no. 8, p. 890.

7 South Korea's international environment and foreign policy

1 Current indicators of the gap between South and North Korea: GNP per head = US$5,569 *v.* $1,064; real growth rate = 9.0 per cent *v.* −3.7 per cent; and total foreign trade = US$134.9 billion *v.* US$4.6 billion. *The Economist*, 18 April 1992, p. 32.

2 'Global Detente and North Korea's Strategic Relations', *The Korean Journal of Defence Analysis*, 1990, vol. 7, no. 1, p. 48.

3 Park Sang-Seek, 'Northern Diplomacy and Inter-Korea Relations', *Korea and World Affairs*, 1988, vol. 12, no. 4, p. 706.

4 Ahn Byung-Joon notes that the 'term *Nordpolitik*' refers to South Korea's policy towards such communist countries as China, the Soviet Union and Eastern European countries, just as *Ostpolitik* refers to West Germany's policy towards these countries'. 'South Korea's New *Nordpolitik*', *Korea and World Affairs*, 1988, vol. 12, no. 4, pp. 693–705.

5 This fear underlies Moscow's refusal to make concessions on the Northern Territories issue.

6 Ahn Byung-Joon, 'South Korean–Soviet Relations: Issues and Prospects', *Korea and World Affairs*, 1990, vol. 14, no. 4, p. 673.

7 Seoul *Yonhap*, 10 October 1989, in *DR: EA*, 19 October 1989, p. 35.

8 Seoul *Yonhap*, 20 October 1989, in *DR: EA*, 20 October 1989, p. 26.

9 The Soviets do not go so far as to concur with the position of the Republic of Korea, whose outlook has been that the DPRK is 'an anti-state organization which illegally occupies a part of the territory of the Republic of Korea'. Kim Hakjoon, 'Korean Reunification: A Seoul Perspective', *Korea and World Affairs*, 1991, vol. 15, no. 1, p. 8.

10 *Choson Ilbo*, 24 November 1989, p. 9, in *DR: EA*, 29 November 1989, p. 28.

11 *Tong-A Ilbo*, 1 April 1990, p. 17, in *DR: EA*, 6 April 1990, p. 21.

12 *Choson Ilbo*, 12 April 1990, p. 2, in *DR: EA*, 12 April 1990, p. 19.

13 For example, Daewoo announced plans to set up joint ventures with the Soviet Union for fifteen different items. Seoul *The Korea Economic Journal*, 6 May 1991, p. 12, in *DR: EA*, 13 May 1991, p. 20

14 Seoul *Yonhap*, 8 June 1990, in *DR: EA*, 8 June 1990, p. 22.

15 Seoul *Yonhap*, 14 June 1990, in *DR: EA*, 15 June 1990, p. 29.

16 *The Korea Times*, 13 June 1990, p. 9, in *DR: EA*, 15 June 1990, p. 30.

17 Tokyo *Kyodo*, 21 April 1990, in *DR: EA*, 4 April 1990, p. 6.

18 *Far Eastern Economic Review*. 14 February 1991, p. 15.

19 Mette Skak, 'Post-Soviet Foreign Policy: the Emerging Relationship between Russia and North East Asia', *Journal of East Asian Affairs*, 1993, vol. 7, no. 1, p. 176.

20 David Dollar, 'South Korea–China Trade Relations: Problems and Prospects', *Asian Survey*, 1989, vol. 29, no. 12, pp. 1167–1176.

21 Seoul *Yonhap*, 8 November 1989, in *DR: EA*, 8 November 1989, p. 16.

22 Seoul *Yonhap*, 13 December 1989, in *DR: EA*, 13 December 1989, pp. 23–24. The *Hanguk Ilbo* considered the proposal too passive and called for more rapid normalization. 12 June 1990, p. 2, in *DR: EA*, 14 June 1990, p. 23.

23 *Chungang Ilbo*, 23 November 1989, p. 1, in *DR: EA*, 24 November 1989, p. 28.

24 Pyongyang KCNA, 9 June 1990, in *DR: EA*, 11 June 1990, p. 10.

25 *The Korea Times*, 11 May 1990, p. 11, in *DR: EA*, 11 May 1990, p. 37.

26 Seoul Television Service, 4 July 1990, in *DR: EA*, 5 July 1990, p. 39.

27 19 September 1990, p. 2, in *DR: EA*, 26 September 1990, p. 29.
28 Taipei CNA, 17 February 1990, in *DR: EA*, 21 February 1990, p. 51.
29 *Tong-A Ilbo*, 6 January 1990, p. 1, in *DR: EA*, 14 March 1990, pp. 26–27.
30 *Choson Ilbo*, 26 April 1990, p. 3, in *DR: EA*, 4 May 1990, p. 8.
31 *The Korea Herald*, 13 October 1988, p. 1.
32 Tokyo *Kyodo*, 20 December 1989, in *DR: EA*, 27 December 1989, p. 3.
33 Tokyo *Kyodo*, 4 January 1990, in *DR: EA*, 8 January 1990, 7–8.
34 *The Korea Times*, 13 March 1990, p. 3, in *DR: EA*, 16 March 1990, p. 19.
35 27 March 1990, p. 1; in *DR: EA*, 2 April 1990, p. 27.
36 *The Japan Times, Weekly International Edition*, 19–25 November 1990, p. 4.
37 Seoul *Yonhap*, 8 May 1990, in *DR: EA*, 9 May 1990, pp. 19–20.
38 *Far Eastern Economic Review*, 7 June 1990, p. 11.
39 Tokyo *Kyodo*, 24 May 1990, in *DR: EA*, 24 May 1990, p. 8.
40 Tokyo *Kyodo*, 24 May 1990, in *DR: EA*, 30 May 1990, p. 2.
41 Seoul *Yonhap*, 14 July 1990, in *DR: EA*, 17 July 1990, pp. 19–20.
42 At that time it was estimated that their forces numbered about 800,000, while the south numbered about 600,000.
43 The two leaders agreed to increase trade from its current level of $900 million to $10 billion by the mid-1990s.
44 The Agreement on Reconciliation, Non-aggression and Co-operation, and the Joint Declaration of the Denuclearization of the Korean Peninsula.
45 *The New York Times*, 16 September 1992, p. A8.
46 The Nuclear Proliferation Treaty was signed in 1968 by the United States, the Soviet Union and over 100 other countries. It remains in force, and seeks to limit the spread of nuclear weapons by restricting their transfer by the signatories. It also limits the non-nuclear-weapon states to the pursuit of only peaceful uses of nuclear power.
47 Soon after Sino-South Korean normalization, the government of the ROC announced it might seek relations with Pyongyang in retaliation for Seoul's actions, but no materialization of this has occurred.

Selective bibliography

Ahn, B.J. (1987) 'Korea: A Rising Middle Power in World Politics', *Korea and World Affairs*, 11, 1: 7–17.
—— (1988) 'South Korea's New *Nordpolitik*', *Korea and World Affairs*, 12, 4: 693–705.
—— (1990) 'South Korean–Soviet Relations: Issues and Prospects', *Korea and World Affairs*, 14, 4: 671–686.
Ahn, B.M. (1978) 'Korean Political Parties and Political Development: Crucial Elections and the Process of Institutionalization of the Political Party System', *Korea Journal*, 18, 1: 30–41.
Ahn, C.Y. (1986) 'Economic Development of South Korea, 1945–1985', *Korea and World Affairs*, 10, 1: 91–117.
Amsden, A.H. (1989) *Asia's Next Giant: South Korea and Late Industrialization*, Oxford: Oxford University Press.
An, T.S. (1983) *North Korea in Transition: From Dictatorship to Dynasty*, Westport, Conn.: Greenwood.
Area Studies (Taipei, Taiwan).
Arnold, W. (1988) 'Science and Technology Development in Taiwan and South Korea', *Asian Survey* 28, 4: 437–450.
Asiaweek.
Baek, J.C. (1984) 'Probe for an Alternative Strategy of Conflict Resolution in the Korean Peninsula', *Asian Perspective*, 8, 1: 120–158.
Batbayar, T. (1993) 'Mongolia in 1992: Back to One-Party Rule', *Asian Survey*, 33, 1: 61–66.
Bedeski, R.E. (1984) *South Korea's Modernization: Confucian and Conservative Characteristics*, Toronto: Joint Centre on Modern East Asia, University of Toronto, Working Paper 21, 'Canada and the Pacific: Agenda for the Eighties'.
—— (1992) 'State Reform and Democracy in Korea', *Journal of East Asian Affairs*, 6, 1: 141–168.
—— and McLean, C. (1984) 'Canada, Korea, and the Pacific Community', *Asian Perspective*, 8, 1: 1–12.
Berton, P. (1986) 'The Soviet Union and Korea: Perceptions, Scholarship, Propaganda', *Journal of North East Asian Studies*, 5, 1: 3–28.
Bienen, H. ed. (1992) *Power, Economics and Security: The United States and Japan in Focus*, Boulder: Westview.
Billet, B.L. (1990) 'South Korea at the Crossroads: An Evolving Democracy or Authoritarianism Revisited?', *Asian Survey*, 30, 3: 300–311.

184 *Selective bibliography*

Bond, D.G. (1988) 'Anti-Americanism and US–ROK Relations: An Assessment of Korean Students' Views', *Asian Perspective*, 12, 1: 159–190.

Burmeister, L.L. (1988) *Research, Realpolitik, and Development in Korea: The State and the Green Revolution*, Boulder: Westview.

Calder, K. (1988) *Crisis and Compensation: Public Policy and Political Stability in Japan*, Princeton: Princeton University Press.

Cha, Y.K. (1986) 'Strategic Environment of Northeast Asia: A Korean Perspective', *Korea and World Affairs*, 10, 2: 278–301.

Chee, C.I. (1992) 'South Korea's Security in the Age of the New World Order', *Korea and World Affairs* 16, 1: 82–99.

Cheng T.J. (1993) 'Distinctions between the Taiwanese and Korean Approaches to Economic Development', *Journal of East Asian Affairs* 7, 1: 116–136.

Choi, K.H., T.H. Kim, and C.R. Cho. (1991) 'The Impacts of Anti-Americanism on U.S.–Korean Relations', *Korea Observer* 22, 3: 311–334.

Choy, B.Y. (1988) *A History of the Korean Reunification Movement*, Seoul: Seoul International.

Christian Science Monitor.

Clark, D.N., ed. (1986) *Christianity in Modern Korea*. New York: Asia Society.

—— (1988) *The Kwangju Uprising: Shadows over the Regime in South Korea* Boulder: Westview.

Clough, R.N. (1987) *Embattled Korea: The Rivalry for International Support*, Boulder: Westview.

Cotton, J. (1987) 'The Prospects for the North Korean Political Succession', *Korea and World Affairs* 11, 4: 745–768.

—— (1989) 'From Authoritarianism to Democracy in South Korea', *Political Studies* 37, 2: 244–259.

Cotton, J. (1992) 'Understanding the State in South Korea', *Comparative Political Studies* 24, 4: 512–531.

Cumings, B.G. (1974) 'Is Korea a Mass Society?' *Occasional Papers on Korea*, 1: 65–81.

—— (1981) *The Origins of the Korean War: Liberation and the Emergence of Separate Regimes 1945–1947*, Princeton: Princeton University Press.

—— ed. (1983) *Child of Conflict: The Korean–American Relationship, 1943–1953*, Seattle: University of Washington.

Daily Report: East Asia.

Darcy, R., and S.H. Song (1986) 'Men and Women in the South Korean National Assembly: Social Barriers to Representational Roles', *Asian Survey*, 26, 6: 670–687.

Deliusin, L.P. (1988) 'Reforms in China: Problems and Prospects', *Asian Survey*, 28, 11: 1101–1116.

Deyo, F.C., ed. (1987) *The Political Economy of the New Asian Industrialism*, Ithaca: Cornell University Press.

Diamond, L., J.J. Linz and S.M. Lipset (1990) *Politics in Developing Countries: Comparing Experiences with Democracy*, Boulder: Lynne Rienner.

Dollar, D. (1989) 'South Korea–China Trade Relations: Problems and Prospects', *Asian Survey*, 29, 12: 1167–1176.

Eckert, C.J. (1991) *The Koch'ang Kims and the Colonial Origins of Korean Capitalism, 1876–1945*, Seattle: University of Washington Press.

Economist.

Epstein, L.D. (1967) *Political Parties in Western Democracies*, New York: Praeger.

Evans, P., D. Rueschemeyer, and T. Skocpol, eds (1985) *Bringing the State Back In*, Cambridge: Cambridge University Press.

Far Eastern Economic Review.

Foreign Broadcast Information Service. *Daily Report: East Asia*. Springfield, Va.: National Technical Information Service. *Free China Journal.*

Fukuyama, F. (1992) *The End of History and the Last Man*. New York: Free Press.

Gibney, F. (1992) *Korea's Quiet Revolution: From Garrison State to Democracy*, New York: Walker.

Godley, M.R. (1989) 'Labour Strategy for Industrialization in South Korea', *Pacific Affairs* 62, 3: 3–17.

Gong, G.W. (1984) *The Standard of 'Civilization' in International Society*. Oxford: Clarendon.

Gregor, A.J. (1990) *Land of the Morning Calm: Korea and American Security*, Washington: Ethics and Public Policy Center.

Haggard, S. (1990) *Pathways from the Periphery: The Politics of Growth in the Newly Industrializing Countries*. Ithaca: Cornell University Press.

Hahn, B.H. (1986) 'A Reflection on the Demise of the Authoritarian Park Regime', *Asian Perspective*, 10, 2: 289–310.

Hall, J.B. (1988) 'Urbanization and Dependency Reversal in the ROK', *Asian Perspective*, 12, 1: 84–106.

Halliday, J., and B. Cumings. (1988) *Korea: The Unknown War*, New York: Pantheon.

Hamilton, C. (1986) *Capitalist Industrialization in Korea*, Boulder: Westview Press.

Han, S.J. (1974) *The Failure of Democracy in South Korea*, Berkeley: University of California.

—— (1988) 'South Korea in 1987: The Politics of Democratization', *Asian Survey*, 28, 1: 52–61.

—— (1989) 'South Korea in 1988: A Revolution in the Making', *Asian Survey*, 29, 1: 29–38.

Han, S.J., and R. Myers, ed. (1987) *Korea: The Year 2000*, New York: University Press of America.

Hatada, T. (1969) *A History of Korea*, Santa Barbara: ABC Clio.

Henderson, G. (1968) *Korea: The Politics of the Vortex*, Cambridge, Mass.: Harvard University Press.

Henthorn, W.E. (1971) *A History of Korea*, New York: Free Press.

Hinton, H.C. (1983) *Korea under New Leadership: The Fifth Republic*, New York: Praeger.

Hong, Y.L. (1992) 'South Korea in 1991: Unprecedented Opportunity, Increasing Challenge', *Asian Survey*, 32, 1: 64–73.

Howe, R.W. (1988) *The Koreans: Passion and Grace*, New York: Harcourt Brace Jovanovich.

Hwang, I.K. (1987) *On Korea Via Permanent Neutrality*, Cambridge, Mass.: Schenkman Books.

International Cultural Foundation (1982) *The Legal System of Korea*, Seoul: Si-sa-yong-o-sa.

Iriye, A., and W. Cohen, ed. (1990) *American, Chinese, and Japanese Perspectives on Wartime Asia*. Wilmington: Scholarly Resources.

Jacobs, N. (1985) *The Korean Road to Modernization and Development*, Urbana: University of Illinois Press.

186   *Selective bibliography*

Jewell, M.E., and C.L. Kim (1976) 'Sources of Support for the Legislature in a Developing Nation', *Comparative Political Studies*, 7, 4: 461–489.

Johnson, C.A. (1982) *Revolutionary Change*. Stanford: Stanford University Press.

Kang, C.W. (1992) 'The Pros and Cons of the Political Choice between the Presidential System and the Cabinet System for Korea's Political Development', *Korea and World Affairs*, 16, 4: 695–713.

Kendall, L., and G. Dix, ed. (1987) *Religion and Ritual in Korean Society*, Berkeley: University of California.

Kennedy, P. (1987) *The Rise and Fall of the Great Powers*, New York: Random House.

Kihl, Y.W. (1979) 'Politics and Agrarian Change in South Korea: Rural Modernization by "Induced" Mobilization', in R. Hopkins, D. Puchala and R. Talbot (eds), *Food, Politics and Agricultural Development: Case Studies in the Public Policy of Rural Modernization*, Boulder: Westview.

—— (1984) *Politics and Policies in Divided Korea: Regimes in Contest*, Boulder: Westview.

—— (1990) 'South Korea in 1989: Slow Progess Toward Democracy', *Asian Survey*, 30, 1: 67–73.

Kim, A.J. (1981) 'Korean Economic Development and External Linkages', *Journal of East Asian Affairs*, 1, 1: 228–254.

Kim, B.W., and Rho W.J., eds (1982) *Korean Public Bureaucracy*, Seoul: Kyobo.

Kim, C.L., and Pai S.T. (1984) *Legislative Process in Korea*, Seoul: Seoul National University.

Kim, D.C. (1989) 'South Korea's Northward Diplomacy', *Area Studies*, 10, 1: 35–42.

Kim, D.J. (1987) *Prison Writings*, Berkeley: University of California Press.

Kim, H.J. (1990) 'U.S.–South Korean Security Relations: A Challenging Partnership', *Korean Journal of Defence Analysis*, 2, 1: 149–160.

—— (1988) 'The American Military Government in South Korea, 1945–1948: Its Formation, Policies, and Legacies', *Asian Perspective*, 12, 1: 51–83.

—— (1991) 'Korean Reunification: A Seoul Perspective', *Korea and World Affairs*, 15, 1: 5–20.

Kim, H.N. (1989) 'The 1988 Parliamentary Election in South Korea', *Asian Survey*, 29, 5: 480–495.

—— and Sunki Choe (1987) 'Urbanization and Changing Voting Patterns in South Korean Parliamentary Elections', *Journal of North East Asian Studies*, 6, 3: 31–50.

Kim, I.J., and Y.W. Kihl, ed. (1988) *Political Change in South Korea*, New York: Paragon House.

Kim, K.D. (1979) *Man and Society in Korea's Economic Growth: Sociological Studies*, Seoul: Seoul National University.

Kim, Q.Y. (1988) 'Korea's Confucian Heritage and Social Change', *Journal of Developing Societies*, 4, 2: 255–269.

Koh, B.C. (1985) 'The 1985 Parliamentary Election in South Korea', *Asian Survey*, 25, 9: 883–97.

—— (1988) 'North Korea in 1987: Launching a New Seven-year Plan', *Asian Survey*, 28, 1: 62–70.

—— (1989) 'North Korea in 1988: The Fortieth Anniversary', *Asian Survey*, 29, 1: 39–45.

Koo, Y.N., and Han S.J., ed. (1985) *The Foreign Policy of the Republic of Korea*, New York: Columbia University Press.

Korea Herald.
Korea Report. Embassy of the Republic of Korea, Ottawa, Canada.
Korean Overseas Information Service (1987) *A Handbook of Korea.* Seoul: Korean Overseas Information Service.
Kuk, Minho (1988) 'The Governmental Role in the Making of Chaebol in the Industrial Development of South Korea', *Asian Perspective*, 12, 1: 107–133.
Kuznets, P.W. (1985) 'Government and Economic Strategy in Contemporary South Korea', *Pacific Affairs*, 58, 1: 44–67.
Kwak T.H. (1992) 'Current Issues in Arms Control in the Inter-Korean Peace Process', *Korea Journal*, 32, 2: 42–57.
Kwak, T.H., C.H. Kim and H.N. Kim, eds. (1984) *Korean Reunification: New Perspectives and Approaches*, Seoul: Kyungnam University.
—— W. Patterson and E. Olsen, eds. (1984) *The Two Koreas in World Politics*, Boulder: Westview.
Lee, H.B. (1968) *Korea: Time, Change and Administration*, Honolulu: East–West Center.
Lee, J.T. (1988) 'Dynamics of Labour Control and Labour Protest in the Process of Export-oriented Industrialization in South Korea', *Asian Perspective*, 12, 1: 134–158.
Lee, K.B. (1984) *A New History of Korea*, Cambridge, Mass.: Harvard University Press.
Lee, S.H. (1987) 'An Analysis of Military Expansion in South Korea, 1945–1980', *Asian Perspective*, 11, 2: 264–284.
Lee, Y.H. (1988) 'The Seoul Olympics: What they Mean to the Korean People', *Korea and World Affairs*, 12, 2: 253–269.
Levin, Norman D. (1990) 'Global Detente and North Korea's Strategic Relations', *Korean Journal of Defence Affairs*, 7, 1: 48.
Lie, J. (1990) 'South Korean Development: The Elusive Reality of Conflict and Contradiction', *Pacific Affairs*, 69, 3: 366–372.
Lim, H.C. (1985) *Dependent Development in Korea, 1963–1979*, Seoul: Seoul National University.
Lim J.H. (1991) 'Tradition in Korean Society: Continuity and Change', *Korea Journal*, 31, 3: 13–30.
MacDonald, C.A. (1986) *Korea: The War before Vietnam*, New York: Free Press.
MacDonald, D.S. (1988) *The Koreans: Contemporary Politics and Society*, Boulder: Westview.
McNamara, D.L. (1990) *The Colonial Origins of Korean Enterprise, 1910–1945*, New York: Cambridge University Press.
Mann, A.J., and R. Smith (1987) 'Public Transfers, Family Socioeconomic Traits, and the Job Search Behaviour of the Unemployed: Evidence from Puerto Rico', *World Development*, 15: 6, 831–840.
Mikheev, V.V. (1991) 'New Soviet Approaches to North Korea: A Problem of Morality in Foreign Policy', *Korea and World Affairs*, 15, 3: 442–456.
Miller, David M., ed. (1985) *Popper Selections*, Princeton: Princeton University Press.
Moody, P.R. (1988) *Political Opposition in Post-Confucian Society*, New York: Praeger.
Moon C.I. (1991) 'The Political Economy of Defense Industrialization in South Korea: Constraints, Opportunities, and Prospects', *Journal of East Asian Affairs*, 5, 2: 438–465.

188   *Selective bibliography*

Morley, J.W. (1986) 'The North's Dilemma is the South's Opportunity', *Korea and World Affairs*, 10, 4: 695–727.
Mukherjee, S. (1992) 'Dependency Theory Revisited: South Korea's March towards an Independent Development', *Korea Observer*, 23, 1: 19–44.
Nahm, A.C. (1987) *Korea: Tradition and Transformation*, Seoul: Hollym.
Nam, J.H. (1987) 'US Forces in Korea: Their Role and Strategy', *Korea and World Affairs*, 11, 2: 268–285.
Niksch, L.A. (1989) 'Future Issues in US–ROK Security Cooperation', *Korean Journal of Defense Analysis*, 1, 1: 59–80.
Oh, K.C. (1990) 'The Military Balance on the Korean Peninsula', *Korean Journal of Defense Analysis*, 2, 1: 95–110.
Okonogi, M. (1989) 'The Korean Peninsula: The Revival of the Old Equilibrium in the New Context', *Journal of Northeast Asian Studies*, 8, 1: 56–69.
Olsen, E.A. (1986) 'The Arms Race on the Korean Peninsula', *Asian Survey*, 26, 8: 851–867.
—— (1988) *U.S. Policy towards the Two Koreas*, Boulder: Westview.
Overholt, W.H. (1987) 'Korea's International Roles: A Move toward Prominence', *Korea and World Affairs*, 11, 1: 43–62.
Pae, S.M. (1986) *Testing Democratic Theories in Korea*, New York: University Press of America.
Pak, C.Y. (1980) *Political Opposition in Korea, 1945–1960*, Seoul: Seoul National University Press.
Palais, J.B. (1975) 'Stability in Yi Dynasty Korea: Equilibrium Systems and Marginal Adjustment', *Occasional Papers on Korea*, 3: 1–18.
—— (1991) *Politics and Policy in Traditional Korea*, Cambridge, Mass.: Harvard University Press.
Palley, M.L. (1990) 'Women's Status in South Korea: Tradition and Change', *Asian Survey*, 30, 12: 1136–1153.
Park, C.W. (1988) 'Legislators and their Constituents in South Korea: The Patterns of District Representation', *Asian Survey*, 28, 10: 1049–1065.
—— (1988) 'The 1988 National Assembly Election in South Korea: The Ruling Party's Loss of Legislative Majority', *Journal of Northeast Asian Studies*, 7, 3: 59–76.
Park, M.K. (1987) 'Interest Representation in South Korea: The Limits of Corporatism', *Asian Survey*, 27, 8: 903–917.
Park, S.I. (1988) 'Labor Issues in Korea's Future', *World Development*. 16, 1: 99–120.
Park, S.S. (1988) 'Northern Diplomacy and Inter-Korea Relations', *Korea and World Affairs*, 12, 4: 706–736.
Park, T.W. (1986) 'Political Economic Approach to the Study of NICs' Foreign Policy Behavior: The Case of South Korea', *Journal of Northeast Asian Studies*, 5, 2: 53–74.
Park, U.K. (1987) 'A Bird's Eye View of Korean Economic Development', *Korea and World Affairs*, 11, 1: 137–148.
Park, Y.O. (1986) 'Korean–Japanese–American Triangle: Problems and Prospects', *Korea and World Affairs*, 10, 4: 748–775.
Pfaltzgraff, R.L. (1987) 'Korea's Emerging Role in World Politics', *Korea and World Affairs*, 11, 1: 18–42.
Pollack, J.D. (1984) 'U.S.–China Relations and the Security of Korea', *Asian Perspective*, 8, 1: 106–119.

Polomka, P. (1986) *The Two Koreas: Catalyst for Conflict in East Asia?* Adelphi Paper No. 208, London: IISS.

Rhee, K.S. (1987) 'North Korea's Pragmatism: A Turning Point?' *Asian Survey*, 27, 8: 885–902.

—— B. Ross-Larson and G. Pursell(1984) *Korea's Competitive Edge: Managing the Entry into World Markets*, Baltimore: The Johns Hopkins University Press.

Ro, S.T. (1989) 'The Korean Economy: Performance and Prospects', *Area Studies*, 10, 1: 43–56.

Roskin, M.G., R.L. Cord, J.A. Medeiros and W. S. Jones (1989) *Countries and Concepts: An Introduction to Comparative Politics*, Englewood Cliffs: Prentice Hall.

Roy, K.C. (1991) 'Development, Income Inequality, and Poverty in LDCs Revisited', *International Studies Notes*, 16, 2, 55–59.

Scalapino, R., and S.J., Han, eds (1986) *United States–Korea Relations*, Berkeley: Institute of East Asian Studies, University of California.

Skillend, W.E. (1978) 'The Political Opposition in South Korea', *Asian Affairs*, 65: 13–22.

Sohn, H.K. (1989) *Authoritarianism and Opposition in South Korea*, New York: Routledge.

Sorensen, C.W. (1988) *Over the Mountains are Mountains*, Seattle: University of Washington Press.

Steinberg, D.I. (1988) 'Sociopolitical Factors and Korea's Future Economic Policies', *World Development*, 16, 1: 19–34.

—— (1989) *South Korea: Economic Transformation and Social Change*, Boulder: Westview.

Stevenson, H.W. (1992) 'Learning from Asian Schools,' *Scientific American*.

Suh, D.S. (1988) *Kim Il Song: The North Korean Leader*, New York: Columbia University Press.

Suh, G.M. (1987) 'The Class Character of the Korean Middle Strata', *Korea Journal*, 27, 8: 20–26.

Takesada, H. (1990) 'Korean Security and Unification in the Detente Era', *Korean Journal of Defense Analysis*, 2, 1: 179–190.

Taylor, W.J., M.J. Mazarr and J.A. Smith. (1990) 'US Troop Reduction from Korea 1970–1990', *East Asian Affairs*, 4, 2: 256–286.

Tucker, R. (1977) *The Inequality of Nations*, New York: Basic Books.

Wakefield, D.H. (1980) 'Religious and Cultural Wellsprings of Korean Women', *Korea Journal*, 20, 5: 5–16.

Walzer, M. (1986) *Spheres of Justice: A Defense of Pluralism and Equality*, New York: Basic Books.

Wang, I.K. (1988) 'Saemaul Undong as a Korean-Version Rural Development Program', *Korea Observer*, 19, 2: 193–211.

Weede, E. (1988) 'The Seoul Olympics, Korea, and World Politics', *Korea and World Affairs*, 12, 2: 303–321.

Weiner, M., and S.P. Huntington, ed. (1987) *Understanding Political Development*, Boston: Little Brown.

Whang, I.J. (1988) 'Rural Development and Central–Local Relations in Korea', *Korea Observer*, 19, 2: 182–192.

Whitehead, Barbara D. (1993) 'Dan Quayle was Right', *The Atlantic*, 271, 4: 47–84.

Wilson, R.W. (1988) 'Wellsprings of Discontent: Sources of Dissent in South Korean Student Values', *Asian Survey*, 28, 10: 1066–1081.

Wright, E.R., ed. (1975) *Korean Politics in Transition*, Seattle: University of Washington Press.
Wu, Y.S. (1989) 'Marketization of Politics: The Taiwan Experience', *Asian Survey*, 29, 4: 382–400.
Yager, Joseph A. (1984) 'The Security Environment of the Korean Peninsula in the 1980's', *Asian Perspective*, 8, 1: 85–105.
Yang, S.C. (1981) *Korea and Two Regimes. Kim Il Song and Park Chung Hee*, Cambridge, Mass.: Schenkman.
—— (1987) 'The Evolution of Korean Nationalism: A Historical Survey', *Korea and World Affairs*, 11, 3: 424–470.
—— (1992) 'United Germany for Divided Korea: Learning from Euphoria and Dysphoria', *Korea and World Affairs*, 16, 3: 436–462.
Yong, R.K. (1992) 'Korean Labour Movement and Political Participation', *Korea Observer*, 23, 1: 1–18.
Yoon, Y.O. (1986) 'The Structure and Process of the Korean National Assembly', *Korea Observer*, 17, 1: 3–30.
—— (1986) 'Policymaking activities of the South Korean National Assembly' *Journal of North East Asian Studies*, 5, 1: 29–48.
Youm, K.H., and M.B. Salwen. (1990) 'A Free Press in South Korea: Temporary Phenomenon or Permanent Fixture?' *Asian Survey*, 30, 3: 312–325.
Young, J.K. (1992) 'The Integration of the Two Koreas: Problems and Prospects', *Korea Observer*, 23, 3: 275–308.

Index